Doin' the
CHARLESTON

Black Roots of American Popular Music
& the Jenkins Orphanage Legacy

Mark R. Jones

EAST ATLANTIC
EAP
PUBLISHING

First Edition
First Printing 2013

ISBN: 13:978-0615852034

Front cover illustration:
20 *Franklin Street* by Judy Beschta.

Book design by Mark Jones & Kari Jones
Edited by John Young & Rebel Sinclair

Printed in the United States of America

TABLE OF CONTENTS

ACKNOWLEDGEMENTS

My wife, Kari Jones, and also my girlfriend, Rebel Sinclair. Thankfully, they are the same person. Thanks for allowing me to disappear into my cave to work on this for 10 hours a day for five years, and for reading and editing early versions of this manuscript. But mostly, thanks for your enduring love and support. I strive every day to be worthy of you.

James Brain (the only Brain in Charleston) for reading sections of this manuscript in early and later stages. And for always digging the music.

John Young, yielder of the unflinching red pen! We had long discussions over the use (or non-use) of an apostrophe.

Joe Mathieu for the great Jabbo Smith drawing.

Pete Faint for the Queen's Dance Orchestra photo.

Dr. Karen Chandler of the Charleston Jazz Initiative for reading and critiquing the (almost) final version of this manuscript. And also, thanks for the amazing Jenkins Band photos.

Lastly, thanks to Jabbo Smith, Cat Anderson, Freddie Green, Tommy Benford, Edmund Jenkins, Tom Delaney, James Reese Europe, Jelly Roll Morton, Noble Sissle, Eubie Blake, James P. Johnson, Duke Ellington and Count Basie for the music. Your genius has become part of the soundtrack of my life.

All mistakes are mine.

AUTHOR'S NOTE

I am not a musician. I am a music lover, a history geek, writer and tour guide always looking for another great story to tell. My formal musical training ended with my years in the Barnwell High School (S.C.) Scarlet Knights marching band. I was a decent snare drummer, a passable percussionist and 1st chair East Regional on the timpani drum. The main reason I made 1st chair was that I was the *only* person to try out for the timpani! Of course, during the heyday of the 1970s glam rock 'n rock, the chicks didn't really dig a guy who played the timpani, so in college I taught myself 25 guitar chords and learned to strum along with the Eagles and Jackson Browne. My musical training has not progressed any further, except with my ears, which steadily led me back in time to the 1920s.

This is the one of the greatest untold stories in American musical history. The Jenkins Orphanage Band was an incubator for several towering musical talents who helped transform American culture through music. Bits and pieces of this story are known to some musicologists and historians. The Jenkins story has been woefully neglected by most writers, except as a backdrop to another story. I have attempted to insert the history of the Jenkins Band into its proper place - its role in the development of America's most significant contribution to human musical culture – jazz.

Enjoy.

CAST OF CHARACTERS

The Orphanage

♪ REV. DANIEL JENKINS: Freed slave and founder of the Orphan Aid Society in Charleston, S.C. A tireless worker, he became internationally known as the "Orphan Man."

♪ ELLA HARLESTON JENKINS: From a prominent Charleston black family, she defied her father to become Rev. Jenkins' secretary, mistress and second wife.

♪ EDMUND THORNTON JENKINS: Son of Rev. Jenkins. Brilliant musician and composer who studied at the Royal Academy in London and lived most of his adult life in Europe.

♪ FRANCIS EUGENE MIKELL: First director of the Jenkins Band. Later a sergeant in the U.S. Army and assistant band director of the Harlem Hellfighters during World War I.

♪ AMOS GAILLARD: Jenkins Band member who later became its director. Also a member of the Harlem Hellfighters.

♪ TOM DELANEY: First member of the Jenkins Band to become a successful professional musician when Ethel Waters recorded several of his songs.

Composed more than 300 songs, including the standard, "Jazz Me Blues."

♪ JABBO SMITH: Jenkins Band member who was the hottest trumpet player in New York City from 1925-29. Was considered a rival to Louis Armstrong and recorded still-influential records for the Brunswick label. Became a Broadway sensation during the 1980s in *One Mo' Time*.

♪ TOMMY BENFORD: Jenkins Band ace drummer who recorded with Jelly Roll Morton, Coleman Hawkins and Django Reinhardt.

♪ FREDDIE GREEN: Jenkins Band member who played guitar for the Count Basie Orchestra for 50 years. Basie considered Green his "right hand."

♪ CAT ANDERSON: Jenkins Band member and lead trumpet player in the Duke Ellington Orchestra for over 20 years. Considered one of the greatest all-time high-note trumpet players.

♪ HERBERT WRIGHT: Jenkins Band drummer and member of the Harlem Hellfighters. Convicted of murder in 1919.

In Charleston

♪ DUBOSE HEYWARD: Charleston author and poet whose novel *Porgy* became the basis for *Porgy and Bess*, America's first folk opera.

♪ OLIVE HARLESTON JENKINS: Illegitimate daughter of Rev. Daniel Jenkins and Ella Harleston.

In New York

♪ JAMES REESE EUROPE: Founder of the Clef Club in New York. Music director for the Castle Society Orchestra and conductor of the Harlem Hellfighters, often called the "first big band." First black American officer to lead troops into battle during World War I.

♪ NOBLE SISSLE: Singer, songwriter and band leader who managed the Clef Club for many years. Also a member of the Harlem Hellfighters.

♪ EUBIE BLAKE: Ragtime pianist and member of the Clef Club. With Noble Sissle, Blake became one of the most popular songwriters of the 1920s and 30s, including the classic, "I'm Just Wild About Harry."

♪ WILL MARION COOK: Brilliant musician and composer of the early 20th century. Member of the Clef Club.

♪ VERNON AND IRENE CASTLE: White couple who changed American culture by introducing black style jazz dancing to an elite white audience. The Castle Society Orchestra featured prominent black musicians and black conductor James Reese Europe.

♪ GEORGE GERSHWIN: American composer of hundreds of popular songs, including America's first folk opera, *Porgy and Bess*.

♪ JAMES P. JOHNSON: Stride pianist in Harlem and

composer of the song "Charleston."

♪ WILLIE "THE LION" SMITH: Ragtime pianist in 1920s Harlem.

♪ BERT WILLIAMS: First black superstar of the American musical stage. Star of the Ziegfeld Follies for more than a decade.

"I am now satisfied that the future music of this country must be founded upon what are called the negro melodies. In the negro melodies of America I discovered all that is needed for a great and noble school of music. They are pathetic, tender, passionate, melancholy, solemn, religious, bold, merry, gay and what you will."

— Antonin Dvorak, 1893.

Carnegie Hall, New York City, circa 1900. *Courtesy of the Library of Congress.*

PRELUDE
The Most Important Day in American Musical History

"The 'greatest hit' of 20th century popular music was not the creation of Michael Jackson, the Bee Gees or even the Beatles. Anyone with a sense of history will realize that the once-ubiquitous dance tune called the 'Charleston' fueled a craze that has never been matched."

– Leslie Stifelman, *Columbia Journal of American Studies.*

THURSDAY, MAY 2, 1912. THE CONCERT THAT NIGHT was a curious affair, a benefit by black musicians for Harlem's institution for artistically gifted children. the Music School Settlement for Colored People. This would be the largest assemblage of African-American artists ever gathered together in New York to perform in America's most famous white-owned, white-operated theater - Carnegie Hall. More than three hundred black American musical artists were scheduled to play before a mixed race audience, on the same stage that had hosted the likes of Tchaikovsky, Rachmaninoff and Arthur Rubinstein.

Although Emancipation was fifty years in the past, blacks were still viewed as a lower class of people by the majority of white Americans, and black musicians were held in even lower esteem. However, David Mannes, concert-master of the New York Symphony, considered music a universal language. He believed that this concert would bring together whites and blacks in an unconceivable way.

In reality, Mannes was a bit naïve and more hopeful than most white Americans at the time. Whites simply did not understand black music, derisively calling it "coon" music. It was considered vulgar, crude and primitive, little more than chants brought over by African slaves to sing on the plantations. Certainly black music was not equal to symphonies of the current European masters. Coon music obviously had no Brahms, no Puccini, no Gilbert and Sullivan. It probably didn't even have a John Philip Sousa.

The Carnegie Hall concert was a risky venture for Mannes. Barely 1000 tickets had been sold two days before the performance and the Hall held 2800 people. Mannes feared the concert would play to a half-empty house which would not benefit the school, and be a public relations disaster for himself. Despite his secret fear and reservations, Mannes maintained confidence in the talents of the black musician he had chosen to host the event – James Reese Europe.

Jim Europe was head of the first black music society in New York, the Clef Club. Although some members of the Clef Club were professional musicians, Mannes also knew many were "barbers, waiters, red caps, bell-hops," and could only attend rehearsals when they were free from their jobs. Even the discovery that many of these "musicians" could not read music did not weaken his faith in Jim Europe. However, he secretly admitted that his deepest fear was that the concert would be a production of "chaos."

Will Marion Cook was even more skeptical. A brilliant violinist and composer who had studied in Germany and performed for the British royal family, he was moody and quick-tempered. Several years before, Cook became enraged when a newspaper reporter called him "the world's greatest Negro violinist." He sought out the reporter at his office and declared, "I am *not* the world's greatest Negro violinist. I am the greatest violinist in the world!" Cook was hesitant to participate in the Carnegie Hall concert due to his fear that it might "set the Negro race back fifty years." But, he also respected and trusted Jim Europe's musical talent, vision and determination, so Cook decided to take his place in the string section of the Clef Club Orchestra and hope for the best.

The night before the show the New York *Evening Journal* published a story which concluded:

> The *Evening Journal* hopes that many of its readers will attend the concert, enjoy it and perhaps find prejudice based on ignorance give place to sympathy and good will.

The concert sold out. More than one thousand people showed up at the box office that evening. The audience contained the elite of white and black New York society. Music editors from major papers were in attendance. Prominent black ministers, lawyers and businessmen were present. Most of the well-known New York white musicians arrived in a show of support. Hundreds of people were still gathered in front of the box office half an hour before the performance, with more arriving by foot, cab, subway, and bus. All elegantly dressed, blacks and whites were seated together in the grand hall. In most theaters at that time, blacks were still forced to sit in the far left wing or in the balcony. No one was sure what to expect, or how to behave.

When James Reese Europe walked on the stage before the 125 piece Clef Club Orchestra there was palpable anticipation in the audience. He raised his baton to cue his musicians and the first notes of

Reese's composition, "The Clef Club March," filled the hall. American music was never to be the same again.

Gunther Schuller wrote that Reese "had stormed the bastion of the white establishment and made many members of New York's cultural elite aware of Negro music for the first time."

During the first decades of the 20th century America experienced amazing transformations. The country doubled in size, admitting twelve new states. Seven new constitutional amendments became law. The population doubled, as did the number of foreign-born residents. Americans were more diverse, urban and mobile. The Harlem section of New York City became a vibrant neighborhood of African culture. Chicago transformed itself from a dirty immigrant railroad town into the world's sixth largest city and Hollywood's cinematic illusions helped draw thousands of starry-eyed dreamers west to golden California.

But in the stagnant, shabby old city of Charleston, South Carolina, most of the tried and true 19th century conventions still applied. Despite the encroachment of modern life, Charleston preferred that the formal, well-defined rules of conduct be strictly enforced. Manners, decorum and polite conversation in the white parlors were all components of fine southern lifestyle. For descendants of the pre-Civil War aristocracy, these rules of etiquette defined civilized society. Blacks were relegated to secondary roles and still expected to address whites as "massa" and "missus." If they were employed by a white family, blacks were to only use the back door, never the street entrance.

For almost two hundred years racial slavery had

been the most distinctive feature of Charleston life. The slave system was the whole of existence for nearly four million black Southerners. Slavery was so important to the Old South that Confederate Vice-President Alexander Stephens pronounced it the "cornerstone of the new nation." The Jim Crow era of early 20th century America was merely an altered continuation of that same "cornerstone." White Charleston was most comfortable while in charge of the rules with everything - and *everybody* – in its proper place.

No one could anticipate how strongly the political and social shock waves from this Carnegie Hall concert would resonate across America, and ultimately, the world. It changed American music forever as the first step in legitimizing African-American music in the eyes of the general public. The concert was also the catalyst for America's greatest decade of social change by igniting the largest dance craze the world would ever witness.

To prove God possesses a rich sense of irony, the most overt symbol of this social and musical upheaval would bear the name of America's "most mannerly city," Charleston - a city so proudly out-of-step with the times for most of the 20th century that her white citizens preferred looking backward through a distorted lens to the golden past rather than forward to an uncertain future. Within a decade of the Carnegie Hall concert, a fiery maelstrom of change would sweep the world and millions of people would be "doin' the Charleston."

Charleston, S.C., Broad Street, circa 1900. *Courtesy of the Library of Congress*

PART ONE:
THE ORPHAN AID SOCIETY

ONE
Black Lambs

"We do not intend to submit to Negro domination and all the Yankees from Cape Cod to hell can't make us submit to it."
                          - South Carolina Governor Ben Tillman, 1890.

CHRISTMAS TIME IN CHARLESTON RARELY INCLUDED ICE and snow, yet on December 13, 1891 it was bitterly cold. The wisps of snow fluttering from the sky were rare as a full belly and a good job, and about as comforting. Daniel Jenkins trudged against the biting winds with inadequate clothing to insulate his thin frame and stomach growling.

Jenkins worked hard to feed his wife and four children. His most consistent source of income came from his wood-selling business. With bone-chilling cold clamping down on the Holy City, he had another wood order to unload so he hunched over against the wind and plodded toward the railroad yard, unaware he would soon find his true life's calling.

Jenkins opened the box car to stack the wood and discovered four small black children huddled in the box car. Their large, round eyes stared up at him warily from the darkness.

"What are you doing in here?" he asked.

The oldest child, no more than ten, answered, "Suh, we're just trying to stay warm."

"Why aren't you at home?"

"We have no home, suh."

"How long have you been on the streets?"

The children just shrugged. The concept of traditional time did not apply to a street urchin. Hour-by-hour, day-by-day survival was how they measured time.

"You're coming home with me," Jenkins told them. It was the kind of instant decision that defined his life.

Daniel Jenkins was born to slave parents in 1862 in Barnwell County, South Carolina. He was given the surname of his white owners, Dickinson (or Dickson, the records are confusing). What he lacked in formal education was compensated by a nimble mind and innate intelligence. A deeply religious boy, he read the Bible dozens of times and committed many scriptures to memory. He grew to be a tall, physical young man with a strong work ethic.

After Emancipation, many freed blacks took on new names of their own choosing. Daniel chose the surname Jenkins to illustrate his freedom. In September 1881, he married Lena James and worked a farm in Ladson, South Carolina for a few years. He then operated a store and when that failed, Jenkins moved to Charleston and opened the wood-selling business. He found an outlet for his religious convictions by becoming a deacon of the New Tabernacle Fourth Baptist Church on Palmetto

Street. By 1891 Jenkins relied on his religion more than ever to remain hopeful despite the ill winds of change that were blowing across South Carolina for blacks. Emancipation had not flung open the gates to the promised land of freedom. After the initial surges of hope after the Civil War, change quickly stagnated for many blacks.

In March 1867, Congress passed the Reconstruction Acts. No state government existed in the South, except for Tennessee which immediately rejoined the United States. Instead, five military districts were created – North and South Carolina comprised the 2nd Military District.

Requirements for a state's readmission to the Union included: Voter rolls opened to all male citizens; a new state constitution written and submitted to the public for approval; and ratification the 14th Amendment which granted citizenship rights to any person born in the United States.

White Charlestonians were in a state of shock from the flood of post-War changes to their lives. Every taxpayer or voter, black or white, was now eligible to serve on a jury. Judges who refused to seat black jurors were removed from the bench. In all the other Southern states, whites adopted the strategy of electing as many white delegates as possible to their constitutional conventions in order to have some influence on the proceedings. South Carolina whites attempted a different strategy.

The Reconstruction Acts required that a majority of registered voters cast their ballots in favor of a constitutional convention. South Carolina whites registered in large numbers and then boycotted the election, hoping to prevent the required majority. The plan failed by a slim margin, mainly because 85% of black voters did turn out. Native white Carolinians, who had held absolute power for over 200 years, now little influence in writing of the new state constitution.

The 1868 South Carolina Constitution was a remarkable document, bestowing voting rights and educational opportunities "without regard to race or color." However, since the document had been written predominantly by blacks, most white citizens refused to acknowledge its legitimacy. They had no intention of obeying "a Negro constitution, of a Negro government, establishing Negro equality." The white press called it the "Africanization of South Carolina."

The document was ratified by citizens in an 80% black vote. During the first general election the newly organized Republican Party was triumphant throughout South Carolina. Of the 124 delegates to the 1868 Constitutional Convention, seventy-three were black. The thirty-one members of the newly elected Senate included ten blacks. In the House, seventy-eight of the 124 members were black.

Blacks achieved greater political power in South Carolina than any other southern state. From 1867 to 1876, blacks won 52% of the state elections. During that nine year period, six of the fifteen blacks serving in the U.S. Congress were from South Carolina. Whites reacted to the rise of black power with shock and horror. The Assembly was called "the crow congress" or "the monkey show."

A distressing change had struck Charleston. Blacks were living in mansions along the Battery, not as servants, but as legitimate residents while whites were standing in food lines. Former Confederate officers were forced to take employment as trolley drivers and bricklayers, while their former slaves were elected to public office. The War was lost; the Cause was doomed. The entire world had been turned upside down. It was a thunderous earthquake of change whites were determined to challenge.

There are many kinds of warfare and armed combat is only one. The white South may have taken off its uniforms, but the fight continued. A decade after the War, Southern whites conducted a subversive and prolonged attack on what they considered an illegal government foisted on them by interlopers.

In 1882, the "Eight Box Law", written by Charlestonian Edward McCrady, Jr. was passed by the state assembly. The law got its name from the requirement that, on Election Day, there were to be eight separate ballot boxes for different offices. A voter had to be able to read in order to know where to place his ballot at a time when the illiteracy rate among blacks was five times greater than whites. Another provision of the law was that every voter must re-register before June 1, 1882, or be forever banned from voting. Within four years, tens of thousands of black voters in South Carolina were disenfranchised. Voting districts were redrawn, leaving only one majority black district. The state's last 19th century black congressman was defeated for re-election in 1896.

As blacks began to lose their grip on political power, violence against them increased. Lynching became commonplace. A white woman who accused a black man of rape was essentially condemning him to a death sentence. The Newberry *Herald* considered the rape of a white woman by a black man too serious to merit the niceties of a legal trial. Elizabeth Porcher Palmer wrote that she hoped lynching would "have a good effect." In 1889 a mob of whites stormed the Barnwell County jail and murdered eight black prisoners accused of killing a white man.

The winner of the 1890 South Carolina gubernatorial election was racist "Pitchfork" Ben Tillman. He proclaimed:

We do not intend to submit to Negro domination and all the Yankees from Cape Cod to hell can't make us submit to it ... we of the South have never recognized the right of the Negro to govern white men, and we never will.

In 1895 South Carolina ratified yet another State Constitution - the third in thirty years. This constitution was written by the white majority legislature and laid the groundwork for the infamous Jim Crow Era. It defined a black person as anyone having "one-eighth or more Negro blood." In 1896 when the U.S. Supreme Court in *Plessy v. Ferguson* pronounced the doctrine of "separate but equal," South Carolina was ready to implement the policy with zeal.

In 1897 Charleston installed electric streetcars which were segregated. Two years later the legislature mandated legal segregation throughout the state in all public facilities. After 1902 only qualified voters could serve as jurors, meaning few blacks were ever called for duty.

What was not segregated by law was done so by custom. Blacks and whites quickly re-learned the steps of this intricate social dance. A black woman could push a baby carriage for a white family around Colonial Lake, but could not sit on any of the benches. The Battery was off limits to blacks except on the Fourth of July. Blacks were expected to go to the back doors of houses and businesses, and address whites as "Massa, Master, Miss, Missus or Boss." Had they used "Mr." or "Mrs." they would have been considered impudent or "uppity."

In Charleston blacks accounted for 56% of the city's population, the highest black-to-white ratio of any Southern city, but their living conditions were generally second rate and often squalid. According to Dr. Henry Horlbeck, Charleston's chief health officer, deaths among blacks skyrocketed, mainly due to consumption of tainted meat. Unemployment among blacks was rampant, leading to increased "loafers" and a heavy-handed police response to "negro idleness."

Charleston street life at the back door, circa 1900.
Courtesy of the Library of Congress.

This backlash against Negroes was part of the combative atmosphere in which Daniel Jenkins was attempting to raise a family and conduct his wood-selling business. Although he was a forward-thinking man of positive attitude, he found it more difficult to navigate these treacherous societal waters. Despite the reemergence of the white south, Jenkins was optimistic about his immediate future. Not even the discovery of four black waifs in a railroad boxcar a few days before Christmas could damper his spirit.

After delivering the wood, Jenkins walked the children to his home in the gathering dusk and cold. He discovered the children were not blood related; they had banded together out of need. None of them knew where their families were. They had been abandoned, "black lambs" left to fend for themselves in a harsh and cruel world.

Imagine Lena Jenkins' surprise when her husband arrived home with four cold, hungry children and announced, "These children need food and we've got to find them a place to sleep tonight."

Their small house barely had sleeping room for Daniel, Lena and their four children, much less four more children's mouths to feed. Lena managed to serve bowls of thin hot stew with stale cornbread. It was a feast for the street urchins.

The next Sunday Jenkins preached a special sermon at the New Tabernacle Fourth Baptist Church. Titled "The Harvest is Great but the Laborers Are Few," it was a passionate appeal to the congregation "to help these and other unfortunate children." The donated money did not last long; it paid for some food and clothing and the rental of a small shack at 660 King Street. It was a place for the children to sleep, but that was all. More money was needed but most of the members of the Fourth Tabernacle Church were just as poor as Jenkins.

For several months the fledgling orphanage operated day-to-day with few funds. On July 21, 1892

Jenkins received a charter from the state of South Carolina to operate the Orphan Aid Society. At this point Jenkins and Lena were taking care of several dozen black lambs. Jenkins knew he needed help; the Society needed a substantial and dependable source of money. He hoped the city of Charleston would be a significant benefactor. After all, city authorities and elite citizens had a 100-year history of generously supporting the Charleston Orphan House.

Charleston Orphan House (for whites) established in 1790.
Courtesy of the Library of Congress

The Orphan House, built in 1790, was the first municipal orphanage in the United States. It was charged with the task of providing a structured and safe environment for needy, abandoned and orphaned white children. Jenkins hoped the city would be halfway as generous toward the black lambs of the fledging Orphan Aid Society.

He approached the Charleston City Council and told them of his plan to rid the streets of its roaming, thieving, "Wild Children" by establishing the Society. He told the council the children in his care would receive food and clothing, Christian instruction and training in an honest trade in order to prepare them to be productive citizens.

The council voted to give him a one-time $50 donation.

TWO
Growing Pains

"Hard work and plenty of corn bread and molasses produce
healthy children."   – Rev. Daniel Jenkins.

IN OCTOBER 1892 THE NEW TABERNACLE FOURTH
Baptist Church promoted Jenkins from deacon to
minister, but his main focus remained the Orphan Aid
Society. Dismayed by the paltry gift of $50 from the
city of Charleston, Rev. Jenkins had no recourse other
than to scrounge for alternative sources of money. His
ultimate dream for the Society was to establish a self-
sufficient community, where his black lambs would be
able to produce their own food on a farm, make their
own clothes and bake their own bread. He aimed to
not only teach the children reading and arithmetic,
but also practical trade skills such as sewing,
blacksmithing, printing and shoemaking. He wrote:

> To allow orphan and destitute children to sit up in long
> dresses on public charity with a flower garden around
> them, doing nothing, is not in my mind. I have worked
> from a boy all my days. Hard work and plenty of corn
> bread and molasses produce healthy children.

This idea was no doubt inspired by the similar
approach taken by Booker T. Washington and his
Tuskegee Institute, but to realize his dream, Jenkins
needed money, to purchase land. His monthly appeals
to the city, churches, and other local charities
produced little in the way of hard cash. So Jenkins

made a personal appeal to several local white men known for their charitable ways – in particular, Major Augustine Smythe and George W. Williams.

Smythe had a colorful career during the War Between the States. As a teenager he procured a seat in the balcony of Charleston's South Carolina Institute Hall on the night of December 20, 1860. Over the next three hours Smythe watched the members of the South Carolina legislature sign the Ordinance of Secession, officially removing the state of South Carolina from the Union and establishing an independent republic, ultimately called the Confederate States of America. The raucous celebration after that historic event spilled into the Charleston streets, with men whooping, drinking whiskey and shooting pistols in the air. Smythe had the calm foresight to make his way through the crowd to the stage and remove the inkwell and pen which had been used to sign the Ordinance. These items today are in the collection at the Confederate Museum, housed in Market Hall on Meeting Street.

Smythe then joined the signal corps in Charleston, and was stationed as a lookout in St. Michael's church steeple. He managed to dodge Union artillery shells passing within ten feet of his roost. He related the conditions of Charleston during the War in a series of wry and eloquent letters to family members. Having led a charmed life, by 1890 he had become a successful lawyer and a man widely known for his generous spirit to the less fortunate.

George W. Williams was one of the richest men in post-war Charleston. He began his business career as a young man by importing sugar and molasses from the West Indies, branching out into shipping and banking. During the War he financed several successful blockade running enterprises, surviving the conflict with his fortune intact; his net worth in 1865 was estimated to be at $1 million – a staggering sum in the defeated South. In 1876 he spent $200,000 for the construction of a 24,000 square foot home at 16 Meeting Street, today called the Calhoun Mansion. A devout Methodist, adamantly opposed to slavery, Williams gave huge sums of money for construction and restoration of several churches, both white and black congregations.

Rev. Jenkins hoped these two white men could help him in his quest for financial stability for his Orphan Aid Society, and indeed Smythe and Williams came through. They convinced Rev. Parker, Dean of the South Carolina Medical College, to grant Jenkins the use of the abandoned Old Marine Hospital, at 20 Franklin Street.

The Old Marine Hospital, considered Charleston's first Gothic Revival structure, was constructed in 1831 by Robert Mills, a Charleston-born architect who later became internationally renowned for designing the Washington Monument. The building was designed as a hospital for sick and disabled merchant sailors. During the War the Between the States it became a Confederate military hospital and subsequently a teaching hospital for the Medical School. By the 1890s the facility sat empty.

The Marine Hospital was not an ideal location for an Orphan House due to its proximity to the City Jail and Lunatic Asylum. The nocturnal sounds of the imprisoned and infirm could be easily heard by the orphans, but the Marine Hospital was a solid building, and Jenkins was past the point of refusing any legitimate offer.

After some minor repairs. Jenkins moved the Orphan Aid Society into its new home. He had an office on the first floor, and the former hospital wards became children's dormitories. Jenkins now had a roof over the heads of his black lambs, but he still had to clothe, feed and educate them.

Corner of Franklin & Magazine Streets, Charleston, SC., circa 1857. Oldest images the jail (left) and Marine Hospital (right). *Courtesy of the Library of Congress*

Not all Jenkins' kids were technically orphans. Some were babies of single women who dropped their children off at the front door on Franklin Street. Others were unruly, wild children who could no longer be controlled by their parents. Jenkins took responsibility for these kids, attempting to instill discipline and teach them a useful skill.

Jabbo Smith (b. 1908, trumpet, and coronet), himself an unruly child, recalled:

> Jenkins was strict. At six o'clock in the morning there would be a prayer meeting, and after that the roll would be read, and if you did anything bad the day before you'd be called up and tied to a post and whipped with a rope or a piece of rein.

Tommy Benford (b. 1905, drums) started on the alto-horn and trombone before becoming the Orphanage Band's ace drummer. He remembered:

> Discipline was strict, but fair. If one of the kids did something wrong and got caught we had a system just like a courthouse with the old man ... Mr. Jenkins, he was beautiful, as judge, and some of the older boys as jury. And you went before them and got tried, and if you got convicted, you got so many lashes. My brother was *always* in trouble; he was in court practically every other day!

Cat Anderson, (b. 1916, trumpet) played with Duke Ellington for more than 20 years. He recalled:

> The teaching was stern, and we got many whippings. We had to do exactly what the teachers said. To kids today the way they used a whip might seem cruel, but it was part of the times. Having gone through that it always seemed a damned shame to me that so many fine musicians gave up afterwards.

In the first two years the Orphanage enrollment increased to 360 boys and girls. By 1896 that number had grown to 536, with a staff of eight teachers and two laborers. Local newspapers called the institution the "Jenkins Orphanage" and referred to the reverend as "the Orphan Man." Jenkins became famous around Charleston for constantly soliciting donations, promoting various ideas for fund-raising. The hand-to-mouth existence was physically and spiritually taxing for everyone involved, not the least Jenkins, who carried on his shoulders the welfare of so many people.

Desperate people often make impulsive decisions and in 1894 Jenkins' latest fundraising idea was a particularly audacious one for a non-musician: teach some of the children to play brass instruments and have them perform on the streets for coins.

Two views of the Old Marine Hospital, 20 Franklin Street, Charleston.
TOP: Front view with jail in background. BOTTOM: Side view.
Courtesy of the Library of Congress

Jenkins made a public appeal for old musical instruments which proved to be more productive than his previous calls for money. As the old brass instruments and broken drums were delivered to the Marine Hospital, he now had the dilemma of teaching the children how to play. With absolutely no musical knowledge himself, Jenkins hired two local musicians as tutors: P.M. 'Hatsie' Logan and Francis Eugene Mikell whose ideas of musical instruction would become the standard among jazz players in the early 20th century.

Mikell had studied and graduated from the Avery Institute, the premiere school for blacks in Charleston. He was a versatile musician who played proficiently in several families of instruments – reeds, brass and percussion. Hatsie Logan was a brilliantly instinctive musician. Together the two men began to lead classes in traditional music reading skills. One of their instructional innovations was to teach actual instrumental techniques as a group, rather than in private sessions. Thus several students at a time would listen to the instructions for the coronet, trombone, clarinet, and tuba resulting in dozens of children becoming adept on several different instruments. These multi-instrumentalists served as a great inspiration for jazz artists of subsequent generations.

In *The Music of Black Americans: A History* by Eileen Southern, Mikell is described as a "master teacher ... highly regarded for both his original compositions and his arrangements."

Alonzo Mills was one of their first students, and when he inherited the teaching position at the Jenkins Orphanage early in the 20th century, he continued to use Mikell and Logan's musical instruction method. One of the Orphanage's most famous students, Jabbo Smith (trumpet and coronet) recalled:

> When we were being taught we would get our lessons in together. Mr. Mills would explain things on a blackboard, and we'd have to sing the notes he'd written, then each player had to play their instruments and you

sat there while he learnt - so, everyone in the band ended up by knowing almost as much about the instrument that the other fellow played. I guess everyone in the band could play trumpet, trombone, alto-horn, baritone horn and tuba if they needed to.

Tommy Benford (drums) remembered:

They did things right at the Orphanage and the first thing they did was teach you to read music ... that's what I tell the kids today, get your groundwork right, and you can go anywhere. When you start on a black-board as a beginner, reading notes from the boards like you're reading a story, then taking the next step forward, that's a sound start. If you can play that next step, you take the next step, and so on. After a while, you can play anything. They also gave us a good general education and you worked at different trades like shoe-making and tailoring.

Cat Anderson (trumpet) recalled:

I began on trombone, but my arms weren't long enough for the sixth and seventh positions. From that, I went to the baritone horn and the upright bass horn. I also played drums, cymbals, kettle drums, and the alto and E flat horn, and the melephone.

Alonzo Mills was tall, and strict. Mr. Blake was short and fierce. I kept well out of his way. Amos Gaillard was also a strict disciplinarian, and he had a louder voice than any of them. He would come into band rehearsal and put a brick down on the table, then he'd roar, "I'll throw this at the first boy who makes a mistake." It was tough training and no short cuts.

As I look back on the teaching now, I know that it was inadequate in some places, that even rudiments were not always taught properly. But the school was run on charity and the pay was small, so there was a limit to what could be expected.

They sat you in front of a blackboard on which were the scales and the five lines and spaces of the staff. I don't remember them teaching about breathing or correct embouchure, but we all helped one another, and to a large extent we were self-taught. We'd sit down and talk, and find things out ourselves. That accounts for a lot of individuality.

Under Mikell and Logan's strict tutelage, the ragtag brass band was soon ready to make an appearance on the Charleston streets, and what a sight they must have been to the public: A group of a dozen black children, all knobby knees and sharp elbows, wearing ill-fitting tattered military uniforms rescued from the trash heap at the South Carolina Military College of South Carolina, The Citadel; carrying percussion instruments with their drumheads repaired by tape and cloth; coronets, tubas and trombones that were dented and green with tarnish.

What they played that afternoon on the Charleston sidewalks to a bemused and astonished crowd of shoppers and businessmen no one knows. But after the performance, Rev. Jenkins stepped forward and asked for donations, holding out his hat. The money collected must have been enough to give him confidence, because soon these impromptu performances became daily occurrences on the streets, and while they helped infuse some cash into the Orphanage coffers, the lack of money continued to weigh heavily on his mind.

As another source of income Jenkins purchased a used printing press in 1893. Soon, the Society was printing advertisements and brochures for local businesses. Within a year Jenkins began to publish his own newspaper - the *Charleston Messenger* - and marketed it toward the black population. The *Messenger* created another stream of income and helped keep the Orphanage in the public's mind.

Charleston, S.C., circa 1900. *Courtesy of the Library of Congress*

THREE
A Trip To England

"…to let loose a brass band of thirteen Negro children upon an urban population suffering from nerves is likely to create almost as many orphans as it would relieve."

- London *Daily Telegraph*, September 9, 1895

JENKINS' IDEA FOR AN ORPHANAGE BRASS BAND WAS inspired by two 19th century traditions - the minstrel show and the municipal brass band.

In the 1880s and 90s the typical touring black minstrel show usually had a brass band as part of its act. The popular show, *In Old Kentucky*, featured a boys' brass band called the Whangdoodles - a Pickaninny Brass Band. On many occasions the Jenkins Orphanage Band would bill itself as "A Pickaninny Band." Rev. Jenkins would have certainly been aware of these types of shows.

There was also the tradition of municipal brass bands. Due to the enormous popularity of John Philip Sousa and the U.S. Marine band, brass band music became the era's most popular form of musical entertainment. Well into the 20th century almost every town in America had its own brass band that gave concerts and marched in parades, often performing Sousa-written tunes. In fact, one of Broadway's great musicals, Meredith Willson's *The Music Man,* is built around the idea of a municipal band.

Most municipal bands were an extension of

regimental or military bands. During the War Between the States several black regiments in the Union army organized their own regimental bands. After the war they became independent, touring and performing public concerts. The Jenkins Brass Band playing on Charleston streets before 1910 fit firmly within this tradition.

107ᵗʰ U.S. Colored Infantry Band, circa 1865. *Courtesy of the Library of Congress*

In the fall of 1893 a tropical storm swept along the Carolina coast. The Orphanage building sustained significant damage, and Rev. Jenkins faced a debt of $1700 (about $10,000 at present) for roof repair. It was a major blow. He'd scraped for three years to fund the Aid Society. It always seemed as if one thing after another knocked him back. Desperate times called for desperate and creative solutions. Jenkins wrote:

> I took 18 of the orphans North, to play and give entertainments, all being green we scarcely made our expenses, and the big debt looked up before me. I felt I would rather die than return to Charleston without the money to cancel the debt.

With a band master and the kids, Jenkins boarded a steamship in Charleston to New York for financial gain. The ship line's standard stops along the way included Wilmington, Norfolk, Baltimore and Philadelphia and the band performed at each stop. However, in New York Jenkins realized that he had only managed to dig himself into a deeper hole. In addition, on April 9, 1894 back in Charleston, Lena gave birth to another son, Edmund Thornton, which only added to the minister's monetary burden.

Listening to the counsel of "some good white friends while in a spirit of despondency", Jenkins decided to take the band to England. Friends had advised that he "would get barrels of money."

Although having "only half enough to pay our way," Jenkins "leaped without a dollar." The ship's captain agreed to transport the orphan band to England at half fare. In exchange the boys would entertain passengers during the voyage. However, most of the boys became so seasick it was impossible for them to perform regularly. Jenkins stated "in less than half hours' time after getting on the ship we became seasick and remained so until the day before we landed."

London of 1895 was city of contrasts. Queen Victoria had been on the throne for fifty-eight years and the city's population was more than 4 million. Oscar Wilde's *The Importance of Being Earnest* was a big hit on the London stage. H.G. Wells' *The War of the Worlds* was released to great acclaim. Newspaper stories about Jack the Ripper were still common, seven years after the killings had stopped.

The city was also suffering growing pains from the Industrial Revolution - affluent developments and modern office buildings stood side-by-side with disease-ridden slums. More than half the citizens lived in horrific circumstances. The air was heavy with foul smoke from coal-fired furnaces; raw sewage dumped straight into the Thames River lead to poor sanitation and widespread disease.

The Jenkins' kids found the London streets colorful and crowded. London street entertainment consisted of adult acrobats, donkey rides, organ grinders with performing monkeys, hurdy-gurdy musicians and low rent Punch and Judy shows.

What a sight the Jenkins band must have been! An interesting diversion for the locals: A group of black American orphan children dressed in ill-fitting and faded uniforms, playing military marches, sonatas, popular songs and Irish jigs, all accented by African dancing and drumming. The "bandmaster" was a seven year old boy, who marched at the head of the musicians with a baton in his hands. To the hooting amusement of the crowd, he danced, cavorted and gyrated in his attempts to "direct" the band, who mostly ignored his instructions and played wildly. The crowds were usually large and unruly, boisterous and often blocked traffic on the already congested streets and sidewalks. A more exotic show could not be found. Between songs Rev. Jenkins would step forward and appeal for money.

Coincidentally, Major Augustine Smythe, who had been instrumental in helping Jenkins procure the Old Marine Hospital for housing, was on holiday in London with his family. One day the Smythe family was taking a stroll in London when they heard music on the street. The two Smythe boys, Cleves, 13, and Austen, 11, recognized the familiar sound. "That's the Jenkins band!" they shouted, racing around the corner and fighting their way through the throng of people. In Charleston the social and racial codes would have prevented the two Southern men from ever greeting one another, but in London, Smythe and his family were happy to acknowledge their fellow "home folks." Jenkins was also happy to accept a donation from the Major.

London, England, circa 1900. *Courtesy of the Library of Congress*

Not long after the Smythe family departed some London police - Bobbies - arrived to disperse the crowd. Jenkins was issued a subpoena to appear before a magistrate. The charge: "Exploitation of child labor."

Jenkins wrote, "On the next morning every newspaper published that we were stranded."

Major Augustine Smythe, a lawyer, read about the trouble in the paper. He composed a letter to the English authorities vouching for the Reverend's character and loaned Jenkins money to tide him over until the court date. From that day forward, the Smythe family law firm handled the Orphanage's legal business pro bono.

On September 8, 1895 Reverend Jenkins appeared in the magistrate's courtroom on Bow

Street, followed by more than a dozen of his charges, all under the age of fourteen. The next day the London *Daily Telegraph* filed the following story:

> Just before the rising of the court, a coloured man entered with a troupe of thirteen little Negro boys whose ages ranged from five to about fourteen years. The man in charge of the boys said he was the Reverend D. J. Jenkins, a Baptist Minister of Charlestown [sic], America, and he wished to make an application to the magistrate.
>
> On entering the witness box, the appellant stated that he had come over to this country to raise funds for an Orphanage with which he was connected in Charlestown. He had brought with him his boys, who all played on brass instruments, and his object was to let the boys play their band in the public streets, after which he lectured and collected money for the Orphanage. He had been stopped that morning whilst thus engaged, and told that he was liable to be taken into custody for what he was doing, and he wished to be informed whether that was so.
>
> Sir John Bridge told applicant that of course he must not cause an obstruction in the public thoroughfares or the police would interfere. Inspector Sara, who was on duty in the court, pointed out that under an Act of Parliament no child under the age of eleven years was allowed to sing, play or perform for profit in the public streets.
>
> **Applicant:** But could not an exception be made in my case, seeing the object I have in view?
>
> **Sir John Bridges:** Certainly not, the law makes no exceptions.
>
> Applicant then said he was without money to take the children back to America. Sir John Bridge said he had no fund which was available for such a purpose, and advised applicant to apply to the American consulate. Inspector Sara said he would send an officer with the Applicant to the Society for the Prevention of

Cruelty to Children where probably he could obtain assistance, and Sir John Bridges gave a sovereign to applicant for present necessities, for which he appeared very grateful.

This news item provoked an editorial on Page 4 of the same issue, which concluded:

Much may be done, no doubt, to raise money for an Orphanage; but to let loose a brass band of thirteen Negro children upon an urban population suffering from nerves is likely to create almost as many orphans as it would relieve.

After the court appearance and publicity, Jenkins was approached by the owner of a local London theater who offered to feature the Orphan Band on stage. Jenkins agreed, but then changed his mind once he appealed to local churches who eagerly invited him to speak during their services. From the pulpit of the Metropolitan Tabernacle, Jenkins pled for help and more than £100 was raised in a matter of moments. He repeated this successful appeal at several more churches before steaming back home to Charleston, where he paid off the debt.

Christmas morning of 1895, Jenkins awakened the band members before dawn and marched them across town to Major Smythe's house on Legare Street. They played traditional Christmas music on the sidewalk, honoring him for his assistance. Without his help they would have remained stranded in London. For several decades, this became a Christmas tradition - the Jenkins Band arriving at the Smythe house on Christmas morning, and according to Jane Wells, Major Smythe's grand-daughter – performing a "marvelous noise."

Jenkins Band in Florida. *Author's Collection*

FOUR
The Jenkins Band Across America

"On the street corner it was every tub on its bottom, every kid doing his own thing. All you needed to know was the melody, and then you'd take off from there. They've been saying all these years that jazz started in New Orleans, and all that, but what were we doing?"
— Jabbo Smith

THE JENKINS ORPHANAGE BAND RETURNED FROM ITS London adventure with a reputation. Once back in Charleston they discovered that the entire *Daily Telegraph* editorial and story of Reverend Daniel Jenkins' arrest had been published in the local *News & Courier* on Sept. 21, 1895. It was the most local publicity the band and Orphanage had ever received and raised the awareness of its cause among most of the prominent citizens.

More white families began to donate money and food to the Orphanage but it was still not enough. Jenkins realized that in order to raise the kind of money they needed, the band would have to travel. Due to the influx of visitors to Florida during the holidays and winter months, Jenkins asked his sister Dora, who lived in Jacksonville, to help plan a trip. She obtained permission for the visiting musicians to be housed with members of local black churches. Official permits were procured from the Mayor, Chamber of Commerce and Police to ensure that all street performances were legal.

The Florida trip was such a financial success that

Jenkins and his staff began to plan tours to other states. Always an opportunist, Jenkins established a touring schedule that took them regularly north to New York and other east coast cities in the summer and south to Florida during the winter.

During this time the band's music became more ragtime oriented. The kids began to match their physical performances to the music, creating a minstrel-style vaudeville show on the street corners – a prancing "director" and a dozen or so kids dancing and gyrating.

Jabbo Smith (trumpet) recalled:

> We played on street corners all over Charleston, and we'd get sent to New York and Jacksonville and Savannah and suchlike to do the same. We also gave concerts at the churches in those places, at eight o'clock in the evening … overtures and marches. On the street corner it was every tub on its bottom, every kid doing his own thing. All you needed to know was the melody, and then you'd take off from there. They've been saying all these years that jazz started in New Orleans, and all that, but what were we doing?

Trombonist Trummy Young, who played with Charlie Parker and Louis Armstrong, claims that two of his first musical heroes were Jenkins' musicians, John Nick and Sylvester Briscoe. Briscoe especially became something of a legend. Young remembered, "Briscoe was a left-handed player. He could blow, and drink lightening, and he was the marryingest man, married about eight women."

Pianist Mary Lou Williams worked with Briscoe, and in 1954 she gave a description of his unusual skills and playing style to writer Max Jones:

> On trombone we had the fabulous Sylvester Briscoe

who could - and did - play more horn with his foot on the slide than most cats can do with their hands. Our Tiger Rag featured Briscoe's crazy act of playing trombone with both hands behind his back, the instrument somehow wedged between his mouth and the floor. This may sound impossible, but it is the truth. I never knew how he did it, and never saw anyone who could imitate him.

Dickie Wells, a former trombonist for the Count Basie Orchestra, remembers the first time he saw the Jenkins Band:

I first saw and heard it [Jenkins Band] in Louisville, Jabbo Smith and Gus Aiken were in it. Briscoe was a short, tubby, left-handed guy, and he used to throw his horn around and play louder than the whole band. All the kids followed him. When he played dances he would sometimes put his right hand behind him, hold his horn with his left, then bend over and go along pushing and skidding the slide on the floor. Briscoe would also take the horn apart and play with just the mouthpiece, then assemble it bit by bit until he had it all together again.

By the turn of the 20th century the Orphanage's finances were stable. The biggest positive change occurred when Deacon Joseph Wild of Brooklyn donated a 100 acre farm in Ladson, South Carolina to the Orphanage, about 40 miles north of Charleston. This gave Jenkins the opportunity to branch out. The farm was called the Jenkins Institutional Reform-atory and operated like a boot camp. Jenkins convinced Charleston judges and court officers to hand over youthful black offenders to him instead of sending them to jail. Boys who were rough, defiant and violent were sent to the farm to work and the Orphanage began to grow much of its own food. This allowed Jenkins to take in more children and expand the training and education of his charges. By 1900 the children were able to learn the following trades: carpentry, tailoring, shoe-making and repair, laundering, printing and dress-making. Jenkins also opened a bakery called the Poor Boy Bread Company which produced a thousand loaves of bread a day and were sold in stores throughout the city

Jabbo Smith remembered, "The Orphanage was famous all over that part of the South. Mothers used to use it as a weapon: 'You watch out, now, or I'll send you to Jenkins!'"

Tommy Benford recalled: "The Reverend was alright to me, but if anyone got out of line, then he'd whip their ass."

However, the main fund-raising operation continued to be the band, taking in more than $9000 in six months on the road. Competition was fierce to join the band, due to the prestige and fun. No matter how hard the musical tutors were, or how tough the discipline was on the road, most kids would rather play in the band than work the farm in sweltering southern heat. During rehearsal, an older musician holding a drumstick would stand behind the younger boys. Each time the beginner made a mistake, he would be cracked in the head with the drumstick, but it was better than the Reformatory farm.

But there were also perks for being in the band. Tommy Benford recalled that:

> We didn't get any pocket money in those days, but people listening to the band, who had missed the official collection, or those who didn't want to wait, used to toss money at our feet, on the sidewalk. If it fell near you, you picked it up and kept it. The Orphanage knew this was going on, but they turned a blind eye, they knew none of the boys were buying whisky or cigarettes, they were just using the money for candy,

soda and food.

The band was divided into two or three different marching groups according to musical ability. Jenkins #1 got the prime assignments to New York, Chicago and Boston. Jenkins #2 traveled to Baltimore, Washington DC, Jacksonville, and St. Augustine. Jenkins #3 played in Charleston and across South Carolina. Each band traveled as a unit consisting of a manager (often a minister), a cook and valet to take care of the uniforms and equipment. As the years progressed, a girls' choir also traveled with the bands to sing religious hymns and spirituals; the girls had their own female chaperones.

Tommy Benford recalled:

> We played all types of music. Any type of music you can mention, we played - from rags to marches to hymns; different songs, different types of music. Everyone you know who came out of that school was a wonderful musician ... we played all over America and all over the world.
>
> They had three bands in the Orphanage, and we made it into the top band, the Jenkins Orphanage Number One Band they called it. Bill and I were in that band along with the three Aitken [Aiken] brothers, Lucius, Gene and Gus ... and we played all those marches and overtures –*Poet and Pleasant, William Tell* and so on ... That band was so far advanced, and this was around 1914 to 1916. They used to call us a jazz band, and we used to feature blues too ... so the first band I was ever in in my life played jazz and blues!

Although the band often traveled on the Clyde Line ships, with passenger service between New York and Charleston, Jenkins purchased used buses and trucks to haul the children and equipment around to cities that were not along the coast.

A routine was established. When they arrived in

town the band manager checked with the mayor and
chief of police to get permission to perform. The
typical stay lasted for two days. The kids played until
a crowd gathered and then the manager collected
money. They would march several blocks in another
direction and perform again, concentrating their
performances in white neighborhoods because blacks
had little money. They also discovered the more the
kids hammed it up for the whites, the more money
was collected. Kids began to work on their own
routines, dancing and prancing, juggling their drum
sticks and tossing their instruments to each other as
they played, switching from trombone to trumpet and
back to trombone.

When the collections faltered they moved to
another town. This went on for two months at a time,
six days a week, taking Sundays off. On the Sabbath
the manager found a black church to visit and the
kids would perform during the service. Usually, a
special collection was taken for them. In the Jim Crow
South band members were forced to sleep in churches,
in the homes of church members or many times on the
bus itself.

Through the years the band developed several
annual routines: a Christmas Eve night concert for
the prisoners next door at the City Jail; the Christmas
morning serenade for the Smythe family and the
Labor Day concert at Abyssinian Baptist Church in
New York City.

Each time the band returned to Charleston they
stopped the bus several blocks away and marched to
20 Franklin Street with as much fanfare as possible –
like triumphant troops returning home. Band
members became hometown heroes. Local children
often begged their parents to enroll them in the
Jenkins Orphanage, so they could play in the band.
Some children were heard wishing they were orphans

so they could join the band.

After almost a decade of holding off poverty by hard work and sheer will, Jenkins himself was now financially comfortable. With the various streams of income successfully pouring money into the Orphanage's coffers, he could pay himself a salary; he become the sole American importer for Collins brand of English band instruments, which also generated a steady income. He lived in a comfortable house with two servants and wore proper clothes befitting a man of his position. He owned a nice automobile and a driver who transported the "Orphan Man" up and down the east coast between Florida and New York to check on the bands out on tour. One newspaper called him "a savior to the abandoned children of the race." He had become a prominent figure in the South, particularly among the blacks and clergy. Even among whites, Jenkins was a man who garnered respect.

However, even though the Orphan Aid Society was stable and successful, a negative turn came for Jenkins' immediate family: his wife, Lena, contracted tuberculosis which left her weak and confined to bed for long stretches of time. Given the nature of the illness, and the threat of exposure to the children, Lena was forced to give up her many duties at the Orphanage – cook, nurse, maid and surrogate mother.

Due to his lack of formal schooling, Jenkins had always relied on more educated people to conduct his correspondence. With Lena's retirement from Orphanage duties, he hired eighteen-year old Ella Harleston as his secretary. Ella's father was Edwin "Captain" Harleston, a successful mulatto businessman, who considered his family to be one of the elite black families in Charleston. He was one of eight children born to William Harleston, white owner of "The Hut" plantation, and his black slave, Kate Wilson. After the

War Between the States, Harleston bought his mulatto family a house in Charleston. The children were raised well above the existing standards of most blacks of that time; they were educated and employed in the few professional jobs available to blacks. Captain Harleston operated a thriving shipping business, hence the nickname, and eventually he founded a successful funeral home.

Ella, the Captain's youngest daughter, had recently graduated from the Avery Institute, the only secondary school in Charleston for blacks. Her older sister Kitty already worked at the Orphanage, and the Reverend was delighted to employ the younger sister also. Ella was a better typist and writer so she soon became Jenkins' personal secretary, handling all his correspondence.

The Captain, however, was adamantly opposed to his daughters working for Jenkins, mainly because the Reverend was poor, uneducated and 100% black - too black to be the equal of the Harlestons. The Captain viewed association with the Orphanage House as a step down in society for his light-skinned daughters.

Ella, however, thrived in her role. She was soon keeping long hours at the Orphan House, often working late into the night with Rev. Jenkins. She admired the Orphan Man and his devotion to his cause. One night when Rev. Jenkins kissed her, Ella did not protest.

"The Charleston Pickaninny Band," as the Jenkins Band was often referred to in the press, appeared at the 1901 Pan-American Exposition in Buffalo, New York to great acclaim. Part of the Expo featured an "OLD PLANTATION", which was described in the program as:

> Reproducing a veritable old plantation in its minutest detail, and giving the visitor an interesting glimpse of the sunny South. The slave quarters and log cabins were brought from the South, and are occupied by genuine darkey families and their pickaninnies. Dancing and other pastimes dear to the old Negro are given at the theater, included in the attraction.

No doubt the presence of the Jenkins Band – *genuine* pickaninnies - raised the popularity of the Old Plantation exhibit.

On September 6, 1901 President William McKinley visited the Expo and attended an organ concert in The Temple of Music. While he was greeting the public after the concert he was shot in the chest and stomach. Following surgery it appeared that McKinley was recovering, but then gangrene set in. Eight days later McKinley died, the official cause of death listed as gangrene of the walls of the stomach and pancreas.

Vice President Teddy Roosevelt was vacationing in the Adirondack Mountains of New York when he learned that the President was not expected to survive. Roosevelt immediately set out on a frantic 15-hour journey to Buffalo. He arrived in Buffalo a few hours after McKinley died. In his haste to reach Buffalo, Roosevelt had not taken time to gather any formal attire. Just prior to the swearing-in as the 26th President of the United States, he borrowed a long frock coat, trousers, patent leather shoes and waistcoat.

A hastily arranged inaugural ceremony was held at the Buffalo home of Roosevelt's friend Ansley Wilcox. The Pickaninny Band from Charleston performed for the assembled crowd, marking an incredible milestone for the Jenkins Orphanage. Ten years before Rev. Jenkins created an orphanage for out of sheer determination and now he had the honor of watching some of his lambs perform for the President of the United States.

Pan-American Expo midway, Buffalo, New York.
Courtesy of the Library of Congress

Their success at the Buffalo Expo led to an invitation for the Band to perform at the 1904 Louisiana Purchase Exposition in St. Louis, opened by Senator William Howard Taft. The future president of the United States was impressed by the antics and music of the band.

Rev. Jenkins immediately took advantage of this newly found success. He persuaded the owners of the Clyde Line to let the band sail at reduced rates, saving the Orphanage money. In exchange, the band entertained the passengers en route to their destinations. The Charleston City Council was so impressed with Jenkins' success that it increased its annual contribution from $200 to $500. Soon, Jenkins set up a Northern headquarters at 147 132nd Street, New York City, where he could live and schedule the band's summer events in Connecticut, New Jersey and Pennsylvania.

It was sometime during 1905 that Rev. Jenkins and his twenty-two year old secretary, Ella Harleston, began a sexual affair, a potentially volatile situation given his moral standing in the community. Then came the inevitable. In the spring of 1906, Ella Harleston informed Jenkins that she was pregnant with his child. It was a scandal of immense proportions which threatened to destroy ten years' of hard work and sacrifice. How eager would people be to support the Orphanage when the Orphan Man himself had impregnated a young woman in his employ, while his wife was slowly dying of tuberculosis?

Pan-American Expo midway, Buffalo, New York.
Courtesy of the Library of Congress

FIVE
Lost Lamb in England

"Many were the miles we pushed buses which broke down, and many were the nights when we slept on the buses."
— Rev. John Dowling of the Jenkins Orphanage

THE ORPHAN MAN'S SON, EDMUND THORNTON JENKINS, had become a serious musician. Edmund, called "Jenks" by everyone, received private music lessons in Charleston from a white man, Mr. Dorsey, and quickly mastered the clarinet, piano and violin. Jenks was a short, frail and seemingly aloof young man who dressed formally. Rev. Jenkins insisted that his son not only work as a musical instructor for the orphans, but also travel with the #1 band, which the young man resented. Jenks felt that leading a group of ragamuffin orphans who mugged and strutted their way through demeaning street performances was beneath him. And just as certainly, the kids in the band made fun of the dandified, serious-minded Jenks.

In 1910, Jenks enrolled in the music program at Morehouse College in Atlanta, Georgia. He was relieved to be free from the day-to-day indignity of spending so much time with the crude and rowdy orphans. He studied under Benjamin Brawley and the violin master Kemper Herrold, whose most famous student was Fletcher Henderson, later the arranger for the Bennie Goodman Orchestra and one of the most legendary figures in jazz. At Morehouse, Jenks was exposed to European classical music more than ever.

Brawley remembered his first meeting with Jenks:

> I well remember him as he came into the room now more than sixteen years later. I can see again the tight little black coat with a dozen medals that even then he had won, all in full array. Evidently here was something different from the ordinary boy who came to enter the academy, and for a moment I could hardly suppress a smile. For him, however, it was serious business; so I examined him and assigned him a class.
>
> He remained at Morehouse for six years. For two of those years I was away. One day, however, on passing down a street in Boston, I saw him leading the little boys of the Jenkins Orphanage Band. He often had to direct them and sometimes he told me that the work was very taxing; yet I could not forget how much it did to give him the all-around equipment that he afterwards possessed. On my return to Atlanta I found that, under the tutelage of Mr. Harreld, he had become even more proficient. With three instruments – the piano, the violin and the clarinet – his acquaintance was not less than masterly. Even so we did not appreciate him sufficiently. But when is genius fully appreciated?

During 1907-1912, the Jenkins band kept a hectic touring schedule, with as many as thirty members traveling during its summer tours. For the winter dates in Florida, the band was less than twenty, so that the younger members could concentrate on their classroom studies and vocational training.

Cat Anderson remembers:

> The Number One and Number Two bands used to travel a lot . . . always with a superintendent from the school in attendance. They would play dance music,

overtures, and marches on the street, and after each tune the superintendent would make a speech, and tell what the school was for and what it was doing. Then a hat would be passed through the audience. It was the same principal as the Salvation Army's. The bands were usually fifteen or sixteen pieces, sometimes more.

Many of these trips for the #1 band included stints in Chicago, which then became the base for trips to Gary, Evanston and other surrounding cities, just as New York was home base for trips to Newark and Hackensack. Tours of the North usually lasted from June to September. Labor Day featured the annual show at the Abyssinian Baptist Church, whose pastor, Adam Clayton Powell, wholeheartedly supported the Jenkins Orphanage. Then they headed back to Charleston for a couple of months before the tourist season in Florida picked up.

Although much improved, the financial situation for the orphanage was always worrisome. Reverend Dowling, one of the teachers at the school remembers that when it was time for a tour Jenkins would tell them, "Alright go!"

Wasn't no use asking for money. He'd tell you, "You got the band, go play music and get the money." We'd do that too. Go right up there after we started travelling by road, stop any time, any town, see the chief of police and get out and play. Made enough money to buy something to eat, and buy your gas and oil, and keep on to the next town. Many were the miles we pushed buses which broke down, and many were the nights when we slept on the buses. Once the bus was stuck in a swamp near the Savannah River and we were stranded for three days in the middle of nowhere. "We got down to only butter and onions to eat," Dowling recalled.

Driving through Florida some local whites tried to run the bus off the road with a car. One of the musicians grabbed one of the wooden guns the bands used for drill practice and stuck the gun out the window. Dowling remembered, "Brother, did they ever get out of the way."

Tommy Benford remembered:

Every winter we used to go down to Florida with the school and the guys always used to kid me because I couldn't stand the heat, and I always used to get sick …
I remember one spring too, they sent us to a farm about 25 miles out of Charleston [the Ladson farm], and we used to steal the melons and all the corn. We got so bad, we had to come back to school.

The Orphanage staff worked tirelessly for their lambs, inspired by the example set by the indefatigable Rev. Jenkins. Dowling recalled, "He was a genius, and never attended school but four months in his life."

Jenkins needed all his genius to deal with the looming problem of his secretary Ella Harleston's pregnancy. The specter of shame and ruin which haunted the pregnancy of any unwed mother of that time was very real. But Ella could not be sequestered anywhere in Charleston without her family learning the truth. Jenkins also did not want or need Captain Harleston's angry disapproval.

The unwanted pregnancy was scandalous, but the delicacy of the situation was heightened by the father's identity. Jenkins already had seven children with his ailing wife, and was internationally known as the Orphan Man. He was described in a newspaper as "among the most influential Negroes in the state," and the Orphanage was called "a splendid monument to his industry. His mind bristles with practical ideas." He was seen as a symbol of Christian virtue and selflessness so the negative repercussions of the pregnancy becoming public would be swift and stern for Jenkins personally, and disastrous for the fortunes of the Orphan Aid Society.

In September of 1906, Rev. Jenkins came up with another of his practical ideas. He and his pregnant secretary accompanied the band on a trip to New York, and then the two lovers sailed for England. What excuse Jenkins used to explain the journey has been lost; perhaps he claimed that the trip was necessary to plan future performances in England, but whatever the explanation, his misdirection was successful.

Upon their arrival in England, Jenkins took Ella by train to Wigan, a mid-sized mill town on the banks of the Leeds and Liverpool Canal in Lancashire. Today, the city is most famous as the boyhood home of British actor Sir Ian McKellen and rock band The Verve. But in 1906 it was a rough and dirty coal-mining city in the middle of the English countryside, halfway between Liverpool and Manchester.

In November with the assistance of a midwife named Alice Layland, a girl named Olive Ashton Harleston was born - the only black child in Wigan, Lancashire, A week later after Ella recovered from childbirth, Jenkins and his secretary sailed back to America. Upon their return, they picked up their life at 20 Franklin Street as if nothing had ever happened. The Orphan Man had left one of his own black lambs behind.

Olive was adopted by Alice Layland's family.

On March 4, 1909, the weather in Washington, DC was cold and bitter. The streets were covered with snow from the previous night's blizzard which slowed the inaugural parade for President-elect William

Howard Taft. Not far from Taft's carriage marched an unusual assemblage – thirty uniformed black boys carrying brass instruments, led by a prancing waif waving a baton with two more boys carrying a banner reading: JENKINS ORPHANAGE BAND. Taft had remembered the antics of the Pickaninny Band from the St. Louis Expo and included them in his inauguration.

President Taft inaugural parade, 1909. *Courtesy of the Library of Congress*

Three years had passed since Olive was abandoned in England, and Ella had paid a very high price. In addition to emotional turmoil from abandoning her daughter, she also bore the brunt of public humiliation. The illegitimate birth had not remained a secret in Charleston's black society and Ella endured endless social scorn. Captain Harleston was mortified by the embarrassment and the family turned their collective back on her.

Propriety in Charleston was not limited to white society. Lena Jenkins was still alive and suffering, keeping a barrier between Ella and Rev. Jenkins. It was a lonely existence for the twenty-six year old secretary. But most importantly, Jenkins had managed to survive the scandal with his reputation intact. He was still revered as the Orphan Man.

Sometime around 1910, the first Jenkins Band member "jumped ship." Thomas Henry Delaney, born in Charleston in 1889, was one of the first lost lambs of the Orphan Aid Society. He studied piano and voice at the Orphanage, performing in the choir. By age twenty, Delaney was anxious to leave the confines of the Orphanage; he was tired of using his musical talents to make money for Rev. Jenkins. He wanted to make his own money. As Jabbo Smith recalled:

> Well, you know, everybody runs away. That's the only way you get out of there (laughter). When they put you in the orphanage, they signed you up until you were twenty-one, so running away was the only method to get out earlier. I started running when I was fourteen and must have run away six or seven times. We got in those little bands around town because somebody was always trying to steal you if they thought you were pretty good. And I'd go. But the orphanage would come and get me.

Delaney escaped north to New York with a goal of making a living playing the piano and singing his own songs. This was just prior to the "Great Migration" of Southern blacks to the Northern cities, so there were very few places for a black musician to play for money. Most of the paying gigs were in white clubs or whites-only parties that hired white musicians. The main alternative for a black musician was to become a "whorehouse professor." For the next few years

Delaney managed to survive playing piano in the saloons, whorehouses and gin joints in the seedy black sections of Manhattan. It would take a decade before he became one of the most successful Lambs.

Tommy Benford recalled when he "jumped ship":

> Then I got the idea I wanted to make some money from playing music, so I ran away. You couldn't leave the Orphanage until you were 21 in those days, so most of the guys used to run away. I ran away four times and each time they caught me and brought me back. When you got hauled back they punished you by stopping all recreation. The first time I left was to join The Green River Minstrels. Gene Aitken [sp] had the band with them ... he was a big fat guy, but a terrific musician on trumpet, bass and trombone. My brother was with me, but I got caught. Next time was a Circus, then a Carnival, and the last one I remember was a Doctor Show. My brother was with me on the Carnival too, but as he was older they didn't worry so much about getting him back. I wanted to learn all types of music, so that's why I did it.

In September 1912, after several years of illness, Lena Jenkins died of tuberculosis. The reverend wished to marry Ella immediately, but feared a wedding so soon after the funeral would be viewed as scandalous and improper. Jenkins waited a few weeks before he approached the Captain to ask permission to marry Ella. The Captain refused; in a rage he complained that marriage to Jenkins would mean a loss of status for the Harleston family – a much larger sin in black Charleston society than Ella's illegitimate pregnancy and possible marriage.

According to Harleston family legend, the Captain was at choir practice one night when his brother ran into the sanctuary screaming "Ella is running off with Reverend Jenkins!" The Captain raced out of the church armed with a pistol followed by several armed friends.

Indeed, Ella and Rev. Jenkins were taking their vows at a hastily arranged ceremony at the New Tabernacle Fourth Baptist Church. As they left the church, they were told that the Captain was in hot pursuit. Jenkins and Ella rushed five blocks to the wharfs and boarded a ferry going up the Cooper River. Captain Harleston arrived as the boat was pulling away. He stood on the dock waving his pistol, fuming with unspent anger. As years passed, the Captain slowly accepted the marriage, but was never more than distantly polite to his son-in-law.

By 1912, Charleston was in an economic malaise. The once-thriving waterfront commercial district had fallen into utter disrepair. The city was a shabby shadow of its former elegance. Before the Civil War, Charleston had been a cultural, political and economic force, but fifty years later stagnation kicked the city into the gutter of history. Most of the white elite in Charleston preferred to reflect upon glories of the past, rather than embrace the promises of the future which demanded too many radical changes.

The election of white supremacist Coleman Blease as South Carolina governor was a desperate gesture by the aristocracy to cling to their former power and glory. It did nothing to improve the lives of blacks across the state. Blease openly referred to blacks as "baboons" and "apes." He refused to use "white men's taxes for black schools." He defended the lynching of blacks by declaring, "whenever the Constitution comes between me and the virtue of the white women of the South, I say the hell with the Constitution." He then promised to pardon any white man convicted of lynching a black.

The two white orphanages in Charleston were generously supported by the public, while the Jenkins Orphanage was granted a pittance from the city - a $1000 annual appropriation. It cost Rev. Jenkins approximately $20,000 a year to operate the Orphan Aid Society. The earnings from the band averaged about $10,000. The rest of the budget was covered by Jenkins' other fundraising operations and donations from people from outside the South, usually from urban centers like Chicago and New York, places where the Jenkins Band was well known.

In February 1917, a group of twenty-nine Charleston blacks founded a local branch of the National Association for the Advancement of Colored People. They were led by artist and mortician, Edwin Harleston, Ella's brother. One of its first public campaigns was to convince the Charleston Navy Yard to hire several hundred black women. The Yard had recently opened a clothing factory to make uniforms, and there were six hundred jobs available. However, black women had been banned from applying.

Ultimately, the NAACP managed to get 200 women employed at the factory. They also undertook a campaign to improve the dismal state of black public schools. For decades, black students had been taught by white teachers who were often incompetent and unmotivated. The NAACP managed to get the city to agree that, for the first time, black teachers would be hired for black students.

Despite these two major successes, the majority of blacks in Charleston refused to join the NAACP. Many blacks worked for the elite white families in the city and they feared that joining the NAACP could put them on the unemployment line. After all, no one in white Charleston liked an "uppity" Negro.

Charleston, S.C., King Street, circa 1910. *Courtesy of the Library of Congress*

At nine o'clock on the evening of Saturday, May 10, 1919, in Charleston, a group of white sailors arrived at a pool hall run by a black man named Harry Police. The pool hall sat at the corner of King and George Streets, a rough, seedy section of town. The sailors were angry and combative. Earlier that evening they had given money to a black bootlegger for a bottle of whiskey, and the man never returned.

Standing outside the pool hall, one of the sailors shouted, "We're looking for the damn nigger we gave $8 for some bug juice!" They started accosting black men who were walking down the street and then a pistol was fired. The sailors stormed into Police's Pool Hall. Within an hour, mobs of whites had joined the sailors and anarchy swept through the streets. Ten hours later, when dawn broke over the city, the riot had been quelled by a combination of Charleston police and marines from the Navy Base. Five black men were dead, with more than twenty other casualties, whites and blacks, taken to the hospital. Dozens of black-owned stores were ransacked and burned.

This was the first of more than thirty race-fueled riots, massacres and lynchings in America during the summer and fall of 1919, all started by whites. The three most violent were in Chicago, Washington, DC and Elaine, Arkansas. The riots were, in part, a white response to post World War I social tensions related to the demobilization of veterans and the competition for jobs among whites and blacks. James Weldon Johnson called it "Red Summer."

World War I altered America forever. With the military mobilization of more than four million American men and European immigration cut off, the industrial cities of the North and Midwest experienced severe labor shortages. By 1919, an estimated 500,000 blacks had moved from the South to help fill the void of labor. It was the first wave of the Great Migration. Southern blacks were fleeing more than just the poor economy of the rural South; they were also escaping the oppression of the vigorously enforced Jim Crow laws. These black workers filled positions formerly held by whites, increasing resentment among the working class of many ethnic whites, immigrants or first-generation Americans. Following the war, rapid demobilization of the military led to high unemployment and inflation that increased competition for jobs.

W. E. B. Du Bois, an official of the NAACP, wrote:

> By the God of Heaven, we are cowards and jackasses if now that the war is over, we do not marshal every ounce of our brain and brawn to fight a sterner, longer,

more unbending battle against the forces of hell in our own land …We return from the slavery of uniform which the world's madness demanded us to don to the freedom of civil garb. We stand again to look America squarely in the face and call a spade a spade. We sing: This country of ours, despite all its better souls have done and dreamed, is yet a shameful land …We *return*. We *return from fighting*. We return *fighting*.

Reports of the Charleston riot ran in newspapers across America. The *State* newspaper in Columbia, South Carolina wrote: "What happened Saturday night, with sailors and Negroes as parties, might have happened anywhere." They placed blame on out-of-town sailors and blacks, not good southern white Charlestonians. The Charleston *News and Courier* made no editorial mention of the event.

Historian Don Doyle wrote that:

Old Charleston, besieged and subverted, retreated to the safe territory South of Broad, with its old mansions and its old ways. As the new century progressed, the old city became a museum, a sanctuary of artifacts and values that no longer ruled the South.

With its proverbial head in the sand, most of white Charleston was too myopic to see, or even understand, the social hurricane taking aim at the ramparts of elite culture across America.

Slave music and dancing, circa 1850s. *Courtesy of the Library of Congress*

PART TWO:
ROOTS OF "THE CHARLESTON"

SIX
An African Jubilee

"Blues is slavery's first child, conceived in the miscegenation between field-holler and big-house hymn ..."
 – David Wondrich, *Stomp and Swerve: American Music Gets Hot*

WHILE ORIGINAL IN THE EYES OF THE GENERAL public, in truth the Jenkins Band was nothing more than the product of a rich heritage. By 1720 Charleston was the undisputed cultural center of the South, and for the remainder of the 18th century, it was the major musical hub on the eastern seaboard. Not only was it the largest slave port in colonial America, it was also the port of entry for most professional artists arriving from Europe. The population of South Carolina at this time was 18,000 people, approximately 11,000 were African. Slaves had been imported from central Africa's Bantu-speaking areas in such large numbers that "the Bankongo culture of the Congo River area was well represented in South Carolina's early black majority." Slaves were the major commodity of the state's planter classes. For that reason Charleston is often referred to as the Ellis Island for African-Americans.

In 1735, the first opera in the Colonies was

performed in Charleston, the one-act ballad, *Flora: Or Hob in the Well*. George Whitefield, a Methodist minister, was shocked by Charleston's opulence. He wrote, "Charleston had achieved a level of prosperity and refinement that often surprised visitors from the northern colonies and abroad." Whitefield questioned "whether the court-end of London could exceed them in affect finery, gaiety of dress and deportment." Governor John Drayton noted that the people of Charleston were "too much prejudiced in favour of British manners, customs and knowledge, to imagine that elsewhere, than in England, anything of advantage could be obtained."

Despite Charleston's small population, as compared to New York or Boston, visitors often remarked that:

> ... the Men and Women who have a Right to the Class of Gentry are more numerous here than in any other Colony in North America ... assemblies, balls, concerts and plays, which were attended by companies almost equally brilliant as those of any town in Europe of the same size.

Johann David Schoepf, a German physician, commented that:

> ... luxury in Carolina had made the greatest advance, and their manner of life, dress, equipages, furniture, everything denotes a higher degree of taste and love of show, and less frugality than in the northern provinces.

By 1762 the white elites of Charleston had organized the first musical society in colonial America - the St. Cecilia Society. Charleston was the most sophisticated city in colonial America, if one was white. This opulence was built on the backs of African slaves whose influence on Charleston culture was more subtle, but just as pervasive.

Richard Jobson, an English sea captain, was sent to Africa by the Company of Adventurers of London in 1620 to explore the Gambia River area. He published *The Golden Trade or a Discovery of the River Gambra and the Golden Trade of the Aethopians.* He observed:

> There is without doubt, no people on the earth more naturally affected to the sound of musicke than these people; which the principall persons do hold as an ornament of their state ... Also, if at any time the Kings or principall persons come unto us trading in the River, they will have their musicke playing before them.

In 1720 James Houstoun wrote, "I visited King Conny in his Castle, who received me with the usual ceremonies of their Country, Musicke, Drums and Horns."

Edward Bowdich gave a description of an African festival in his book *Mission from Cape Coast to Ashantee.* Bowdich was sent to Africa by the African Committee of London to establish commercial relations with the Ashanti people. He was also an amateur musician and recorded African melodies in notation, described instruments and provided detail about musical performances.

> Upwards of 5000 people, the greater part warriors, met us with awful bursts of martial music, discordant only in its mixture; for horns, drums, rattles and gong-gongs were all exerted with a seal bordering on phrenzy [sic]. We were halted whilst the captains performed their Pyrrhic dance in the centre of a circle formed by their warriors. More than one hundred bands burst at once on our arrival, [all playing] the peculiar airs of their several chiefs; the horns flourished their defiance [fanfare melodies], with the beating of innumerable drums and metal instruments, and then yielded for a

while to the soft breathings of their long flutes, which were truly harmonious; and a pleasing instrument, like a bagpipe without the drone, was happily blended.

Slave dancing on Southern plantation, circa 1820s. *Library of Congress*

For almost every occasion in the life of the Ashanti community, there was appropriate music. Music was important from birth to death. Music accompanied celebrations, religious rites and hunting expeditions. There were fishing and boating songs, warrior songs, and cooperative work-songs; music was chanted and sung while performing communal tasks. Many festivals lasted several days. Bowdich observed the Ashanti thought it "absurd" to worship God in any way other than through singing and dancing. Among the peoples of Angola (now the Congo) music was used in court trials - evidence and arguments were often presented with the accompaniment of drums, instruments and songs.

African day-to-day life was filled with music and singing. Every village had master musicians, singers and instrumentalists who provided music for formal activities. Many served a function similar to that of the Irish bard, singing songs of history and culture. Master musicians were highly esteemed in African culture, often seated with royalty.

Percussive instruments were the most common encountered by English travelers to Africa. Fashioned out of hollowed tree trunks, these drums were elaborately carved, open at one end and covered at the head by animal skins.

Other instruments included a variety of bells and xylophones, rattles, flutes, lutes, whistles and trumpets made from elephant tusks. Fiddles were made of narrow wooden boxes, covered by alligator or antelope skin, with strings of horse or cow hair twisted together for different sounds.

The most exotic performances witnessed by the early European travelers were the dance rituals. They observed that dancing was the "diversion of the evenings" and that "all the night the people continue dancing, until he that playes be quite tyred out." When one group of musicians took their rest, they were replaced by others and the dancing continued. Like music, dancing was a form of communication, creative expression and sheer recreation.

John Atkins, author of *A Voyage to Guinea, Brasil, and the West Indies* describes a dance in Sierra Leone:

> Men and Women make a Ring in an open part of the Town, and one at a time shews his Skill in Antick Motions and Gesticulations, yet with a great deal of Agility, the company making the Musick by clapping their hands together during the time, helped by the louder noise of two or three Drums.

During the years of the slave trade, the musical tradition of West Africa varied from nation to nation, but the cultures featured enough in common to constitute an identifiable heritage for Africans in the New World. Although the exact number of Africans transported to the New World on the Middle Passage slave trade will never be known, it is estimated at 10 to 15 million people or more.

By 1700 the "peculiar institution" of slavery was a reality throughout the established twelve American colonies. Slaves were removed from their homes in chains and transported to the New World, usually separated from their families and communities due to the "unholy alliance" – the bartering between English traders and African tribal chiefs.

As author Rebel Sinclair notes in the article, "Charleston and the Unholy Alliance":

> At the time, Africans did not identify on racial or national lines, but rather on local family or lineages. The kings did not "sell their own," nor did Europeans "sell their own;" in those times, slavery was an acceptable fate for enemies, prisoners and outsiders in Africa as well as the rest of the world. They did not see "blacks" sold to "whites;" it was a business transaction.

Each individual who survived the Middle Passage retained memories of the rich cultural traditions from the motherland, and as Africans spread up and down the eastern seaboard in America, their traditions of song and dance were dispersed with them. Blacks in colonial America left few written records of their activities. However, there is some documentation that gives support to the theory that slaves were musical.

Newspapers published accounts of slaves for sale, or notices of runaway slaves which often described musical gifts, such as:

♪ TO BE SOLD. A Negro Indian Man slave, about forty years of age, well known in town, *being a fiddler.* [*New York Gazette-Post-Boy*, June 21, 1748]

♪ TO BE SOLD. A young healthy Negro fellow who has

been used to wait on a Gentlemen (sic) and **plays extremely well on the French horn**. [*Virginia Gazette*, March 1766]

♪ CAESAR: Absented himself from my Plantation . . . **plays well on the French horn.** [*South Carolina Gazette*, April 19, 1770)

♪ RUN AWAY: Dick, a mulatto fellow . . . **a remarkable whistler and plays on the Violin.** [*South Carolina Gazette*, June 4, 1772]

Slave auction. *Courtesy of the Library of Congress*

Many slave owners encouraged their slaves to sing as they worked, thinking it improved morale and increased productivity. For the workers, it did help ease the boredom of field work. It also lifted spirits and soothed the soul. Ex-slave Frederick Douglas wrote:

Slaves are generally expected to sing as well as to work. A silent slave is not liked by masters or overseers. "Make a noise" and "bear a hand," are the words usually addressed to the slaves when there is silence amongst them. This may account for the constant singing heard in the southern states.

Their singing was accompanied by a single drum or other object used for percussion. Since most slaves were often without instruments, clapping and foot-stomping became an integral part of their music-making. The most distinctive component of African music has always focused on rhythm, making African folk styles far more complex than any other ethnic music.

By the time of the American Revolution, blacks were an integral part of colonial society. They participated in musical activities by singing psalms and hymns in the meetinghouses. Although the African had the inclination toward music-making, he arrived in the New World empty-handed so he often had to acquaint himself with new and often strange instruments. To be sure, some of the white man's instruments were similar to those in Africa, but the slave had to adjust to the ways of his masters.

Slaves on the largest plantations or those living in the grand homes of wealthy whites were exposed to America's most cultured society. Many white children were taught an instrument by traveling teachers, such as flute and violin. There is some evidence that in Charles Town, South Carolina, a few slaves were given lessons by professional musicians.

In Charles Town a school for slaves was run by Mr. Boulson in 1740, under the auspices of the aforementioned Methodist evangelist George White-field. A dance school and concert room doubled as a classroom for slaves, where they were taught to play music. In return, slaves often played the fiddle for dancing in the white home and for the white children's dancing classes.

South Carolina Gazette, September 17, 1737:

If any gentlemen living in the Country are disposed to send their children to Charlestown, they may be boarded with George Logan, who also intends to open his School to teach to dance, next Monday being the 19th Instant. He will likewise go into the Country if he meets with Encouragement. Any white Person that plays on the Violin, or a Negro may be employ'd by the said Logan living in Union [State] Street.

In all likelihood, slaves sang and danced in traditional African ways on the plantation, though there is very little written documentation. However, 1739 eyewitness accounts describe the unusual use of African music during a South Carolina slave uprising, the Stono Rebellion

During an attempted escape to Florida, a group of slaves killed a storekeeper, gathered tools and weapons, and according to one account, "halted in a field and set to dancing, Singing and beating Drums to draw more Negroes to them." In less than twenty-four hours they had grown into a mob of "above sixty, some say a hundred." The group then marched ten miles, killing at least twenty-five whites on their way south. A white militia from Charles Town killed forty-four of the slaves, mounting the decapitated heads of slave leaders on posts along the major road to town.

The South Carolina Commons House of Assembly had been debating a Negro Act. After the Stono Rebellion they stopped debating and quickly approved an Act sharply restricting the behavior of slaves: they could no longer travel without written permission; they could not assemble in groups without the presence of whites; they were forbidden to raise their own food, possess money, or learn to read.

One of the most important provisions forbade the use of drums, horns and other "loud instruments" that might be used to communicate with other slaves. Some of these restrictions had been in effect before the Negro Act, but now they were strictly enforced. The punishment for a minor offense was death – hanging followed by decapitation, or being burned alive.

Traditionally, twice a year, slaves were given several days respite from work. Their favorite form of entertainment during these holidays was dancing to fiddle music. White masters also sought out the fiddlers' skills for their own balls, assemblies and other entertainments. As the largest and most elite urban center in the South, Charles Town offered a wide variety of opportunities for developing musical skills.

Nicholas Cresswell, an English traveler, wrote in his journal in 1774:

> Mr. Bayley and I went to see a Negro Ball. Sundays being the only days these poor creatures have to themselves, they generally meet together and amuse themselves with Dancing to the Banjo ... They all appear to be exceedingly happy at these merrymakings and seem if they had forgot or were not sensible of their miserable condition.

But of course, it was in black churches where music truly flourished for slaves. The earliest permanent black congregation in America was the First African Baptist Church in Savannah, Georgia in 1788. In 1808, one of the most famous black American churches was established in the Harlem section of New York City, Abyssinian Baptist.

The Methodist church welcomed blacks from its inception. Music was an integral part of their worship, and blacks embraced the musicality of the service. In 1737 a Methodist hymnal was published in Charles Town, the first in America, *A Collection of Psalms and Hymns*. Charles Wesley, composer of over 6000 hymns, was on board a ship bound for America in 1735 when he became inspired by the music of the Moravian passengers. The singing of hymns became an integral part of the Methodist worship service, and thus black services.

In 1785 Bishop Francis Asbury officially established Methodism in Charleston. In Asbury's opinion, Charleston was ripe for the Methodist doctrine. Due to the city's embrace of hedonism – card playing, excessive drinking, gambling, dancing, and worst of all, slavery – Asbury called Charleston "the Sodom of the South." He organized a small group of zealots into the Cumberland Street Methodist Episcopal Church. Due to their public stance against the city's most popular vices, and the city's most important economic force, slavery, the Cumberland Street Church was immediately controversial. The building was vandalized and one of the early ministers was attacked and nearly drowned.

Meanwhile, many of the white Methodists became disturbed by the interpretations of their hymns by black members. John Fanning Watson wrote in 1819:

> We have too, a growing evil, in the practice of singing in our places of public and society worship, merry airs, adapted from old songs, to hymns of our composing ... Most frequently [these hymns are] composed and first sung by the illiterate blacks of the society ... their shouts and singing were so very boisterous that the singing of the white congregation was often completely drowned in the echoes and reverberations of the colored people's tumultuous strains.

William Faux commented in 1820:

> After the sermon they began singing merrily, and continued without stopping, one hour, till they became exhausted and breathless ...While all the time they were

clapping hands, shouting and jumping, and exclaiming, "Ah Lord! Good Lord! Give me Jasus! ..."

The camp meeting became a phenomenon during the "Second Awakening" from 1780-1830, led by Methodists. Often, there were more blacks than whites at the meetings. Swedish novelist Fredrika Bremer in her book, *The Homes of the New World*, [New York, 1853] described a camp meeting:

> A magnificent choir! Most likely the sound proceeded from the black portion of the assembly, as their number was three times that of whites, and their voices are naturally beautiful and pure. On the black side [of the camp] . . . the tents were still full of religious exaltation, each separate tent presenting some new phrases . . . In one, a song of the spiritual Canaan was being sung excellently . . . At half past five [in the morning] the hymns of the Negroes were still to be heard on all sides.

Daniel Payne wrote in his *Recollections of Seventy Years* that:

> After the sermon, they formed a ring, and with coats off sung, clapped their hands and stamped their feet in a most ridiculous and heathenish way. I requested the pastor to go and stop their dancing. At his request they stopped their dancing and clapping of hands, but remained singing, and rocking their bodies to and fro.

The camp meeting also brought about defiance by the blacks against the staid singing of the white religious establishment. Since there were no hymnbooks and the majority of the camp followers were illiterate, a new kind of singing developed.

Choruses and refrains were added, and repeated often, so those among the crowd could join in. Often songs were composed on the spot by enthusiastic blacks in the crowd. Call-and-response shouts were an early form of blues-styled music, a "functional expression, style without accompaniment or harmony and unbounded by the formality of any particular musical structure." This pre-blues music was often heard in slave ring shouts and field hollers.

Methodist Camp Meeting, 1819. *Courtesy of the Library of Congress*

After the Civil War, Negro folk and spiritual songs began to appear in print, but they largely remained unknown among whites until a group of black college students from Fisk University formed a chorus. Established in 1866 in Nashville, Tennessee by the American Missionary Association as the Fisk Free Colored School for education of freedmen, it was named in honor of General Clinton Fisk of the Tennessee Freedman's Bureau. George L. White was one of Fisk's white teachers. He was assigned to devote his leisure hours to music instruction to promising students in standard classical music, but he also allowed them to choose "their own music" to sing. In 1867, under White's direction, the Fisk students presented a concert in Nashville. Encouraged by the positive reception, White began to take the singers on trips to nearby towns. In 1871 he decided to take them on tour in order to raise money to support the school.

Fisk Jubilee Singers. *Courtesy of the Library of Congress*

This was not a low brow minstrel show. The Fisk students did not rely on jokes, dances and catchy tunes. They were not white men dressed up in dark face playing "negro music." They were black college students, performing serious Negro spiritual music for a white audience. It was an audacious idea. As the group began to have success, White decided they needed a name. He found a reference in the book of Leviticus in the Bible that described each fiftieth Pentecost to be followed by a "year of jubilee" in which all slaves would be set free. Since most of the students and their families were newly freed slaves, the name "Jubilee Singers" seemed a proper fit.

Over the next seven years the Fisk Jubilee Singers performed across the world for the crowned heads of Europe, and the common people of Germany, Switzerland and Great Britain. They raised more than $150,000 for their school.

They also raised awareness of a different musical tradition unknown to most white Americans. It was the distillation of African tribal customs, filtered through the shout-and-holler, call-and-response singing used on Southern plantations and brought to joyous exclamation during religious services and camp meetings.

It was the first foot-in-the-door for serious Negro music into mainstream culture. With America standing on the threshold of the 20th century, who could have predicted the turbulence simmering beneath the surface would soon boil over and transform the world?

Black-faced minstrel show with white performers.
Courtesy of the Library of Congress

SEVEN
Minstrel Shows & Cakewalks

"The minstrel show – an institution through which white America stole…the music and the culture of black America."
    – David Wondrich, *Stomp and Swerve, American Music Gets Hot*

FROM THE BEGINNING OF THEIR EXILE IN NORTH America the Africans would have encountered another group of people the English regarded as equally barbarous, uncivilized (and musical) as the Africans - the Celts. Fifty thousand Irish slaves and indentured servants were sent to work the plantations of South Carolina, Barbados and Virginia. The 1790 census lists 200,000 Americans who claimed Scots – Irish ancestry.

African music drastically differs from European music in several major ways. Foremost, it is more rhythmically more complex, and the style of playing the instruments is disparate. European musicians took a stringed instrument, the violin, and isolated the tone, looking for as much resonance and enhancement as possible by caressing the violin string with a bow and allowing it to breathe. The African method was to "corrupt the sound of the strings by plucking the banjo string against a drumhead, again and again." It was in the mix of traditional Celtic and African instrumentation, dance and music that the roots of 20th century American popular music were planted.

Blackface minstrelsy emerged during the 1820s as the white's exploitation of slave music and dancing.

With their faces blackened by burnt cork, whites took to the stage to sing "Negro songs", perform "Negro dances" and tell jokes about slaves. They called it "coon music."

White minstrels in blackface, Gorton's Minstrel poster, illustrating Jim Crow and Zip Coon stereotypes. *Courtesy of the Library of Congress*

Two types of blackface characters developed: Jim Crow - a caricature of a plantation slave, with ragged clothes and a thick childlike dialect and intellect; and Zip Coon - a dandy dressed in fine clothes who flashed money and boasted of his success with women.

By the early 19th century blackface performers such as George Nichols, George Washington Dixon, and Thomas Dartmouth Rice, called "Daddy Rice, Father of American Minstrelsy" were portraying blacks as buffoons and ridiculing their behavior.

Rice, a white man, was inspired by the singing of an old crippled stable-groom. He came up with the idea of a stage show based on impersonation of the old slave. The combination of song and dance, old clothes and blackface was hugely successful, and Rice became a rich man. He traveled from city to city, town to town, theater to theater, becoming known as "Jim Crow Rice." He was one of America's first musical superstars.

The Virginia Minstrels became the first American band playing truly American music. In a New York boarding house in 1842, Billy Whitlock added his percussive banjo to Dan Emmett's fiddle, creating something new, and to some listeners, something dangerous. Before the Virginia Minstrels, white performers kept the fiddle, labeled a white instrument, segregated from the banjo, perceived as a black instrument. Whitlock and Emmett broke that tradition. They were white men with nappy wigs on their heads and layers of burnt cork on their faces playing Negro music. They would dance and sing, pick the banjo and rock the bow, give mangled speeches and tell corny jokes. White American audiences could not get enough of it.

Similar to the jazz age of the 1920s and the rock and roll frenzy of the 1950s and 60s, the Virginia Minstrels kicked off the first American musical craze. In the 1840s the minstrel show swept across America, and in the process it became the most popular form of mass entertainment. By the time of the War Between the States, the minstrel show had become world famous and respectable. Late in his life Mark Twain fondly remembered the "old time nigger show," with its colorful comic darkies and its rousing songs and dances.

The Virginia Minstrels organized a full-length minstrel show featuring a quartet of performers and toured Europe to great acclaim. In 1844, the Christy Minstrels organized, featuring E.P. and George Christy. They became the most popular attraction for the next decade, inspiring hoards of imitators. Hundreds of minstrel shows performed across America and Europe.

Until the turn of the 20th century, minstrel shows were the most popular form of theatrical entertainment in the world. To get new material, performers visited plantations, listened to black men singing in rice and cotton fields, on steamboats and docks and in tobacco factories. They used banjos, tambourines, fiddles and bone castanets to, as E.P. Christy said, "reproduce the life of the plantation darky."

Stephen Foster, the greatest popular songwriter of the 19th century, wrote hundreds of songs for minstrel shows, including "Oh! Susanna," "Camptown Races," "My Old Kentucky Home" and "Old Black Joe." These songs were performed to great acclaim, initially by the Christy Minstrels and later by all the shows. William Henry Lane, called "Master Juba", became the first black performer to travel with minstrel groups. Charles Dickens watched Juba perform in New York and called him "the greatest dancer known."

The popularity of minstrel shows unfortunately established a stereotype of black men that persisted through most of the 20th century on the vaudeville stage, musical comedy, movie screen, radio, and television - shiftless, irresponsible, happy-go-lucky darkies. And yet, despite this extreme racist stereotype, blackface minstrelsy was at its core a tribute to

African music and dance, opening the door a bit wider for black culture to enter the American mainstream.

After Emancipation, black musicians began to open their own minstrel shows – the all-black Georgia Minstrels being the first. They were so successful that the term "Georgia Minstrel" became synonymous with black minstrels. White minstrel groups continued to bill themselves as "Nigger Minstrels." Black meant black, and white meant "nigger." In an ironic twist, in order to be taken seriously as Coons, black minstrels had to use burnt cork on their skins and whiten their lips. The paying public expected all Coons to be a certain consistent shade.

By the turn of the 20th century some of the most famous minstrels were black men - the best known was Bert Williams, who performed in blackface well into the 1920s. At the same time whites performing in blackface was common and accepted. The first talking picture, *The Jazz Singer* (1927), was a blackface film starring Al Jolson. Judy Garland performed in blackface in three movies, *Everybody Sing* (1938), *Babes In Arms* (1939) and *Babes On Broadway* (1941). Bing Crosby did a blackface sequence in 1943 singing a version of "Dixie." As late as 1960, Frank Sinatra and Dean Martin appeared in blackface for comedic effect in the movie, *Ocean's Eleven*. More recently, the 1976 blockbuster movie *Silver Streak*, (with Gene Wilder and Richard Pryor) and 1983's *Trading Places*, (with Dan Ackroyd and Eddie Murphy) both feature white characters (Wilder and Ackroyd) in blackface playing outrageous black stereotypes for comedic effect.

Black minstrel shows differed from white minstrels in one important detail – they were better! Black performers could be successful, as long as they portrayed the stereotypical plantation darkie singing and jive shucking, Of course, it was demeaning, but when a post-Civil War black man could make $50 a week as a minstrel performer, many of them swallowed their pride, took the money, fed their families and went on with the show.

By the late 1870s minstrel shows introduced a new element: dancing in pairs – a male and female flinging their legs up in the air and throwing their heads back in wild abandon. The Cakewalk was born. Leigh Whipple related a story told to him by his childhood nanny in 1901:

> Us slaves watched white folks' parties where the guests danced a minuet and then paraded in a grand march, with the ladies and gentlemen going different ways and then meeting again, arm in arm, and marching down the center together. Then we'd do it too, but we used to mock 'em every step. Sometimes the white folks noticed it, but they seemed to like it; I guess they thought we couldn't dance any better.

In 1950 ex-ragtime entertainer Shepard Edmonds remembered stories told to him by his parents from Tennessee:

> The cake walk was originally a plantation dance, just a happy movement they did to the banjo music because they couldn't stand still. It was generally on Sundays, when there was little work that the slaves both young and old would dress up in hand-me-down finery to do a high-kicking, prancing walk-around. They did a take-off on the manners of the white folks in the "big house," but their masters, who gathered around to watch the fun, missed the point. It's supposed to be that the custom of a prize started with the master giving a cake to the couple that did the proudest movement.

In the *Journal of Social History* (1981), B. Baldwin states the Cakewalk was meant:

... to satirize the competing culture of supposedly 'superior' whites. Slaveholders were able to dismiss its threat in their own minds by considering it as a simple performance which existed for their own pleasure.

As previously related, post-Civil War America had also fallen in love with military band music. In the 1880s these military bands began to mix their music with minstrel shows. Each minstrel show paraded into town prancing behind a brass band. W.C. Handy, bandleader of Marhara's Minstrels, stated:

> ... the procession circled on the public square, and the band played a program of classical overtures plus a medley of popular airs for the throngs that assembled there in the open.

Gradually the minstrel brass band began to play more and more "Coon" music, and less classical. The next step forward into mainstream culture was taken by a pair of vaudeville veterans George Walker and Bert Williams.

Walker & Williams started as a song-and-dance act on the vaudeville circuit. The pair performed in burnt-cork blackface, billing themselves as "Two Real Coons," to distinguish their act from the many white minstrels also performing song-and-dance numbers, comic dialogues, skits and humorous songs in blackface. Originally Williams portrayed Zip Coon, the slick conniver, while Walker played the Jim Crow buffoon who was the victim of Williams' schemes. However, they soon discovered that the audience responded better when they switched roles. The sharp-featured and slender Walker eventually developed a persona as a strutting dandy, while the stocky Williams brilliantly played the languorous, deadpan oaf.

Walker & Williams – "Two Real Coons."
Courtesy of the Library of Congress

In late 1896, Walker & Williams were added to the cast of *The Gold Bug,* a struggling vaudeville musical. The show was weak, but their spirited performance of the cakewalk as easily the nightly highlight. On the strength of that success they were booked as headliners at New York's Koster & Bial's vaudeville house for a 36-week run in 1896-97. The cakewalk routine brought the house down every night. Soon the dance was so popular in New York that most people believed that Walker & William's had invented it. They wasted little time taking advantage of their success. Williams wrote:

> Long before our run terminated, we discovered an important fact: that the hope of the colored performer must be in making a radical departure from the old time "darky" style of singing and dancing. So we set ourselves the task of thinking along new lines. The first move was to hire a flat in 53rd St., furnish it, and throw our doors open ... The Williams and Walker flat soon became the headquarters of all the artistic young men of our race who were stage struck ... By having these men about us we had the opportunity to study the musical and theatrical ability of the most talented members of our race.

Within a couple of years they produced their own revue, *In Dahomey*, which featured music written by Will Marion Cook. It was a satire of the "back to Africa" movement and became a rousing success. In 1903 they performed *In Dahomey* in England for eight months, including a command performance for King Edward IV in London. Walker was then forced to retire due to illness, and Williams continued on as a solo performer. In 1910 he became the first featured black performer in the Ziegfeld Follies and during the next decade Williams became one of America's most popular performers.

Change is always difficult, and frightening. The idea of a black featured performer in an otherwise all-white show was shocking in 1910 and Williams' initial reception was mixed. Half of the audience loved him, and the other half was offended. Several cast members delivered an ultimatum to Florenz Ziegfeld: they wanted Williams fired. Ziegfeld told them, "I can replace every one of you, except him." Williams stayed and soon became the star of the Follies.

During his time with the Follies, Williams was making as much money as the President of the United

States, $75,000 ($1.9 million in 2012 dollars.) His stage character has been described as a black counterpart to Charlie Chaplin's Little Tramp, a bumbling but good-hearted simpleton.

Despite his enormous popularity, Williams continued to face racism almost everywhere he went. Once, in the elegant Hotel Astor in New York City, the white bartender tried to get rid of Williams by telling him he would be charged fifty dollars for a drink, a standard ploy to keep undesirables out of fashionable places. Williams calmly produced a thick roll of hundred dollar bills out of his pocket and placed the wad on the bar. "How about a round for everybody, then?" he asked the bartender.

Bert Williams in blackface at the height of his popularity.
Courtesy of the Library of Congress

In 1910, Booker T. Washington wrote of Williams, "He has done more for our race than I have. He has smiled his way into people's hearts; I have been obliged to fight my way."

Gene Buck, who discovered W.C. Fields in vaudeville and hired him for the Follies, wrote, "Next to Bert Williams, Bill [Fields] was the greatest comic that ever lived." W.C. Fields called Williams "the funniest man I ever saw, and the saddest man I ever knew." He was also the first major Negro entertainer in America, pushing the vaudeville barn door open wide. Soon he was followed by a stampede of actors, writers and musicians.

The first practical sound recording and repro-duction device was the mechanical phonograph cylinder patented in 1878 by Thomas Edison. His first device used tin foil wrapped around a hand-cranked cylinder, but soon discovered that foil was not durable enough for everyday use and commercial production. Within a few years Edison developed wax cylinders, licensed by Charles Sumner Tainter and Alexander Graham Bell, which became known as the Columbia Phonograph Co. The wax cylinders had sound record-ings in the grooves on the outside which could easily be removed and replaced on the machine which played them. There were several flaws to this system. First, after less than 100 plays, the wax cylinder deteriorated so badly that it was useless; and second, in order to get multiple recordings the performer would have to record the same song over and over.

The American recording industry truly started in 1890 when a distributor of Edison phonographs began attaching coin boxes to the devices that played the wax cylinders. They were set up in locations guaran-teed to have high pedestrian traffic, chiefly saloons and drugstores, creating the first jukeboxes. The selections were limited, the sound was atrocious and customers had to listen through a rubber ear-tube, but the jukeboxes caught on immediately. People stood in line to listen. One New Orleans drug store took in about $500 a month from a single jukebox. The cylinders wore out so quickly that some distributors sent around a boy on a bicycle to change them three times a day.

Unfortunately, the first thirty-five years of the recording industry are lost to history. Most cylinders were produced in miniscule quantities, and those copies have all since been broken, erased or eaten up by mildew. Many discs were melted down in World War II for recycling drives.

By 1891, there were suddenly two worlds of American music: one that was made on record and one that wasn't. The first was mainly Northern, civilized, middle class and white; it was sweet, safe and unoriginal. The unrecorded world was mostly Southern, rural, poor and black; it was rough, dangerous and exhilarating.

Musical history scholars contend that this unrecorded rough music first reached mass audiences at Chicago's World Columbian Exposition of 1893. The Expo drew almost thirty million people during the six months it was open, including almost every con man, pool hustler and whore in the Midwest. Along with the whores came the so-called "whorehouse professors," the black gentlemen whose jangly piano playing was the soundtrack of the saloon night life. Their music was called Ragtime.

EIGHT
Ragtime & Blues

Society has decreed that ragtime and cake-walking are the thing,
and one reads in amazement and disgust of historical and
aristocratic names joining in this sex dance, for the cakewalk is
nothing but an African *danse du ventre* (belly dance), a milder
version of African orgies.

- Musical Courier, New York City, 1899.

BLUES IS OFTEN CONSIDERED THE ORIGINAL PROTEST
music, "colored folks' opera." Imported from Africa
and nurtured on the plantations, it was mournful,
spiteful, negative and devoid of hope. By the turn of
the 20th century the Negro spiritual style of singing
and the call-and-response mode of field hollering had
transformed itself into blues music, performed almost
exclusively in saloons and roadhouses in poor, rural
America.

Ragtime was its far removed cousin, joyful, fun
and exuberant, more readily acceptable to a mass
audience. It was a synthesis of African syncopation
and European classical music, and it brought renewed
vigor to African music, especially when John Philip
Sousa began integrating ragtime style arrangements
into his popular military marches. Ragtime is often
referred to as the American equivalent of Mozart's
minuets and Brahms' waltzes.

A popular ragtime song, "Syncopated Sandy"
written in 1897 by Ned Wayburn and Stanley
Whiting, described the new sound in the preface of its

sheet music:

> RAG-TIME … originated with the negroes and is
> characteristic of their people. The negroe [sic] in playing
> the piano, strikes the keys with the same time and
> measure that he taps the floor with his heels and toes in
> dancing, thereby obtaining a peculiarly accented time
> effect which he terms RAG-TIME.

Sheet music cover of "Syncopated Sandy."
Courtesy of the Library of Congress

If minstrel music was black banjo music, then
ragtime was black piano music, a natural development of the Africanized jigs and reels that the
minstrels exploited in the 1840s.

The rhythm was the same for minstrel music and
ragtime, but minstrel songs always relied on the banjo

as the main instrument. Since it is impossible to hold a note on the banjo, the player has to hit a lot of notes. When brass bands were added to the minstrel shows the music became less reliant on the chunky banjo rhythm and more melodic. Ragtime was developed on the piano and combined the banjo's numerous notes with the brass band's march-like feel. Saloon and brothel pianists needed music that was lively, loud and swinging. By taking simple syncopations of the minstrel tunes, complicating them and playing the cross rhythms against each other these pianists begin develop the style called ragtime. It's most brilliant practitioner was a pianist named Scott Joplin.

When he was still a young child, Joplin's family left the farm on which his father (formerly a slave) worked as a laborer. They moved to Texarkana where Joplin's musical talent was noted by a local music teacher, Julius Weiss. He instructed Joplin further, placing special emphasis on European art forms, including opera. This teacher's influence instilled into Joplin a lifelong desire for recognition as a classical composer.

The first documented sign of Joplin's musical career is in the summer of 1891 when, as reported in newspapers, he was back in Texarkana working with a minstrel troupe. In 1893, he was in Chicago at the time of the World's Fair, leading a band and playing cornet. After the fair he returned to Sedalia, Missouri and established it as his home. He played first cornet in the Queen City Cornet Band, for about a year and then he formed the Texas Medley Quartette, working dances and other events.

In 1895 he traveled as far east as Syracuse, NY, with the Quartette, a vocal group. His performances so impressed several businessmen in Syracuse they issued his first two publications, the songs "Please Say You Will" and "A Picture of Her Face."

Sheet music cover for "Maple Leaf Rag."
Public Domain

When not traveling, Joplin worked in Sedalia as a pianist, playing at various events and sites, including the town's two social clubs for black men, the Maple Leaf and Black 400 Club (both founded in 1898). He also taught several of the local young musicians in town, most notably Scott Hayden and Arthur Marshall, with whom he later wrote collaborative rags. Before Joplin published his next rag, he obtained the assistance and guidance of a young lawyer, Sedalia resident Robert Higdon. In August 1899, they contracted with Sedalia music store owner and publisher John Stark to publish "Maple Leaf Rag," which became the greatest and most famous of piano rags. The contract specified Joplin would receive a one-cent royalty on each sale, a condition that rendered him a small, but steady income for the rest of his life.

Sales in the first year were slight, only about 400. This is probably because at the time Stark was only a small-town publisher, and the *Maple Leaf Rag* was a difficult piece to play. But the sales steadily increased. By 1909, approximately a half-million copies had been sold and the song would remain popular for the next twenty years.

Early in 1903 Joplin filed a copyright application for an opera, *A Guest of Honor*. A few months later, he formed a thirty person opera company, rehearsed at the Crawford Theatre in St. Louis and embarked on a tour scheduled to take him to towns in Illinois, Missouri, Iowa, Kansas, and Nebraska. Early in the tour, someone associated with the company stole the box office receipts, seriously damaging the company's financial position. Furthermore, unable to pay for the company's board at a theatrical boarding house, all of Joplin's possessions were confiscated, including the music from the opera. Copies of the score were never filed with the Library of Congress and the music has never been recovered.

Following the failed opera tour, Joplin returned to Arkansas to visit relatives. There he met Freddie Alexander, a 19-year-old woman. Joplin was so enchanted by Freddie that he dedicated the song "The Chrysanthemum" to her. Since ragtime was considered a disreputable art form, Joplin endowed this rag with more dignity by portraying it as "An Afro-American Intermezzo."

In June Joplin and Freddie married in Little Rock. Tragically, Freddie developed a cold that progressed into pneumonia, and she died at the age of 20 on September 10, 1904, ten weeks after their marriage.

After Freddie's funeral, Joplin left Sedalia and never returned. Through the next few years his career

106 / Mark R. Jones

floundered. Having lost much of his money on the failed opera, he was in poor financial condition. He spent most of the time in St. Louis, picking up insignificant musical jobs that paid little money. His "Binks' Waltz" was written as a commission from a local businessman. During this period however, he still issued several outstanding works including the ragtime waltz "Bethena," "Sarah Dear," "Leola," "The Rose-Bud March," "Antoinette," "Ragtime Dance" and "Eugenia."

Joplin published only one rag in 1910, "Stoptime Rag," but completed an opera called *Treemonisha.* He told his friends that he had turned it over to Irving Berlin at Snyder Seminary, but that Berlin rejected it a few months later. The following spring, in 1911, Irving Berlin published his greatest hit song up to that time, "Alexander's Ragtime Band," and Joplin complained to friends that the song's verse was taken from the "Marching Onward" section of "A Real Slow Drag" in *Treemonisha.* Joplin then altered that section and published the opera himself in mid-May, 1911.

The opera's story, written by Joplin, takes place in a rural black community in Arkansas, not far from his childhood home of Texarkana. In part, the opera is a tribute to both his mother, for the way that Treemonisha obtains her education, and to Freddie, his deceased wife, with the opera's action occurring in September 1884, the month and year of Freddie's birth. The opera's story relates how Treemonisha, the only educated member of her community, leads her townspeople out of the bondage of ignorance and superstition. The story is an allegory of how Joplin viewed the problems of the African-American community of his time, proposing the view that racial equality would come with education.

Joplin gave a copy of the score to the editor of

the *American Musician and Art Journal*, an important music magazine. In the June issue the magazine published a lengthy review of the score, declaring it to be the "most American opera ever composed."

In 1911, in an attempt to win financial backing, Joplin mounted an unstaged run-through of the opera with piano accompaniment, but it failed to win over any support His futile efforts to have the opera produced detracted from his other creative work. In 1913 Joplin formed his own publishing company with his new wife Lottie. Over the next two years, Joplin composed several new rags and songs, a vaudeville act, a musical, a symphony, and a piano concerto, but none of these were published and the manuscripts have been lost.

By 1916, Joplin was experiencing the devastating physical and mental effects of tertiary syphilis, a disease he had contracted almost two decades earlier. By mid-January, 1917, he was hospitalized, and soon transferred to a mental institution where he died on April 1, 1917.

Scott Joplin called himself "King of Ragtime Writers" revealing his recognition that not all his musical skills were on the same level. His piano playing was described as mediocre, perhaps due to early effects of syphilis. He also played cornet and violin, but put little effort into developing himself on those instruments. He is reported to have had a fine singing voice, and performed at times as a singer. He also had perfect pitch and, on becoming proficient at music notation, composed away from the piano. But, his most unique talent was composing ragtime tunes.

But exactly what is ragtime? Is it jazz or blues? Is it jazz *and* blues? What is jazz and what is blues? Jazz is American and blues is African. Or maybe, blues is American and jazz is African. Certainly jazz is city and blues is country ...

All of the above is correct. Ragtime + Blues = Jazz. If there had been no blues, there would be no jazz. If jazz was a brick wall, then blues would be the mortar.

David Wondrich, in his 2003 book *Stomp and Swerve: American Music Gets Hot* says:

> Blues is slavery's first child, conceived in the miscegenation between field-holler and big-house hymn, born in a cotton field, raised in a juke joint, nursed on knife-drawn blood and cheap corn whiskey, as old as the swamps and young as last Saturday night. There is a spoonful of blues in every ragtime, jazz, country, soul, rock 'n roll and rap song ever written.

William Christopher Handy was born in Alabama in 1873, the son and grandson of AME ministers. His earliest musical influences were found in the church music. As a teenager he secretly bought his first guitar from local shop window. His father was angry when he discovered the guitar. "What possessed you to bring a sinful thing like that into our Christian home?"

Handy enrolled in classical organ lessons and learned to play cornet. He found music in almost everything, including the clanging of shovels tossing coal into a furnace. He later wrote that he found joy in:

> ... whippoorwills, bats and hoot owls and their outlandish noises, the music of every songbird and all the symphonies of their unpremeditated art ... Southern Negroes sang about everything ... They accompany themselves on anything from which they can extract a musical sound or rhythmical effect ... In

this way, and from these materials, they set the mood for what we now call blues.

At age 23 Handy joined W. A. Mahara's Minstrels, as its bandleader. He stayed with the group for several years and ended up in Memphis where encountered a "piano thumper." In 1940, Handy remembered:

As I was walking down Beale Street one night, my attention was caught by the sound of a piano. The insistent Negro rhythms were broken first by a tinkle in the treble, then by a rumble in the bass; then they came together again. I entered the cheap café and found a colored man at the piano, dog tired. He told me he had to play from seven at night until seven in the morning, and rested himself by playing with alternate hands.

In 1903 while traveling in the Mississippi Delta, Handy had several musical experiences which affected him deeply:

A lean loose-jointed Negro had commenced plunking a guitar beside me while I slept ... As he played, he pressed a knife on the strings of the guitar in a manner popularized by Hawaiian guitarists who used steel bars. The singer repeated the line three times, accompanying himself on the guitar with the weirdest music I had ever heard.

They struck up one of those over and over strains that seem to have no beginning and certainly no ending at all. The strumming attained a disturbing monotony, but on and on it went, a kind of stuff associated with [sugar] cane rows and levee camps. Thump-thump-thump went their feet on the floor. It was not really annoying or unpleasant. Perhaps "haunting" is the better word.

By 1900 most brass bands had embraced the new

sound of ragtime. John Philip Sousa, the undisputed king of white popular music, famously stated that "there was no hierarchy in art." However, most musicians still perceived the brass band inferior to a symphony orchestra. The intellectual bourgeoisie thought a brass band sounded liked "a threshing machine through which live cats are being chased." Scott Joplin and W.C. Handy ultimately became known as "King of Ragtime" and "Father of the Blues," and are now universally recognized for their genius, but at the turn of the 20th century they were just two more Negro musicians.

Claflin College (South Carolina) Brass Band, circa 1900.
Courtesy of the Library of Congress

Despite the low reputation of black syncopated music, Sousa began to introduce popular polkas, cake walks and raggy tunes in his musical programs for white audiences. And more boldly, his trombone player, Arthur Pryor, began to smear and slur his notes in a most unconventional way for white audiences, coming up with ragged musical arrangements. The white audiences loved it. After all, if Sousa approved of it, it must be okay, right?

It may not have been jazz yet, but it was close, and the door for black music respectability cracked open slightly wider.

Traveling Minstrel Show. *Courtesy of the Library of Congress*

PART THREE:
DOIN' THE CHARLESTON

NINE
James Reese Europe & the Clef Club

"The Negroes have given us the only music of our own that is American – national, original and real."
— New York *Evening Journal,* 1912.

DURING THE LATE 19TH AND EARLY 20TH CENTURY JOHN Philip Sousa was arguably America's most famous and influential musician. He was conductor of the world famous U.S. Marine Band, based in Washington, DC. One of Sousa's most successful community programs involved having members of the Marine Band volunteer their time instructing music to promising black children. Among the gifted children was young James Reese Europe, who received instruction in piano and violin.

Europe's parents had moved to the capitol in 1889 when Jim was nine years old. His father procured a position with the Federal government and within a few years, the elder Europe was a supervisor in the Mail Equipment Division and a law student at Howard University. Jim began to study the violin under Joseph Douglass, the grandson of the famous abolitionist, Frederick Douglass.

Two years later, Sousa moved in a few doors down the street from the Europe's house. Jim and his younger sister Mary were both accepted in the Marine Band's musical program. Brother and sister received piano and violin instruction from Enrico Hurlei, Sousa's assistant director.

John Philip Sousa. *Courtesy of the Library of Congress*

As teenagers, both Jim and Mary showed promise. They performed violin duets around the city for churches and other social events. In 1894 fourteen-year old Jim entered a citywide competition for musical composition and came in second. Mary finished first.

After his father's death in 1899, nineteen-year old Jim Europe was left with the obligation of helping to support his mother and sister. In those days there were few opportunities for a young black man to make a living as a musician. Jim held down a series of low-paying, temporary jobs while performing and practice-ing music when time allowed, expanding his repute-tion as an exceptional violinist. Four years later Mary graduated from the Miner Normal School for teachers and began to teach in Washington City Schools. With some of the family's financial burden lifted from his shoulders, Jim decided to move to New York to pursue a career as a professional musician.

In the early twentieth century, the New York music world was an informal one for blacks; musicians got their foot in the door by playing in saloons, brothels and other dives, hoping for a better job. The pinnacle employment was a slot in the orchestra of a successful musical theater production. The most talented musicians were also hired to play at private parties for wealthy white socialites. To be hired for any of these jobs, it was necessary to have previously held a musical job somewhere in the city. For several weeks Jim lived hand-to-mouth as he auditioned around town on the "stringed box." He learned the same lesson Jenkins Orphanage alumni Tom Delaney learned - the money was in the saloons. After each audition Jim Europe was told matter-of-factly that despite his obvious skill, there was very little call for violin music in a whorehouse.

Desperation forced Europe to switch to the piano, an instrument far more common in a saloon. Jim landed a job in a cabaret named the Little Savoy, on West 35th Street, where he unknowingly influenced a future songwriting and musical genius. George Gershwin remembered being seven years old and sitting on the curb outside the Little Savoy in Harlem, listening for hours as Jim Europe played the piano.

During that period, it was customary for stars of the New York stage and musical world to frequent low-rent saloons in the early morning hours after the shows had closed. Jim's musical skills and vibrant personality quickly drew notice. He also began to meet other artists who shared his musical vision. In 1942 singer, songwriter and band leader Noble Sissle remembered those days:

> Most notable among those of the colored places was that of the late Baron Wilkins when he was down on Thirty-Seventh Street. Every white and colored performer of reputation in those days would at some time drop down in Baron's place and sing or dance, or in some way display their talent. It was to such saloons that theatrical producers and managers would go look for talent. Many a Broadway star today owes his or her success to his appearing in one of those underworld dives.

Jim Europe's first major step towards success was meeting John Love at the Marshall Hotel on West 53rd Street in 1903. The Marshall was one of three nice hotels on the street and it became the center of a fashionable black life that had never before existed in New York. On Sunday evenings these hotels served dinner with musical entertainment, attracting large crowds of well-dressed diners. The Marshall served as a mecca of Negro talent - actors, musicians, composers, writers, singers and dancers. They all gathered there to perform, and to watch others. Many fashionable whites patronized the Marshall restaurant, not just for the good food, but for the outstanding entertainment. John Love was one of those customers.

Love was the personal secretary of Rodman Wanamaker, son of one of the wealthiest and most socially prominent families in Philadelphia. Rodman's father, John Wanamaker, had opened the world's first department store in 1861 and later served as President Harrison's Postmaster General. Love hired Jim Europe to supply a string quartet for Rodman's three day birthday celebration in Atlantic City. The Wanamakers were so impressed with Europe that, for the next sixteen years, he was part of every important Wanamaker family function. More importantly, it introduced him to the inclusive world of the East Coast white social elites, leading to musical engagements for some of the most glamorous families in America.

Five months later Europe was hired by the John Larkins Company to direct the orchestra and chorus for a black musical titled *A Trip to Africa*. A year later, he was the musical director of Cole and Johnson's successful production of *Shoo-Fly Regiment*. He also received his first taste of songwriting success when one of his songs, "On the Gay Luneta," was featured in the second act. Two years later he performed the same duties for Bert Williams' *Mr. Lode Of Coal*. Williams by this time had been a featured performer in the Ziegfeld Follies for a decade, and was the most famous black entertainer in the world. Jim felt his career as a professional musician had finally arrived!

However, as successful as black musical theater was in New York City, on the road the performing companies often ran into trouble across Jim Crow America. During the early 20th century, riots erupted throughout the county, particularly in the South and Midwest during the time called Red Summer. Traveling black musical shows were often easy targets for white frustrations.

The growing popularity of motion pictures also began to cut into ticket sales of traveling black theatrical shows. The number of touring companies dwindled down to a mere handful. Jim Europe had finally ascended to the top level of his profession only to see these musical theater jobs disappear. He was determined, however, not to allow success slip from his grasp.

On April 10, 1910 a group of black musicians, dancers and singers met at the Marshall Hotel and formed a new organization - the Clef Club of the City of New York. Jim Europe was elected its first president and conductor of its symphony orchestra. Their goals were simple, which they spelled out in their charter:

> We, the members of said organization, have established, organized, and incorporated the Clef Club of the City of New York, in order to inculcate the science of vocal and instrumental music, technique, and execution of vocal and instrumental music, and to promote good fellowship and social intercourse.

Simply put, the Clef Club was going to function as a fraternal organization, musician's union and booking agency for its members. Jim Europe also envisioned the Clef Club as a showcase to prove to the world that an ensemble - an orchestra! - of black musicians was capable of performing music in a dignified manner, while also reflecting the unique qualities of the African musical tradition.

Within a few weeks the Clef Club had more than 100 members and purchased a building on West 53rd Street to serve both as a club and booking office. Two of the most important early members were pianist-composer Eubie Blake and singer-lyricist Noble Sissle.

These two became Europe's right hand men in running the Clef Club.

Noble Sissle. *Courtesy of the Library of Congress*

Sissle became de facto office manager for the Clef Club, hiring musicians, finding engagements and keeping the books, while Europe and Blake were more involved on the performance side. Over the next two years, the Clef Club Symphony Orchestra performed concerts to great acclaim throughout New York City. Europe wisely limited the performances to light classics, military-style Sousa numbers and a few compositions by Clef Club members, including his own "The Clef Club March." As the first all-black orchestra in America, the Clef Club Orchestra consisted not only of traditional symphony instruments like violins, cellos, brass and wind, but it also featured more than twenty strummed instruments - mandolins, banjos, ukuleles and guitars.

However, many of the musicians could not read music. During a performance, Jim placed the musicians who could sight read in the center, so the surrounding musicians could pick up and play off the reader. In one of the best early descriptions of jazz music Europe stated that:

> Good musicians can catch anything if they hear it once or twice, and if it's too hard for 'em the way it's written, why they just make up something else that'll go with it.

From the beginning, the Clef Club Orchestra was an odd mix of traditional symphonic music played by musicians who typified, and invented, loose ragtime sensibility - the first Jazz Orchestra.

One of the most prominent members of the Clef Club was Will Marion Cook. Born in 1869, Cook was the son of two black college graduates. His musical talent was so obvious that by age 15 he was sent to study violin at the Oberlin Conservatory and then at the National Conservatory of Music in New York with Antonin Dvorak. Despite his obvious talent and academic pedigree, cultured white America was not ready to allow a black man, even a light-skinned one, to storm the halls of the symphonic world in the 19th century.

So he began to write Coon music to support himself. In 1898, Cook composed *Clorindy, or the Origin of the Cakewalk,* the first all-black musical to

be performed in a Broadway house – the Casino Roof
Garden. One of the promoters flatly told Cook,
"Broadway audiences will not listen to Negroes
singing Negro opera."

When the show opened its first night at 11:45 pm,
Cook remembers that:

... there were only about fifty people on the Roof. When
we finished the opening chorus, the house was packed to
suffocation. What had happened was that the show
downstairs in the Casino Theater was just letting out. The
big audience heard those heavenly Negro voices and took
to the elevators. At the finish of the opening chorus, the
applause and cheering was so tumultuous that I simply
stood there transfixed, my hand in the air, unable to move
... the Darktown finale was of complicated rhythm and
bold harmonies ... My chorus sang like Russians, dancing
meanwhile like Negroes, and cakewalking like angels, black
angels! When the last note was sounded, the audience stood
and cheered for at least ten minutes ... It was pandemonium
... I was so delirious that I drank a glass of water, thought it
wine and got gloriously drunk. Negroes were at last on
Broadway, and there to stay. Gone was the uffdah of the
minstrel! Gone the Massa Linkum stuff! We were artists
and we were going a long, long way!

During the next ten years, Cook helped write,
produce and conduct half a dozen musical shows.
James Weldon Johnson said, "Cook was the first
competent composer to take ... rag-time and work it
out in a musicianly way."

Cook's mother, however, was unimpressed. "I've
sent you all over the world to study and become a
great musician, and you return such a nigger!" she
admonished him.

Even though Cook continued to write successful
Coon musical shows, he also composed "serious" music
and carried a chip on his shoulder. It galled him that
in order to be successful he had to collaborate with

what he considered lesser talents like Bert Williams and Jim Europe.

Europe may not have had Cook's burning musical genius, but he had something Cook did not – practicality and flexibility. Cook was universally considered one of the finest musicians in America, but he had also acquired a huge reputation of being a prickly personality, a diva. Europe, on the other hand, was more practical, always an energetic and cheerful person open to compromise.

On May 27, 1910, six weeks after the formation of the Clef Club, they hosted a "Musical Melange and Dancefest" at the Manhattan Casino in Harlem, on 155th Street and 8th Avenue. The performance of a "large and efficient body of colored musicians," one hundred members of the Club, singers, dancers and musicians, created a stir among the New York musical community. For the next two years, under Europe's musical direction, the Club prospered and raised the professional reputation of dozens of black artists, including Sissle and Blake.

During this same period Europe also became involved with the Music School Settlement for Colored People of Harlem. The school was organized by David Mannes, concertmaster of the New York Symphony. Mannes had received his early musical instruction from the black violinist John Douglass and wanted to do something to honor his former teacher. Mannes convinced several New York philanthropists, including George F. Peabody, to establish the school for the musical education of black students. Mannes stated that "through music, which is universal, the Negro and the white man can be brought to have a mutual understanding."

Jim Europe and a staff of black volunteer Clef Club music teachers were soon giving daily lessons in piano, violin, voice, sight reading and musical theory

— at twenty-five cents per lesson. Europe also suggested to Mannes that the Clef Club Orchestra perform a benefit for the school. He was stunned when Mannes recommended the concert be performed at Carnegie Hall.

James Reese Europe, with baton in hand.
Courtesy of the National Archives

The Carnegie board of directors had been looking for one of New York's student orchestras to perform a concert that consisted entirely of music by Negro composers. Mannes convinced the Carnegie board that the Clef Club Orchestra was an outstanding

Negro Orchestra and its director, "Big Jim Europe," was the man who could make the concert a success. The Carnegie Hall performance was set for May 2, 1912.

If the reality of being responsible for conducting the first Negro orchestra to perform at the greatest concert hall in America was not daunting enough, the colossal task of preparing the musicians for the concert left Jim with little choice but to work harder than ever. As he told his good friend, Noble Sissle:

> Day and night for months I sat and rehearsed each one of the individual sets of instruments in their parts – I tell you Sissle, half of the boys didn't read music, and I would have to take the guitar and mandolin players and place their fingers on the different strings, and correct them time and time again, till I finally taught them the entire program chord by chord, note by note. You see the thing that made it doubly hard was the fact that at no two rehearsals was there the same set of men. I could not compel them to rehearse ... I was not paying them ... so I only could get results by patiently coaxing them.

Tickets sales were anemic. Less than one thousand of the 3000 seats sold. But on the day of the concert, the New York *Evening Journal* published an editorial.

> The Negroes have given us the only music of our own that is American – national, original and real. This concert, which is organized for tonight at Carnegie Hall, will be from beginning to end a concert by Negro musicians. The musicians volunteer their services. The proceeds of the concert will be devoted to the Music School Settlement for Colored People. This school is intended to encourage and develop musical talent in Negroes, and there is no doubt that those taught by it

will contribute to the pleasure of the public and make valuable additions to the musical works of this country.

The concert sold out the day of the event. Thousands of people showed up at the box office that evening. The audience contained the elite of white and black New York society.

It is difficult to overstate the importance of the Clef Club concert in the history of American music. This was twelve years before the Paul Whiteman-George Gershwin "Rhapsody in Blue" concert at Aeolian Hall and twenty-six years before Benny Goodman's famous jazz concert at Carnegie Hall. Jazz, blues and ragtime music were still living in the cultural gutter. Jim Europe spent all of his considerable energy and talent organizing an event that would present Negro music to the larger musical world. He wished to convince them the music was as worthy as the works of the accepted European classical masters.

Carnegie Hall was jammed to capacity when Big Jim Europe strode onto the stage and led the 125-member orchestra through its opening number, the symphonic ragtime number, "Clef Club March."

James Weldon Johnson described the night in his book, *Black Manhattan*:

> New York had not yet become accustomed to jazz; so when the Clef Club opened its concert with a syncopated march, playing it with a biting attack and an infectious rhythm on the finale bursting into singing, the effect can be imagined. The applause became a tumult.

The concert's success elevated Jim Europe to unimagined heights. He was now considered one of America's best composers and conductors. The *New York Tribune* reported that his music was "worthy of the pen of John Phillip Sousa." It also gave the Clef Club Orchestra greater respectability among white society. This led to lucrative engagements at many of the most elite functions in New York, London, Paris, and aboard yachts traveling throughout the world.

The club functioned as a clearing house not only for musicians but for all types of black entertainers, and under Europe's leadership, it was actively involved in improving the entertainers' working conditions. Prior to this era, some establishments hired black musicians primarily as waiters and bartenders but also expected them to entertain the guests between serving food, drinks and washing dishes. However, when an act was booked through the Clef Club, the musicians were hired solely as entertainers, receiving a salary, transportation expenses, room and board. The Club proved exceptionally successful, generating over $100,000 a year in bookings.

The Clef Club musicians were well treated and well paid, but often did not receive their due as true professionals, much to Eubie Blake's consternation. He remembered:

> Now the white bands all had their music stands, see, but the people wanted to believe that Negroes couldn't learn to read music but had a natural talent for it. So we never played with no music. I'd get the latest Broadway music from the publisher and we'd learn the tunes and rehearse 'em until we had 'em down pat. Never made no mistakes.
>
> All the high-tone, big-time folks would say 'Isn't it wonderful how these untrained, primitive musicians can pick up all the latest songs without being able to read music?'

Jim Europe used the Carnegie Hall success to secure a recording contract with the Victor Talking

Machine Company in 1913-14. Those recordings now represent some of the best examples of the pre-jazz ragtime style of the 1910s, but unlike Europe's post-World War I recordings with the Harlem Hellfighters Band, the Victor songs were not called nor marketed as "jazz." Jim Europe was a black musician working under a different set of rules - making black music with black performers for upper class whites. The most important fact was that his foot was in the door. Despite itself, America was about to change forever.

America learns a new style of dancing to a new style of music.
All images courtesy of the Library of Congress

TEN
America Learns To Dance

"It is good for a man not to touch a woman."
- 1st Corinthians 7:1

DURING THE SUMMER OF 1912, EIGHTEEN-YEAR OLD New York City black pianist James P. Johnson made the daily trip to Far Rockaway, a beach resort near Coney Island. He remembered:

> It was a rough place, but I got nine dollars and tips, or about eighteen dollars a week over all. That was so much money that I didn't want to go back to school. That fall, instead of going back to school, I went to Jersey City and got a job in a cabaret run by Freddie Doyle.

James Price Johnson was born in New Brunswick, New Jersey, in 1894. His mother taught him to play the upright piano in the family parlor. At age nine he started lessons with Bruto Giannini, a strict musician from Italy, who corrected Johnson's fingering but didn't interfere with his playing rags and stomps. The Johnson family moved to New York City when Jimmy was twelve, and by 1910 he was called the "piano kid" at Barron Wilkin's Cabaret in Harlem. It was at Barron's that he met the legendary ragtime pianist Charles L. "Lucky" Roberts, who taught Johnson how to strengthen his right hand playing.

In 1912 Johnson met Willie "the Lion" Smith, a first-class pianist who became one of his closest friends. Smith played in a joint called Randolph's, in the tough section of Newark known as "the Coast." Johnson and Smith very quickly made their way back to New York and began to work the clubs in the "Jungle," the Tenderloin area of Harlem between 60th and 63rd streets.

Johnson attracted the attention of the music industry and by 1916 he was recording piano rolls for the Aeolian Company. There he befriended another up-and-coming, hot-shot pianist, a young, white Jewish teenager named George Gershwin.

James P. Johnson, composer of "Charleston."
Courtesy of the Library of Congress

Johnson often played at a Harlem club called The Jungles. In a 1959 interview with Tom Davin he recalled:

> The people who came to The Jungle Casino were
> mostly from around Charleston, S.C., and other places
> in the South. Most of them worked for the Ward Line
> as longshoremen, or on ships that called on southern
> coastal ports. There were even some Gullahs amongst
> them. They picked their [dance] partners with care to
> show off their best steps, and put sets, cotillions and
> cakewalks that would give them a chance to get off. It
> was while playing for these Southern dancers that I
> composed a number of Charlestons, eight of them, all
> with the same dance rhythm. One of these later became
> my famous 'Charleston' when it hit Broadway.

The Great Migration of blacks to the North
transformed Harlem, a section of Manhattan about
fifty blocks long and seven or eight blocks wide. By
1920 more than 200,000 Negroes lived in Harlem. It
bustled with energy. Streets clogged with traffic and
new businesses opened on a daily basis. It was new-
found prosperity for tens of thousands of blacks.

With the sudden population explosion, property
took an immediate upward boom. Many of the whites
living in Harlem, however, were panic-stricken by this
black invasion. They quickly abandoned their
neighborhoods and fled to Brooklyn, the Bronx,
Queens and Westchester. Property owners doubled
and tripled their rents, but the Negro influx to New
York continued. With as many as five to seven
thousand people residing in a single block, living
conditions were often anything but wholesome and
pleasant. Harlem deteriorated into slum conditions,
little different from many others in New York.

In many instances, two entire families occupied
space intended for only one. Large rooms were
converted into two or three small ones by building
solid partitions. These cubbyholes were then rented at

the same price as full sized rooms. In many houses, dining and living rooms were transformed into bed rooms after midnight, like a hotel. "Shift-sleeping" was common. During the night a day-worker used the room and soon after dawn a night-worker moved in.

Even this creative apartment sharing was often not enough to meet the doubled and tripled rents. Another solution developed: a few days before the rent was due, you would advertise a party and make your "guests" pay a cover charge. Thus, the Harlem "rent-party" was born. Many of the working class Negroes were maids, porters and elevator operators, paid on Saturday and not required to work on Sunday. Saturday became the logical night to party until dawn. Party-goers would squeeze into a five-room flat until the walls swelled. Card and dice games kept the action hot in the back rooms, but the center of attention was the piano in the front parlor, where a piano "tickler" sat on a stool—hands poised above the keyboard—like a king on his throne.

Very quickly, Johnson and Smith became kings of the rent parties. Piano ticklers were in great demand for cheap entertainment. The better pianists, like Johnson, Smith and Fats Waller, would move from party to party playing for several hours at each, trying to outplay and out class each other. Johnson recalled:

Each tickler kept these attitudes even when he was socializing at parties, or just visiting. It was designed to show a personality that women would admire. With the music he played, the tickler's manner would put the question in the lady's mind: 'Can he do it—like he can play it?'

Willie "the Lion" Smith recalled those days:

A hundred people would crowd into one seven-room flat until the walls bulged. Plenty of food with hot maws [pickled pig bladders] and chitt'lins with vinegar, beer, and gin, and when we played the shouts everybody danced.

By 1913 the Jenkins Band was a well known quantity in New York City. The Band's antics on the streets and the quality of its music were noticed by musicians and professional theatrical agents. James Johnson and Willie Smith watched the band perform on occasion. Smith recalled:

They had a kind of circus band that marched up and down the streets of Harlem. They'd play concerts on the street corners and pass the hat. They sometimes had as many as twenty pieces and none of the kids were over fifteen years of age.

Several more of the black lambs "jumped ship" while in New York. As the kids approached the age of twenty, they were more interested in finding work in the big city than remaining in the Orphanage system. A paying job in a Harlem band was better than traveling the back roads in a cramped bus with twenty other kids.

Freddie Green (b. 1911, ukulele, banjo and vocals), played guitar for the Count Basie Orchestra for more than fifty years. He remembers traveling with the Jenkins Band:

We had a bus. It was a homemade bus; a truck that was made into a bus. Listen, I can't describe it. But it was very uncomfortable. We used to have to get up around noon and play all through the streets...a parade, you know. We were in the small towns of Maine. And we had dress uniforms that we wore. I wanted to go. I wanted experience. I wanted to get on the road.

Advertising poster for *Uncle Tom's Cabin*.
Courtesy of the Library of Congress

Rev. Jenkins signed a contract for one of the bands to perform in a new musical production of *Uncle Tom's Cabin*. The show's white producers believed that, in order for a white audience to sit through a show about Negroes, the Negroes had to dance, play music and generally act the fool. So the Jenkins Band debuted on Broadway, playing the part of jiving coons, an act they long ago perfected during their extensive tours of small towns and cities up and down the eastern seaboard. The band in the show consisted of:

♪ **Conductor:** *JOHNNY GARLINGTON*, ten years-old, who pranced and cavorted on stage with his baton.

♪ **Band Leader:** Twenty year-old *ALONZO MILLS* played the cornet and served as the real leader of the band. A talented musician, Mills would later become the head music teacher at the Jenkins Orphanage; his legacy to American music is the large number of professional musicians he nurtured in the Orphanage Band, including four of the 20th century's greatest jazz trumpet players -Jabbo Smith, Cat Anderson, Gus Aiken and Peanuts Holland.

♪ **Trumpets** *HORANCE HOLMES, EUNICE BRIGHAMS* and twelve-year old *AUGUSTINE "GUS" AIKEN* (often misspelled as Aitken). Gus would later perform with the Charlie Johnson Paradise Band, Louis Armstrong, Sidney Bechet, Dickie Wells and Duke Ellington.

♪ **Tuba:** Eleven year-old *BILL BENFORD*. As an adult Benford would play with Ethel Waters and Jelly Roll Morton and lead his own band during the 1940s.

♪ **Trombone:** *JOSEPH WATSON* and *JACOB FRAZIER.*

♪ **French Horn:** *GEORGE THAYER.* This was his first trip with the band.

♪ **Drums:** *STEPHEN WRIGHT*, thirteen or fourteen years-old, and *CLINTON BROWN*.

Jules Hurtig was a booking agent with an office at 1545 Broadway, New York. He caught the Jenkins Band in the *Uncle Tom's Cabin* production and realized its commercial potential. He had been hired to supply some of the acts for the Anglo-American Exposition, scheduled to be held in London in 1914. The Expo was to be a celebration of a century of American-British peace and progress from 1812 to present day.

Hurtig discussed with Rev. Jenkins the possibility of hiring the band as one of the featured performers for the London Expo. Hurtig's idea was to use the band only for concert purposes. He offered Jenkins a contract that paid $100 a week for a ten week engagement, in addition to new uniforms for the band, all transportation and board for the band and caretakers.

Jenkins agreed immediately. He realized this would be a golden opportunity to visit his abandoned daughter, Olive.

By 1913 public dancing had become all the rage in New York City and the two most famous dancers were Vernon and Irene Castle. The Castles became wildly popular among New York Society, charging more than $1000 an hour for dancing lessons. They taught white America a new way of dancing, introducing and popularizing the ragtime-style "fox trot" and the sultry tango. They taught white America how to dance from the waist down.

Up to this time, ragtime dancing and music were considered vulgar and crude, only for lower "black" tastes. Classical musician Edward B. Perry described ragtime as "a dog with rabies." The magazine *Musical America* stated, "It exalts noise, rush and street vulgarity. It suggests repulsive dance-halls and restaurants." Forty years later the same complaints would be leveled at Frank Sinatra, then at Elvis Presley, then The Beatles as well as hip-hop.

The majority of early American colonists were opposed to dancing. Puritans equated it with promiscuity and sin. They were particularly opposed to "mixt" dancing between men and women which led to temptation and ultimately, adultery. Some hard-liners even spoke out against the time-honored Maypole tradition – young ladies dancing around a pole wrapping flower garlands. It was considered a pagan ritual, sacrilegious and therefore, evil.

Evils of Modern Dancing.
The indecent attitudes in modern dancing and the exotic music can only tend to develop all that is bestial and low in man.

Caption reads: "Evils of Modern Dancing. The indecent attitudes of modern dancing and the exotic music can only tend to develop all that is bestial and low in man."
Author's collection.

Baptists minister preached from their pulpits against the:

> unchaste handling of male or females. The sin of dancing is that it assaults a person's sense and caused them to sin by upon what lust has caused.

Famous fire and brimstone evangelist Billy Sunday railed against drinking and dancing in the 1920s and 30s because the two activities were linked – drinking led to dancing and dancing led to drinking.

It was a fast and vicious path to hell. Sunday declared:

> You sow the dance and the ballroom and you reap a crop of brothels. You sow saloons and you reap a harvest of drunkards. You must want a lot of prostitutes or you wouldn't sow dances.

In an article of the Ladies Home Journal, Anne Shaw Faulkner asked the question: "DOES JAZZ MUSIC PUT THE SIN IN SYNCOPATION?"

In 1925 the Catholic Church in Ireland was so concerned with the evils of new jazz dancing that they released this recommendation to the faithful:

Evils of Dancing

Statement of the Archbishops and Bishops of Ireland issued at their Meeting, held in Maynooth, on 6th October, 1925.

To be read, until further notice, at the principal Masses, in all Churches on the first Sunday of each Quarter of the Ecclesiastical Year

We have a word of entreaty, advice and instruction, to speak to our flocks on a very grave subject. There is danger of losing the name which the chivalrous honour of Irish boys and the Christian reserve of Irish maidens had won for Ireland.

Purity is strength, and purity and faith go together. Both virtues are in danger these times, but purity is more directly assailed than faith. The danger comes from pictures and papers and drink. It comes more from the keeping of improper company than from any other cause; *and there is no worse fomenter of this great evil than the dancing hall.*

We know too well the fruits of these halls all over the country ... dancing halls have brought many a good, innocent girl into sin, shame and scandal, and set her unwary feet on the road that leads to perdition ... imported dances of an evil kind, the surroundings of the dancing hall, withdrawal from the hall for intervals, and the dark ways home have been the destruction of virtue in every part of Ireland ...

Vernon Castle was an Englishman who moved to New York in July 1906. He followed in the footsteps of his actress sister, Coralie, who had landed a role in a Broadway musical, *About Town*. Vernon became a constant presence backstage during rehearsals, entertaining the cast and crew with his magic tricks and comedic banter. The producer, legendary vaudeville showman Lew Fields, was so charmed by Vernon that he gave the young Englishman a small role in the show. One year later Vernon was given a larger role in Fields' next production *The Girl Behind the Counter*, which became a huge hit.

Over the next two years Vernon became a popular comic actor, famous for his graceful and acrobatic pratfalls on stage. As 1910 rolled around Vernon was considered one of the hottest up-and-coming Broadway stars. During that summer, Vernon rented a room in New Rochelle, Connecticut. Many Broadway people summered there. It was only a forty-five minute train ride from New York and offered a quieter and cooler climate than the city. During that summer he met seventeen-year old Irene Foote.

Irene was a short-haired tomboy with a spirit of rebellion and a love of dancing. By age five she was entertaining at local parties and charity balls. When Irene met Vernon at the New Rochelle Rowing Club she later recalled, "I could tell by looking at him he was not my cup of tea." However, upon discovering that Vernon was a successful Broadway actor, she became more interested. "My heart skipped a beat. I turned loose every ounce of charm I could muster to hold his attention."

It must have worked. Vernon managed to get Irene a part in the next Lew Fields' production and one year later they married. They moved to Paris in 1912 when Vernon was offered an opportunity to produce his own show, and the young couple jumped at the chance.

The show, *Finally ... a Review*, was a mixed bag. The first act, a comedic barbershop skit, bombed in front of the French audience. The second act, however, became a sensation - Vernon and Irene dancing wildly to a spirited version of "Alexander's Ragtime Band." Irene recalled the dance as being so acrobatic that "I was in the air much more often than I was on the ground."

The Castles' dancing quickly became the rage of Parisian nightlife, and the couple was invited to perform at Café de Paris, the city's leading elegant club. Suddenly, everyone in Paris society was Castle-mad. These two untrained American dancers were being invited to dance at every club in the city, in private homes and for large lavish balls. Women handed over money to dance with Vernon, and men out-bid each other to take a spin on the floor with Irene. Their dancing technique at the time was "rough and tumble" Irene recalled, more comic and acrobatic than smooth and chic.

Tragedy brought them back home to America. Irene's father died in May 1912. They returned to New York and wasted little time finding employment, landing a job dancing at the Times Square club Café de l'Opera at $300 a week. At midnight, as the spotlight focused on the slim couple near the edge of the bandstand, they sprang up, twirling and swirling across the dance floor – teaching white Americans a new way to dance. Untrained as they were, the Castles made it up as they went along. Irene remembered:

Vernon and Irene Castle. *Courtesy of the Library of Congress*

All we did was write on paper about what we thought we would do. This custom of writing out our dances first was almost adhered to in later days. The first dances we never even rehearsed ... by keeping my eyes firmly fixed on the stud button of his dress shirt I could anticipate every move he was going to make and we made it together, floating around the floor like two people sharing one mind.

What made the Castles unique was their ability to refine dance steps considered too objectionable for polite society – ragtime trots and grizzly bears. The couple's grace and elegance turned low dances into refined entertainment. When the Castles met James Reese Europe at a private society party where the Clef Club Orchestra was playing, they realized they had discovered their perfect band leader – a man who shared their musical sensibilities.

Europe quickly formed the "Castle Society Orchestra" with Eubie Blake at the piano and other members of the Clef Club. The orchestra became internationally famous, accompanying the Castles in concert halls and theaters across the world. Jim composed and arranged several popular songs for them, including "The Castle Perfect Trot" and "Castle House Rag."

The Castle Society Orchestra was not a small "Dixieland" style band, but a full symphonic orchestra with intricate arrangements by Jim Europe, similar in style to Sousa's Marine Band. Europe also added a saxophone to his band, a bold decision. The saxophone had never been considered a serious instrument; for years it had been used mainly as a novelty in musical acts, but Europe's use of the saxophone raised it to the status of a respectable instrument for the first time. Over the next decade the addition of the saxophone to orchestras and combos led to a monumental change in American music.

The Castles' hiring Jim Europe was a culturally defining moment, exposing syncopated Negro dance music to the most elite sophisticated white audience ever. The Castles pushed the mainstream door open with the introduction of the Foxtrot, a slower paced dance that most non-dancers could perform adequately. For the first time "low" Negro music was mixed with black-style dancing but handled with such grace by a respected white couple that it became acceptable for respectable whites, one more fundamental change in American popular music and culture.

For the next two years, Jim Europe and the Castles traveled the world mesmerizing, delighting (and shocking) audiences with their music and performances. They ushered in an era of "animal" dances which included the Foxtrot, Grizzly Bear, Horse Trot, Kangaroo Hop, Chicken Scratch and Turkey Trot.

After two years of dancing to Jim Europe's music the Castles were international celebrities. One night, during the height of their popularity, they danced at the New York Hippodrome, accompanied by the regimented military music of John Philip Sousa. It was a clash of opposite cultures, like pop music before Elvis Presley. Irene Castle remembered that:

> He [Sousa] ignored our frantic signals to pick up the tempo and his uniformed arms flailed away with the precise beat of a man conducting a military march, which was exactly what he was doing.

Which proves the old adage: once you go black you can never go back.

Vernon and Irene Castle, the epitome of early 20th century chic.
Courtesy of the Library of Congress

ELEVEN
Black Lambs in London

"He told me that his father was going to take the band to London and that he would have to leave immediately."
— Benjamin Brawley about Edmund Thornton Jenkins.

ON MAY 2, 1914 REV. JENKINS RECEIVED A TELEGRAM from Jules Hurtig that read "Bring with you the best musicians you have of small boys."

Jenkins was smart enough to bring more than just young boys to the Anglo-American Expo in London. Although the small boys in their uniforms constituted an important aspect of the band - giving them their pickaninny look - for a job as prestigious as this one, the music was more important. The boys would be performing a rigorous five hour program each day in London, on a regular stage in front of thousands of people, so Jenkins decided to bring several seasoned older players who were in their late teens and early 20s. Although billed as "The American Pickaninny Band," Jenkins recognized this was a significant opportunity for the band to prove they were a serious musical entity.

He was also insightful enough to insist that his son, Jenks, who was the best musician associated with the Orphanage, accompany them to England. As much as Jenks hated to leave school and immerse himself once again in the band's chaos, he balanced that with the fact he would be in London and could influence the music selection to include something other than cakewalks and ragtime tunes.

The Jenkins Band that went to London included:

♪ **Leader:** P.M. 'HATSIE' LOGAN (whom the boys called "Fess", short for 'Professor.')

♪ **Deputy Leader:** DANIEL GREEN, coronet.

♪ **Coronet:** ALONZO GREEN AND FRANK WALLACE.

♪ **Trombone:** AMOS GAILLARD, WILLIAM JOHNSON, ED AND JACOB FRAIZER, NATHANIEL JENKINS (one of the reverend's sons.)

♪ **Alto Saxophone:** FRANK MIDDLETON, JOHN BROWN and ISSAC DANTLZER.

♪ **Clarinet:** Edmund Thornton Jenkins (one of the reverend's son.)

♪ **Baritone Saxophone:** ABRAHAM JONES.

♪ **Tubas:** BUTLER GREEN and ALEXANDER STAFFORD.

♪ **Drums:** OSCAR MAZYCK, JOSEPH NESBITT, GENE ANDERSON and GEORGE SCOT.

The above instrument list reveals the Jenkins Band was also using the saxophone at about the same time as Jim Europe's Clef Club Orchestra, long before it was considered a "proper" instrument for symphonic bands.

During the early 20th century, more than a dozen international expositions were organized in the United States, with at least twice that number held in France and England. In 1901-02 Charleston had hosted the South Carolina & West Indian Exposition, so Rev. Jenkins would have been familiar with the Expo format. The London Exposition was similar to the one in Charleston, essentially little more than a professional trade show. Most Expositions constructed elaborate pavilions called "the White City," which housed exhibits of science and industrial invention.

The Anglo-American London Expo was held at Shepherd's Bush, a few miles west of London. It included an amusement park called Merryland, a place where the "great unwashed" could entertain themselves. It was little more than a dirt midway lined with freak shows and carnival rides. Some of the acts the Band appeared with included the A.J. Cummings Wild West Show, magician Harry Houdini, and a bawdy up-and-coming comedian named W.C. Fields. But Jenkins and the boys were determined to do their best. After all, their first musical performance each day was at the Expo's main stage, the Court of Honour where the glamorous His Majesty's Twentieth Hussars military band performed every evening.

The official Expo programme gave their full repertoire, which included military band music, ragtime numbers, popular songs and, at Jenks' urging, some Italian opera.

COURT OF HONOUR 11:45 -12:45
1. March ... *Battle Commander* (Hernandez)
2. Two-Step ... *The Trail of the Lonesome Pine* (Smith)
3. Comedy Waltz ... *Fran Louisa* (Pryor)
4. Medley Waltz ... *The Good Ship Mary Ann* (LeBay)
5. Waltz ... *The Curse of an Aching Heart* (Richmond)
6. Overture ... *The Fall of Jericho* (Maillochand)
7. Cakewalk ... *Coon Band Contest* (Pryor)

MERRYLAND 2:45 p.m. to 4:45 p.m.
1. March ... *National Emblem* (Bagley)
2. Waltz ... *The Charmer* (Whitmark)
3. Two-Step ... *I Love the Ladies* (Berlin)
4. Dance ... *Mimi* (Robinson)
5. Comedy Waltz ... *Peg O' My Heart* (Fischer)
6. Caprice ... *Love's Enchantment* (Losey)
7. Barcarolle ... *Les Contes d'Hoffmann* (Offenbach)
8. Reverie ... *Sliding Jim* (Losey)
9. *You're My Baby* ... Introducing *My Little Bumblebee* (Douglas)
10. Two-Step ... *That Ragtime Regiment Band* (Morris)

MERRYLAND 6 p.m. to 7:30 p.m.
1. March ... *The Gold West* (Losey)
2. Novelette ... *Wooing the Muse* (Brooks)
3. A Joplin Rag ... *The Smiler* (Wenrich)
4. Song ... *Rebecca of Sunnybrook Farm* (Gumble)
5. Two-Step ... *Down in Chattanooga* (Berlin)
6. Caprice ... *Dance of the Nymphs* (Buglio)
7. Song ... *Gaby Glide* (Monaco)
8. Serenade ... *Moonlight* (Moret)
9. One-Step ... *Beaux Espirits* (Tompkins)

MERRYLAND 8:30 p.m. to 9:45 p.m.
1. March ... *United States* (Hernandez)
2. Celebrated Waltz ... from *Il Trovatore* (Verdi)
3. Two-Step ... *The Midnight Choo-Choo* (Berlin)
4. Air De Ballet ... *La Mouche d'Or* (Armstrong)
5. Rag ... *Frozen Bill* (Pryor)
6. Selection ... *The Jolly Elks Patrol* (Frey)
7. Medley ... *You've Got Your Mother's Big Blue Eyes* (Berlin)
8. Song ... *Razzazza Mazzazza* (Pryor)

MERRYLAND 10:15 p.m. to 10:45 p.m.
1. March ... *Captain Cupid* (Pryor)
2. Selection ... *Wonderland* (Douglass)
3. Song ... *The Stars and Stripes* (Sousa)

END OF PROGRAMME

The band mixed serious music with ragtime pieces, which gave the boys their opportunity to play up their "pickaninny" side. If the rough crowd at Merryland was stunned into silence by an American band of Negro boys playing selections from a Verdi opera, they quickly roared with raucous approval when the band broke into a Scott Joplin rag or one of Irving Berlin's two-step tunes, with accompanying dance steps by the prancing conductor.

Within a few weeks the band was the most popular attraction at the fair. Picture postcards of the "Famous Piccaninny Band" sold by the thousands. People flocked to watch them.

Anglo-American Expo postcard – "The Famous Piccaninny Band."
Photo courtesy of the Charleston Jazz Initiative, Avery Research Center for African American History and Culture, College of Charleston.

Sometime during the London trip Jenkins and Ella managed to sneak away for a "vacation." They took a train to Wigan, Lancashire to visit their daughter Olive, who had grown into a quiet seven-year old girl. Olive was as English as any white girl in the city. She played the piano and attended the All Saints School. What Rev. Jenkins and Ella must have made of this young girl, completely different from the reverend's other children, no one knows. And what did Olive think? Who was she? An American girl, with a black family named Jenkins, or an English girl with a white family named Laylands? It was a question that Olive would struggle to answer her entire life.

The highlight of the band's trip occurred on June 25, 1914, when Queen Alexandra, the sixty-nine year old widow of King Edward VII, visited the Expo with the Empress Marie of Russia and Princesses Royal and Maud. The Jenkins Band played a special performance at the Court of Honor for the dignitaries. Queen Alexandra must have been impressed by the boys' performance, because within a few weeks, King George V scheduled a visit to the Expo, and remarked that he was anxious to hear the American Pickaninny Band.

The Expo's promoters immediately asked Rev. Jenkins to extend his contract until October. Jenkins agreed, but ever the astute business man, he negotiated a higher fee for the band and to be paid in gold, not currency.

On June 28, 1914, Archduke Ferdinand, heir to the Austro-Hungarian throne and his duchess Sophie were assassinated by Gavrilo Princip in Sarajevo Bosnia-Herzegovina. Princip was an agent of Serbia, which claimed Bosnia for itself. The assassination prompted an international crisis. Austrian Emperor Franz Josef threatened to invade Serbia and Kaiser Wilhelm II of Germany publically agreed to support Austria-Hungary. This was all shocking news to Jenkins and the adults in the Band's organization, who followed it daily in the newspapers, but it was of little consequence to the on-going events surrounding the Anglo-American Expo.

During the preparations for the King's impending visit, a letter was sent from the Expo's Director to Paul G. Daniels (Rev. Jenkins' assistant).

13 July 1914
Dear Sir,
I shall be glad to know whether your band can play 'God Save The King' and if not will you please learn it well in readiness for the special performance which is to take place shortly.

Yours faithfully,
Gerald Kiralfy

However, even though the band's contract was to run through October 1914, Jenkins and Ella needed to return to the States. The reverend wrote two letters, one to F. Eugene Mikell, the band's first musical director, then living in Jacksonville, Florida.

London, England July 25 1914
Dear Sir,
I would like to have you here to lead the Band, as my boy will have to leave very soon. We are doing well here. This is a great country. I am compelled to go home and would like to have just such a man as you with whom to lead my Band. They play only five hours daily as you will see by the enclosed program; no work on Sunday; everybody goes to Church. This would be the trip of your life if you would come to London. You would be paid in a hundred and one ways I need not mention. We are offered jobs from everywhere over here. If we had ten bands we could have work to do. If you would like to come over and lead my band until within one week at Christmas at which time we will be in Charleston, cable me on receipt of this letter as follows: 'Jenkins, Piccaninny Band, White City, Shepherd's Bush, London England. Can come, Mikell'. On receipt of my reply 'Come at once' buy your ticket to New York via Clyde Line and I will meet you there August 16. I shall be stopping at 147 132nd St., and I shall send you direct to the Band.
Of course it's a long distance and expenses are high, and I won't be able to pay you but thirty-five dollars per month for actual service. The Band will leave here in October and will play three nights in New York, Philadelphia, Wilmington, Baltimore, Washington, Charlottesville, Richmond, Lynchburg, Asheville, Spartanburg, Greenville, Andersonville, Columbia, Charleston. When I meet you in New York, I will begin billing places for this tour. I must take advantage of the

trip over here in raising money for the way back. Although I offer you 35 dollars, if I could ahead when I arrive in Charleston, I will do more for you.

This is one of the greatest opportunities I have ever been able to offer you. I have always liked you and shall never turn my back on you. Now, the money you spend coming to New York, I shall hand back to you when I see you in New York. If you reach there before me just remain there till I come. I leave Liverpool August 8.
Yours respectfully
D.J. Jenkins

The other letter was sent to Brooks Brockman, another former member of the Orphanage's staff, then living in Columbia.

London, England July 25 1914
Dear Brooks,
The boys are making good. This is a fine opportunity for you to display your great talent as a cornetist before thousands of Europeans. I would like to have you come at once. If you can come, on receipt of this letter, wire me as follows, 'Will come, Brockman'. Then go to Charleston at once, get an order from Miss Marshall at the Orphanage for a ticket to New York via Clyde Line. When you reach New York, go to 223 Grand Street, Jersey City. You will find ticket there for London. Now, don't fail to wire me on receipt of this letter so I shall have time to have your ticket there waiting for you. Should you get there before the ticket, just remain there until it arrives. I shall give you twenty five dollars per month and all travelling expenses. Your salary begins with actual service. Trusting you are well, I am.
Yours respectfully,
D.J. J.

On July 23, 1914, Rev. Jenkins sent a letter on his orphanage stationary (deleting "Charleston, S.C." and replacing it with a typed "London, England") to South

Carolina Governor Coleman Blease. Some of the text of the letter included:

> ... the salvation of the South between the white and the black man lies in the careful training of the little negro boys and girls to become honest, upright and industrious citizens ... Teaching the Negro to read, to write and to work is not going to do the white man any harm ... Nine of the Councilmen of London called on me yesterday and congratulated me on the work I am doing for my race. If were able to gain the respect of the people of England, how much more can be done if the Governor and Lawmakers of South Carolina would simply co-operate with me?

Blease had been elected governor in 1910, because he "knew how to play on race, religious, and class prejudices to obtain votes." He was one of the most racist politicians ever elected in South Carolina. He favored complete white supremacy in all matters. He encouraged the practice of lynching, and was opposed to the education of blacks. He even once buried the severed finger of a black lynching victim in the South Carolina gubernatorial garden.

In light of Blease's racist attitude, Jenkins's letter to the governor was an indication of the reverend's fierce determination to raise money, no matter how remote the success.

On July 29, 1914, Austrian artillery began to bombard Belgrade, the Serbian capital. Russia was Serbia's protector and allied by treaty with France. Germany was allied with Austria, which could mean a German invasion of France, its goal capturing Paris. However, a German invasion of France would have to pass through Belgium, a neutral country, allied with

Great Britain. The British government warned Kaiser
Wilhelm that an invasion of Belgium would result in a
state of war between their two countries.

On the day of the Serbian bombardment, Jenkins
and Ella were sailing across the English Channel to
France, for a Parisian visit. Three days after their
arrival the French army was mobilized against
Germany. Ella wrote a note to her brother, Teddy, in
Charleston: "Will return to London Monday, leave for
Liverpool Wednesday and sail for New York
Saturday."

Great Britain declared war on Germany the same
day Jenkins and Ella arrived back in London. The
Anglo-American Expo came to a screeching halt.
Jenkins booked passage to New York for the band
aboard a ship called the *Laconia*, due to depart on
August 8. However, the British government suspend-
ed all civilian ship traffic and all ocean liners were
pressed into service as troop transports. Jenkins, Ella,
Jenks and the eighteen boys in the band had no choice
but to wait patiently for five weeks.

In September 1914, the Jenkins band boarded the
S.S. Campania in Liverpool and sailed to New York –
with one exception.

The reverend's son, Edmund Jenkins, elected to
stay in Europe. Jenks could not bear to return to
America still in the clench of Jim Crow politics. His
father reluctantly agreed to pay for his tuition to
London's Royal Academy of Music. While in England,
Jenks began to feel like a real man for the first time
in his life, a real citizen and, more importantly, a real
musician. Playing ragtime tunes on the street with
orphans was not what he envisioned for his life. He
dreamed of writing music that would be heard in
European concert halls, performed by members of the
finest orchestras in the world.

His role model for this vision was Will Marion

Cook – the prickly violinist who played with the Clef Club Orchestra at the famous Carnegie Hall concert, now revered as a great violinist. Even though Cook had written his share of "coon" music, Jenks considered him true composer and respected serious musician.

On September 21, 1914 Jenks enrolled in London's Royal Academy of Music. Ironically, the campus site had once been an orphanage. His enrollment fee was £14 ($75) which covered only his piano and composition studies. He listed his home address as 20 Franklin Street, Charleston, S.C., U.S.A. He was enrolled to study composition under the direction of Francis Corder, one of the world's leading experts on Wagnerian opera.

For an extra cost Jenks studied the French language and clarinet, taught by Edward J. Augarde. He also had to pay for his other expenses, such as instruments and lodging, but musical students in London could always earn money. Jobs were plentiful playing in pit bands for theatres, small orchestras in restaurants and cafes, or playing the piano for the silent movies. Since Jenks could sight read any music, and perform professionally on the violin, clarinet, piano and all brass instruments, he had little trouble paying his bills. It seemed Europeans were wild about black American musicians.

Opportunity (magazine), New York, Nov. 25, 1925, pp. 338-339:

> He [Jenks] also did a great deal of work in theatrical orchestras in London and the provinces of Great Britain. Chief among these periods with theaters is a season spent as first clarinetist at the Savoy Theater. As well as the holding of the same chair at the Grand Theater in Llandudno, Wales.

Jenks thrived socially and personally in the less

restrictive English racial climate. In 1915, his second year at the school, he won the bronze medal for clarinet, and in July 1916, Jenks' first composition, an overture, "Much Ado" for a production of *Much Ado About Nothing*, was publically performed.

Musical News, London, June 10, 1916:

> The orchestra played some very interesting music during the evening, under the direction of Mr. Frederick Corder, including a new Overture, "Much Ado", written for the occasion by a student, Edmund T. Jenkins. Though not strikingly original in design or treatment, the Overture indicated an engaging knowledge of orchestral effect which should carry the student far. It was splendidly played, and the composer had an enthusiastic call.

Musical News, London, Dec. 9. 1916:

> An interesting programme of music for two pianos was submitted by Messrs. Arthur L. Sandford and Edmund T. Jenkins, who were very much of one mind in their duets, which were rendered with wonderful precision and smoothness of execution.

Musical News, London, March 21, 1917.

> A song, "How Sweet Is Life" by a student, Mr. Edmund T. Jenkins, who is a native of Africa, showed the composer to be possessed of a vein of melody, not original as yet, and of a style which needs unifying, but his effort was full of promise, especially in the matter of orchestration. The song was well rendered by Miss Marjorie Perkins.

On June 22, 1917 Jenks' composition for grand organ and orchestra, *Prelude Religieuse*, was performed at the Queen's Hall at the Royal Academy.

In a mere two years, Jenks had progressed to the point where his compositions were being performed at one of London's leading concert halls. As the war raged across Europe, Jenks had something more important on his mind – his musical future.

***

Despite the death and devastation in Europe, the first two years of the Great War were heady ones for Jim Europe and the Clef Club. In the summer of 1916, almost a year before America entered the war, a new all-black regiment of the New York National Guard was formed; in September, Europe enlisted as a private and was immediately assigned to a machine gun company. Jim explained to Eubie Blake and Noble Sissle that, having lived in New York for sixteen years, he felt the need for an organization of Negro men that could "bring together all classes of men for a common good."

Jim Europe told Sissle:

> Now, some of the most influential men of our race, in Harlem, are going to join this regiment, as they realize the moral effect it will have, being promoted, financially, by the biggest men on Wall Street ... No, New York cannot afford to lose this great chance for such a strong, powerful institution, for the development of the negro manhood of Harlem.

Noble Sissle had been working as the manager of the Clef Club office for six years when Jim Europe convinced him to enlist. Their white commanding officer, Colonel William Hayward, recognized the importance of music and parades in establishing and maintaining military morale. He asked Europe to organize and develop the finest band in the U.S. Army. Although initially reluctant, Europe agreed to organize the band when his requests for both an expansion of the standard complement, from twenty-eight musicians to forty-four, and a handsome increase in the budget were approved. He and Sissle began to look for the best black musicians in the Army, or failing that, those whom they could persuade to join.

According to Noble Sissle, one of the most fortunate events was the recruitment of former Jenkins Band instructor, Eugene Mikell.

> Fate sent along a little, quiet, unassuming fellow, who gave his name as Eugene Mikell, and who turned out to be not only a good coronet player but an instructor of Bands and a good director. Jim made him the Band Master and assistant Conductor. He proved to be Jim's most valuable aid in perfecting the musicianship of the band.

Mikell brought former Jenkins trombonist, Amos Gaillard, into the band. Gaillard had remained in New York as a professional musician after the Orphanage Band's frantic return from England. Mikell also enlisted the two "non-brother" Jenkins' drummers, Steve and Herbert Wright.

Jim's confidence in the band's potential for success was bolstered when Mikell joined. Here was a professional music teacher and arranger, the perfect man to conduct rehearsals and transcribe Europe's arrangements. They immediately placed advertisements in prominent black newspapers across America looking for musicians.

ATTENTION!!!
Negro Musicians of America
Last Call   Golden Opportunity
If you want to do *your* duty in the present crisis

IF you are not in a financial position to give your services as a private volunteer.

IF you would serve you should be able to make a living wage for your family.

IF you are a First Class Musician.

IF you have dreamed of belonging to a famous Military Band.

IF you have longed for the time you could devote All Your Time to your music.

IF you want to belong to a regiment whose officers are sparing no means to make

their regimental band the Best In The World.

IF you want to be in a band that in the time of Peace will devote its time to Concert

Tours.

THEN WIRE OR CALL

Lt. James Reese Europe, care of 15th Regiment, N.Y. Infantry,

Harlem River Park Casino, 127th Street and 2nd Avenue, New York City.

P.S. There Are Only a Few More Vacancies Left, and the Regiment Goes To Camp, Sunday, May 13th.

So Hurry! Hurry! Hurry!

Colonel Hayward later wrote that:

... without the band of 369th U.S. Infantry the regiment never could have performed the long and difficult service it did both in America and in the A.E.F., and without Lieutenant Europe, there would have been no band.

During the tedious tour of Guard duty, in the camps, on the march, in billets and on the edge of the battle fields, the band was my main-stay for preserving moral and keeping up the spirits of our men.

I concur with Irvin S. Cobb who said in the *Saturday Evening Post*, that this was the best band in the American army. Others will write of his [Europe] musical ability, of his uniform good nature, of his sparkling wit and humor, but I will say that he was a brave soldier, a loyal friend and an honorable man.

Eubie Blake was asked to take over the administrative duties of the Clef Club. Unlike Sissle, Jim never pressured Blake to join the Guard. As Blake remembered it:

> Europe is a lieutenant now, see. And everybody knows they're going to war, but they're just gonna be musicians. Ain't none of us was a fighter, you know. But they'd introduce me to girls and they'd say, "This is Eubie Blake, the slacker." Now they don't tell the girls I'm thirty-five years old, see, way over the age for the army.

In May 1916 the 15th Regiment reached their camp near Peekskill, New York, and for eighteen days endured field training, passing their physicals and qualifying as riflemen. Under the strict instruction of Bandmaster Mikell, the regimental band quickly became a first class outfit while Jim spent many hours in New York City assembling the band's music library and working out arrangements. His growing sense of patriotism was remarkable, particularly in light of the persistent discrimination that black American soldiers encountered throughout the country. For example, following America's entry into the war, a request to include the 15th Regiment in the farewell parade down Fifth Avenue was rejected. Jim and the band were upset they were not to be accorded the same honor as a white band. This insult was compounded by a remark made to Europe as they marched off to join the Rainbow Division in France. Someone in the crowd hollered, "Black ain't one of the colors of the rainbow!"

Noble Sissle remembered:

By that time the band had several new members. Most valuable membership had been contributed by Hampton University in the persons of six musicians, who were not only masters of their instruments, but fine gentlemen ... the only exceptions being the drummer boys, Steve and Herbert Wright, who were below the standard educationally. They were practically waifs. Once they were members of Jenkins Orphanage Band from Charleston ... Band Master Mikell had at one time been director of this organization and it was he who got them to enlist ...

When I first saw them they appeared to me a great card. Both of them were of the same height, very dark of color and blessed with a set of pearly white teeth that shone as a flash of ivory against their ebony hue. It was not long before the Colonel and all the regiment were wild over them. And when Jim finally rejoined the band, he too, became equally wild about the boys and would always feature them on every program.

Shortly thereafter, the Army, in its infinite wisdom, announced the 15th Black Regiment would take up its training in Spartanburg, South Carolina. This brought an immediate warning from the mayor of Spartanburg, J. F. Floyd, who was quoted in the *New York Times*:

I was sorry to learn that the 15th Regiment has been ordered here, for with their northern ideas about race equality, they will probably expect to be treated like white men. I can say right here that they will not be treated as anything except negroes. We shall treat them exactly as we treat our resident negroes. This thing is like waving a red flag in the face of a bull, something that can't be done without trouble.

An inevitable series of incidents followed the 15th Regiment during its training in South Carolina, where the Jim Crow laws were strictly enforced and whites were emboldened to flaunt their superiority. Members were roughed up on the streets and refused service in local cafes and diners. The soldiers were forced to walk a narrow line – any retaliation by against the white civilians' threats was a punishable offense. So the black soldiers and musicians had to bear the harassment. However, the band's public concerts were warmly appreciated by many Spartanburg residents. But once again, the Army decided it was best to transfer the all-black regiment. This time, rather than admit defeat by shipping them to another location in the United States, it was determined the unit would be sent to France to complete its training.

TWELVE
Harlem's Hellfighters – Jazz Mad!

"Before we had played two numbers the audience went wild. We had conquered Paris!"   – Lt. Jim Europe

IN 1917 THE CHARLESTON CITY COUNCIL APPROPRIATED $2500 to the Jenkins Orphanage with the logic that without the Orphan Aid Society, the city's black children would "become a burden and menace to the community." The band was the Society's most successful fundraising tool, accounting for more than $10,000 of its $28,000 annual budget.

1917 was also the year the Original Dixieland Jazz Band (ODJB) recorded what are now considered the first jazz records. The ODJB have historically been dismissed as white guys who copied Negro music and called it their own. Although there is much truth in that sentiment, the early recordings of the ODJB are excellent representations of the new music that was creeping into mainstream society.

The ODJB toured in Europe. Their appearance at the London Hippodrome was the first official jazz gig by any band in the United Kingdom. It created furor that would only be matched by Beatlemania forty years later. The band was invited to a command performance at Buckingham Palace for King George V. During the concert the aristocratic audience peered through opera glasses at the band "as though there were bugs on us," according to trumpet play Nick

LaRocco. The British tour ended with the band being chased to the Southampton docks by Lord Harrington whose daughter was being romanced by a member of the band. Louis Armstrong acknowledged the importance of the ODJB. In a 1936 interview he stated:

Only four years before I learned to play the trumpet in the Waif's Home, or in 1909, the first great jazz orchestra was formed in New Orleans by a cornet player named Dominick James LaRocca. They called him 'Nick' LaRocca. His orchestra had only five pieces but they were the hottest five pieces that had ever been known before.

The Original Dixieland Jazz Band introduced black dance music to a larger white audience. *Courtesy of the Library of Congress*

In 1921 the ODJB recorded on of their most famous songs, "Jazz Me Blues," written by whore-house professor Tom Delaney, ten years after his escape from the Jenkins Orphanage.

James Reese Europe and the 15th black Regiment from New York joined a convoy of American soldiers to France, arriving on New Year's Day 1918. They were the first American black combat group to set foot on French soil, and Jim Europe immediately conducted the band in a rousing performance of the "Marseillaise." However, Europe's arrangement of the song was such a rhythmically spirited rendition the French soldiers failed to recognize it. Halfway through the song, everyone on the docks realized these Negro Americans were actually playing the French national anthem! Everyone rushed to stand at attention.

The Americans received orders to proceed to a center where an engineering detachment was busy building facilities to support an overwhelming force. Their musical instruments were exchanged for picks and shovels. Assignments were made even more difficult by the traditional injunction against black soldiers serving with white ones. It was clear that the American Army had no idea what to do with a black regiment.

Eventually American entertainment organizers got word Europe's band was in France, and when they finally heard the group perform they were astounded. Orders followed from General Pershing, transferring the 15th Regiment to a location where they could entertain soldiers who were on a week's leave.

In February-March of 1918, James Reese Europe and his military band travelled over 2,000 miles across France, performing for British, French and American military audiences as well as French civilians. Their programs featured Sousa's "Stars and Stripes Forever" and "plantation" melodies, finishing with "Memphis Blues" which invariably brought down the house. "Jazz spasms" and "ragtime-itis," to use Sissle's words, worked the crowds into a frenzy.

In 1900 France was driven "ragtime wild" by John Philip Sousa's performances, and a few years later it became "Castle-mad." Now, the entire country was infected with the music of the all black Regimental Band.

15th Regimental Band, aka, the Harlem Hellfighters.
Courtesy of the National Archives

Repeated attempts to have the 15th Regiment reassigned to combat duty fell on deaf ears because of America's Jim Crow policies. The unit was given two choices: return to the United States and await assignment to a proposed black division, or accept immediate transfer to the French Army, which had already integrated French colonial troops into its ranks and was now in desperate need of reinforcements. The regiment's commanding officer accepted the latter proposal at once, and at the end of March Lt. Jim Europe's regiment, carrying the colors from the state of New York, marched to the front, becoming the first American unit to join a French combat force. The 15th Infantry Regiment vanished and the 369th Infantry Regiment, U.S. Army, was born. Lt. Europe was given command to Company I, 3rd Battalion. Lt. Europe was impressed with the French soldiers. He wrote to Fred Moore, editor of the *New York Age*:

> Their broad minds are far and free from prejudice, and you, as a great champion of our people, I am sure will be glad to know that ... the French simply cannot be taught to comprehend that despicable thing called prejudice ... "Viva la France" should be the song of every black American over here and over there.

These black soldiers of the new Trois Cents Soixante-Neuvième (369th), as they were dubbed, soon impressed everyone with their adeptness at throwing grenades and in hand-to-hand bayonet combat. The Germans bristled with outrage of being attacked by Negro troops. They charged the Allies had "brought black troops to subdue European soldiers."

Nonetheless, genuine friendships developed between the French and black American soldiers, and the level of cooperation between the two forces seemed nothing short of miraculous in light of the black regiment's recent experiences in the U.S. Army. In the trenches, however, both sides needed each other – a soldier is a soldier.

The 369th were soon ordered closer to the front, and Lt. Europe turned over his music responsibilities to Noble Sissle and Eugene Mikell as director and conductor of the regimental band, which continued to perform concerts for morale. Lt. Europe took charge of instructing his troops in the use of the French machine guns and protection from gas attacks. Then he learned some tragic news – his old friend and employer, Vernon Castle, after flying more than 100 reconnaissance missions behind German lines for the Royal Air Force, had died in an airplane training accident near Fort Worth, Texas.

Vernon Castle's crashed plane. *Courtesy of the Library of Congress.*

Jim Europe grieved deeply for the man who played such an important role in helping to expose the Clef Club Orchestra's black music and dance to middle class white America. Europe considered Castle "one white absolutely without prejudice."

But in a time of war, mourning is accomplished quickly. Within a few weeks Lt. Europe became the first black officer to lead his troops into combat during the War, the first to cross into no-man's land, the area between two enemy trenches that neither side wishes to openly move on or take control of due to fear of being attacked by the enemy. He was the first black officer to conduct a raid on the German lines.

Over the next several weeks Jim Europe gained firsthand experience of the hell called "no man's land." The Germans also became aware of these unusual

American troops, calling them those "blood-thirsty black men." The unit picked up the nickname "the Hellfighters."

Black Troops marching through France, World War I.
Courtesy of the Library of Congress

During the third week in June 1918, Lt. Jim Europe and his machine gunners came under heavy German artillery fire. Lt. Europe was the victim of a gas attack and transferred to a field hospital. When Noble Sissle arrived at the gas ward to visit he was astounded by what he saw:

> When we looked around the little white partition and saw Lieut. Europe sitting upright in his bed, with his knees raised and using them for a table upon which he was writing some words in a little notebook that he had been carrying with him. When he looked up through his big, shell-rimmed glasses and saw it was us, a big broad smile swept across his face, and instead of telling us how seriously he was gassed ... the first thing that he

spoke up and said was: "Gee, I am glad to see you boys, Sissle, here's a wonderful idea for a song that just came to me."

We asked the Lieutenant to show us what he had written. Little did either of us realize that we were listening to a song that has gone down in theatrical history as being a masterpiece of jazz description.

It was the chorus of "On Patrol in No Man's Land," based on the bombardment the night before. It was to become one America's most popular songs after the war.

What's the time? Nine? Fall in line
Alright, boys, now take it slow
Are you ready? Steady! Very good, Eddie.
Over the top, let's go

Quiet, lie it, else you'll start a riot
Keep your proper distance, follow 'long
Cover, brother, and when you see me hover
Obey my orders and you won't go wrong

There's a Minenwerfer [German mortar] coming --look out (bang!)
Hear that roar (bang!), there's one more (bang!)
Stand fast, there's a Very light [flare]
Don't gasp or they'll find you all right

Don't start to bombing with those hand grenades (rat-a-tat-tat-tat)
There's a machine gun, holy spades!
Alert, gas! Put on your mask
Adjust it correctly and hurry up fast

Drop! There's a rocket from the Boche [German] barrage
Down, hug the ground, close as you can, don't stand

Creep and crawl, follow me, that's all
What do you hear? Nothing near
Don't fear, all is clear
That's the life of a stroll when you take a patrol
Out in No Man's Land
Ain't it grand? Out in No Man's Land

Jim Europe was sent to Paris for a few weeks to recover where he was classified as Physical Class B, which meant he could not be sent to active front line duty. In August, the band was ordered back to Paris to give a concert and Colonel Hayward ordered Jim Europe to resume his duties as bandmaster for this concert.

I protested, telling him that I hadn't led the band since February, but he insisted. Well, I went back to my band and with it I went to Paris. What was to be our only concert was in the Théâtre des Champs-Elysées. Before we had played two numbers the audience went wild. We had conquered Paris. General Bliss and French high officers who had heard us insisted that we should stay in Paris, and there we stayed for eight weeks.

During the remaining months of the war the band played hundreds of concerts that held audiences spellbound and thrilled. What made this American black band so different, so better than other bands the French had heard? Was it the novelty of all black musicians? Was it French gratitude for American assistance in the war? Jim Europe wasn't sure.

The supreme moment came in the Tuileries Gardens when we gave a concert in conjunction with [the] greatest bands in the world – the British Grenadier's Band, the band of the Garde Republicain [sic], and the Royal Italian Band. My band, of course, could not compete with these, yet the crowd … deserted them for us. We played to 50,000 people, at least, and had we

172 / Mark R. Jones

wished it, we might be playing yet.

After the concert was over the leader of ... the Garde Republicain came over and asked for the score of one of the jazz compositions we had played. He said he wanted to his band to play it. I gave it to him, and the next day he again came to see me. He explained that he couldn't seem to get the effects I got, and asked me to go to a rehearsal. I went with him. The great band played the composition superbly – but he was right; the jazz effects were missing. I took an instrument and showed him how it could be done, and he told me that his own musicians felt sure that my band used special instruments.

Both band leaders were learning that it was less important *what* the band played, rather it was *how* they played it. In an October 1918 *New York Age* article titled "Jazz Music Makes A Hit With French Officials," the writer commented on French officers being "exceedingly fond of the 'jazz' music furnished by colored bands ... with some of the Negro dance stunts in keeping with the spirit of the melodies."

A few weeks after the Armistice the "Harlem Hellfighters" of the 369th Infantry Regiment were awarded the Croix de Guerre. The December 9, 1918 citation to the French Croix de Guerre with Silver Star reads in part:

This officer (Lt. James Reese Europe), a member of the 369th Infantry Regiment of the 93rd Infantry Division, American Expeditionary Forces, was the first black American to lead United States troops in battle during World War I. The unit, under fire for the first time, captured some powerful and energetically defended enemy positions, took the village of Bechault by main force, and brought back six cannons, many machine guns and a number of prisoners.

It was also discovered that the 191 days the regiment had spent in action was the longest stretch served by any group of American soldiers, black or white, during the War. Yet they had always fought attached to a foreign service, never to an American brigade or division. The Hellfighters were one of the most amazing stories during World War I that has sadly faded away into the mists of American history, unnoticed by the short-sighted public of their age.

Tens of thousands of people line New York City streets waiting for the Harlem Hellfighters to march past. *Courtesy of the National Archives.*

THIRTEEN
Hellfighter's Triumph & Tragedy

"I have come back from France more firmly convinced than ever that Negroes should write Negro music. We have our own racial feeling and if we try to copy whites we will make bad copies ... We won France by playing music which was ours and not a pale imitation of others, and if we are to develop in America we must develop along our own lines."

- James Reese Europe, Literary Digest, 1919

THE HARLEM HELLFIGHTERS ARRIVED BACK IN THE United States on the *S.S. La France* and the band via the *S. S. Stockholm* on 12 February 1919. For their arrival in New York, Col. Hayward asked for his favorite song, "The Army Blues" to be performed. Noble Sissle recalled:

> I had heard the band play with enthusiasm and spirit on several occasions, both on concert and parade, but I never heard such a volume of jazzy syncopated strains as came from their instruments when Lieutenant Europe gave them the signal to play and amid the cheers and yells of the crowd, those dusky heroes came proudly stepping down the gang-plank and drew up in formation. By that time the news had spread all over upper New York and all over Harlem, the home section of most of the boys.

The regiment was then taken to Camp Upton, Long Island for demobilization. Col. Hayward was well aware of the men's bitterness because of being denied a parade when they left New York, so plans were made for a victory parade up Fifth Avenue and home to Harlem.

New York City Mayor John Hylan was in Palm Beach, Florida that day, escaping the winter chill. He had declined to proclaim an official holiday for the Hellfighters, but most New Yorkers took the day off anyway. As one white spectator said, "I just had to see those boys. I never will get another opportunity to see such a sight, and I can get another job."

On February 15, 1919, two days before the big parade, the *New York Age* announced a concert being sponsored at Carnegie Hall by the Clef Club to honor the Hellfighter's Band. W.C. Handy served as a guest conductor for three of his "blues" songs. An exaggerated advertisement in the paper read:

> Hear the songs that the Doughboys of the Fighting Old 15th sang as they went "over the top" and put the Huns to run! Hear the Jazz tunes of Lieut. James Europe's Famous Ragtime Soldier Band which set France whistling and dancing! Hear Sergt. Gene Mikell's great song hit "Camp Meetin' Day" which created such a furor at the big Armistice celebration in Paris, London and Rome.

On February 17, the Harlem Hellfighters marched home on Fifth Avenue. Jim Europe proudly led his band in the nation's first parade for returning World War I heroes. More than a million people watched the famed 369th Infantry strut from Madison Square to Harlem. Noble Sissle remembered:

> There must have been two thousand cans of shoe polish used to shine those Army shoes ... every bayonet was shining like the highest polished steel ...

trousers were creased, coats pressed and helmets shined. All the soldiers that had been complaining of rheumatism and other ailments that heretofore had caused them to be limp and crippled, were now standing erect and in the best marching condition. Jim Europe had swung through his band and made a careful inspection of their instruments ... looking as though they were freshly plated silver.

The command was given, "Forward March!" The band swung out to the time of the rattling drums (of the Jenkins Band Wright boys). There were now forty-five musicians who had jazzed their way from the Hudson to the Rhine and back again, and whose experience had run the gauntlet of human adventures.

Before they were known as Colonel Haywards' "Tin Soldiers", now they were stepping off under the enemy's christened name of "Hell Fighters" and every movement screamed confidence, born of experience. On foot, officers and hundreds of men, all wearing decorations for honor and bravery, paraded proudly.

As the regiment swung along, the entire length of Fifth Avenue, from the windows - from the roofs - from the street — from everywhere, there rose a tumultuous yell ... it was a sight that no one had ever seen before.

As the band marched into Harlem they broke into "Here Comes My Daddy" to the grand delight of the crowd. Major Arthur Little recalled, "For the final mile of the parade about every fourth soldier of the ranks had a girl upon his arm – and we marched through Harlem singing and laughing."

These soldiers were bringing home a new self-confidence, a new lifestyle, a new attitude and a new music that would soon infect America. James Weldon Johnson wrote:

The Fifteenth furnished the first sight that New York has had of seasoned soldiers in marching order. There was no militia smartness about their appearance; their "tin hats" were battered and rusty and the shiny newness worn off their bayonets, but they were men who had gone through the terrible hell of war and come back.

**Harlem Hellfighters' triumphant march through New York.
Courtesy of the *National Archives***

Jim Europe was discharged from active duty on February 25, 1919, and he immediately set about making plans for a national tour with his 369th Hellfighters Band. Several members of the original 15th Infantry Band decided to return home after their discharge, including Sgt. Gene Mikell. Jim got busy augmenting the band with additional musicians.

Before the tour the band recorded about thirty songs for the Pathe Record Company. Today these songs stand as the best illustration of Jim Europe's vision of where popular black music was headed. It included "On Patrol In No Man's Land", the song Europe had written while recovering from his gas attack.

One of the more interesting songs recorded was the already popular tune, "How You Gonna Keep 'Em Down on the Farm (After They've Seen Paree)." It perfectly catches the mood of returning American soldiers: after exposure to the horror of trench warfare and the nightlife of Paris, their lives were forever changed. When performed by Hellfighters Band, their swinging version of "How You Gonna Keep 'Em" becomes nothing short of an early civil rights protest song.

Music historian Gunther Schuller calls these thirty recordings the "first big band," which just happened to feature three former Jenkins band members - Amos Gaillard on trombone and the non-brother drummers, Herbert and Steve Wright. Not to mention the invisible hand of Gene Mikell who arranged and rehearsed these songs with the band during their time in France until playing the notes came as a reflex for the musicians. It may have been the tightest musical outfit at the time.

Schuller said, "White concerts bands could take a ragtime or early jazz piece and make it stiff and polite, while Europe's band could take a polite salon piece and make it swing."

It wasn't *what* they played; it was *how* they played it.

Less than a month after making those recordings the band debuted in front of three thousand people at the renowned Hammerstein's Manhattan Opera House. They were billed as "Lieut. James Reese Europe and His Famous 369th U.S. Infantry Band featuring Superstar Lieut. Noble Sissle."

The New York *Sun* raved:

> There was a flood of good music, a gorgeous racket of syncopation and jazzing, extraordinarily pleasing violin and cornet solos and many other features that bands seldom offer. ... echoes of camp meetings and of the

traditional darkey life that seems almost to have disappeared ...

The only slightly negative part of the show had been during the snare drum duet by the "Percussive Twins," as Herbert and Steve Wright were called. During the solo Herbert dissolved into a fit of uncontrolled giggling, but soon had the audience laughing along with him. It saved an embarrassing moment for the band; however, it just emphasized to Jim Europe what a fool Herbert could be. The boy was unpredictable.

The band took the train to Boston for a sold out performance at the Boston Opera House, and for the next ten weeks they toured Eastern and Midwestern cities, selling out each theater and leaving in their wake exuberant audiences and equally enthusiastic newspaper accounts.

Advertisements proclaimed: 65 BATTLING MUSICIANS DIRECT FROM THE FIGHTING FRONTS IN FRANCE - THE BAND THAT SET ALL FRANCE JAZZ MAD!

"On Patrol In No Man's Land" became one of America's most popular songs, favored by U.S. veterans, both black and white. Riding high artistically and commercially, Europe, Sissle and Blake made plans to organize a National Negro Orchestra and a new musical Broadway production. Meanwhile, they endured the tough grinding two month tour. The days, the towns, the concerts seemed to blend into a blur – two days and four performances in one town and then an overnight train ride to another town. But finally they reached the end on May 9, 1919 back in Boston. There was a large ad in the Boston *Herald* that read: "Return Visit By Popular Demand: Three Jubilee Days of Sunshine in Music by Lieut. 'Jim' Europe and the Famous

Hellfighters' 369ᵗʰ U.S. Infantry Band."

Due to a scheduling conflict at the Boston Opera House, the band's second appearance in Boston was moved to Mechanic's Hall, whose large auditorium was used to host boxing matches, dog competitions and flower shows.

When the train pulled into Boston the morning of May 9, 1919 Jim Europe was exhausted and suffering from a deep cough and cold he could not shake. Since the band had two performances that day – a matinee and an evening show at 8:30 - Europe went to see Doctor Bennie Robinson, who told Jim that he "was a very sick man and if he were not careful, his cold would run into pneumonia and he would have to go to the hospital."

Mechanic's Hall, Boston. *Courtesy of the Library of Congress*

Noble Sissle recalled:

It was raining and very miserable – one of those days that are cold and misty, accompanied by treacherous East winds that Boston is noted for. The Mechanics Hall had no stage facilities and was a very cold and barn-like auditorium, quite different from the warmth and beautiful Boston Opera House … the continuous downpour of rain in the evening likewise affected the attendance of the crowd, and at 8:30 when the opening number was played, there were quite a few empty seats noticeable in the auditorium.

Sissle's part of the musical program consisted of singing "four or five songs near the end of the second half." That left him free to tend to whatever business arose during the concert. The main issue of concern for the first performance was that Herbert Wright wandered off the stage after the second song. Sissle went to look for the drummer and found Herbert lying on a bench in the dressing room. He had taken his uniform coat off. Sissle asked him if he was ill.

"No, I'm not sick," Herbert replied.

"Well, what's the matter?" Sissle asked. "Why don't you go back on the stage? You know it's time for you and Steve to do your drumming bit."

Herbert sat up and Sissle saw that the boy was in a "very sulky and nasty mood."

> Having trooped with him for over two years, in all conditions, I knew that the boy would get sulky moods at times, and I generally being in command of the discipline of the band, would always make allowances for his peculiar nature and humor him into doing whatever I wanted him to do. From his attitude I knew that he would like to get into an argument but I went to him and patted him on the shoulder and asked him what was wrong.

"You know, Lt. Sissle," Herbert said, "I work hard and Steve never does anything right and he makes mistakes and then Lt. Europe looks back in the drummer section and frowns at me."

"Look, Herbert," Sissle replied. "Jim never depends on Steve in any of the heavy numbers and if anything goes wrong in the drummer section, Lt. Europe depends on you to pull the time together."

Herbert reluctantly put on his coat and stood up. "Well, for you, Lt. Sissle, I will go back on the stage but you know I work hard and Jim has no right to frown at me." Sissle walked Herbert back to the stage and the band finished the first half of the show, concluding with the rousing and popular "Percussive Twins" number. Sissle returned to the dressing room to read the newspaper.

During intermission, Jim Europe joined Sissle in the dressing room, followed by Herbert and Steve Wright. Herbert still had his drum fastened to his neck strap. Steve closed the door behind him.

Europe wearily sat down at the table opposite Sissle and said, "Now Herbert, you and Steve know how sick I am. The doctor says that I should be in the hospital right now, but I am trying to keep going in order to finish out this engagement, that all of you may have your money and be able to go home or take your vacations. You two boys above anybody else in the band should cause me the least worry. I have at all times tried to be a father to both of you and there is nothing I wouldn't do to help both of you, and I don't want either one of you to worry me anymore."

Steve was instantly apologetic. "All right, Lieutenant, I promise I will not cause you any more worry."

"How about you, Herbert?" Jim Europe asked.

"Lt. Europe, you don't treat me right. I work hard for you. Look at my hands, they're all swollen where I have been drumming, trying to hold the time and yet, Steve, he makes all kinds of mistakes and you never say anything to him, you don't treat me right."

Before Jim could answer several people entered the dressing room, wanting to meet Lt. Europe. During the intermission, Europe often met with local dignitaries. Sissle could sense that Herbert was still in a foul mood, telling the drummer to return when the visitors left. Sissle escorted Herbert through the door and turned to go back into the room.

A moment later, Herbert burst back into the room and tossed his drum into the corner. He yanked off his coat, throwing it on the floor. He turned and raised his fist toward Jim Europe. Flashing a knife he yelled, "I'll kill anybody that takes advantage of me! Jim Europe, I'll kill you!"

Europe backed up to the wall with a chair in his hands. He held it as a shield between himself "and the menacing dwarf, as he stood there in his distorted position, crouching as a ferocious animal preparing to lunge upon its victim."

Everyone hollered, "Knock the knife out of his hand, Jim!"

Noble Sissle described what happened next:

> Jim grasped the chair in an attitude as though he was about to carry out our warning, when all of sudden there came over him some thought, God knows what, that caused him to completely relax, his whole body and set the chair down and was about to mutter "Herbert get out of here!" when to our amazement, before any of us could move from our track, like a panther Herbert Wright hurled himself over the chair.
>
> As he came through the air, Jim clasped his body and whirled it away from him, but as the demon had made up his mind to carry out his murderous attack with a back-handed blow. He made a wild swing of his knife, brought it down in the direction of Jim Europe's face.

Herbert fell and before the drummer could regain his feet Noble Sissle grabbed him. Sissle hollered, "Herbert, what's the matter with you? Are you crazy to cause this embarrassment here before strangers? Come out of the room!"

Herbert offered no resistance as Sissle led him out into the hall to another dressing room. Just as he was about to confront the drummer for his behavior someone hollered, "Sissle, come here at once! Herbert stabbed Lt. Europe!"

Sissle rushed into the room and saw Europe sitting down, tugging at the military collar around his neck. When the collar was unfastened a stream of blood spurted from the small wound.

They wrapped a towel around Jim's neck. An ambulance was called; a police officer in the audience took Herbert Wright into custody. Europe ordered to be carried out the back door, so no one in the audience would know anything had happened.

As he was carried out on the stretcher, Europe told Sissle:

> Don't forget to have the band down before the State House at 9:00 in the morning. I am going to the hospital and I will have my wound dressed and I will be at the Commons in the morning, in time to conduct the band. See that the rest of the program is gone through with. I leave everything for you to carry on.

They made an announcement to the audience that Lt. Europe had fallen ill during the intermission but the concert would continue. After the concert, Sissle went to the police station to give his statement. Then he rushed to the hospital. He was told by an orderly at the desk that Lt. Europe was in grave condition, the only thing that may save him would be a blood transfusion. Sissle volunteered to give blood, and a few minutes later he was told there would be no need.

"Lt. Europe is dead," the orderly told him.

After surviving a gas attack in the trenches of "no man's land," Jim Europe ironically failed to live through the Harlem Hellfighter's triumphant national concert tour. After facing German machine gun fire

186 / Mark R. Jones

and bayonet attacks, Europe was killed by a stab wound rendered from a pen knife by a simple-minded drummer.

The next day, newspapers across America screamed the headline: KING OF JAZZ MURDERED! W. C. Handy was living in Harlem and remembered the disbelief that ran through the community when they heard the news. In his biography, *Father of the Blues: An Autobiography*, Handy wrote:

> The man who had just come through the baptism of war's fire and steel without a mark had been stabbed by one of his own musicians during a band performance in Boston. No wonder I couldn't sleep ... the sun was in the sky. The new day promised peace. But all suns had gone down for Jim Europe and Harlem didn't seem the same.

New York's black community was not alone in their shock. Lt. James Reese Europe was held in such respect among white society his murder was considered a national tragedy and he was given a public funeral – the first for a black American in New York City.

On Tuesday, May 13, 1919 thousands of people filed past his casket at Paris Undertakers on 131st Street. Just after 11:00 am the funeral procession began. Led by a squad of police from the 38th Precinct the procession slowly wound through the streets of Harlem – to 7th Avenue, north to 140th Street, east to Lenox and South to 125th Street, following the same route of the victory parade just three months earlier.

Six cars carried flowers sent by hundreds of Americans. Following the flowers was the new 15th Infantry Band veterans of the "Old 15th," then the hearse, eight members of Lt. Europe's Hellfighters machine gun unit and a dozen honorary pall bearers.

The streets were lined with thousands of citizens, often four or five people deep on the sidewalk for block after block. Europe's body was taken to Philadelphia Station and transported to Washington, D.C. for burial with full military honors at Arlington National Cemetery.

Harlem Hellfighters Band. James Reese Europe (extreme left) with the "Percussive Twins" sitting behind him. *Courtesy of the National Archives*

On the day before Europe's funeral, Herbert Wright was indicted for first degree murder in Boston. He pled self-defense. Two doctors for the defense examined Wright and found him in their opinion, insane. The state of Massachusetts hired its own medical experts to examine Wright and found him, "of such low type mentality that there was a question as to his entire responsibility."

Herbert Wright pled guilty to manslaughter and was sentenced to ten to fifteen years in the Massachusetts State Penitentiary. He was paroled eight years later on April 1, 1927 - April Fool's Day.

In July 1919, the Hellfighter's Band was reorganized under the leadership of Gene Mikell. They played a successful concert at the Manhattan Casino and served as the headliner at one last Carnegie Hall concert as "a tribute to the late leader of this band."

Noble Sissle and Eubie Blake hit the vaudeville circuit as the "Dixie Duo" ending their shows with their rendition of "On Patrol In No Man's Land." In 1920 they met the comedy-dancing team of Flournoy E. Miller and Aubrey Lyles. Together, these men decided to resurrect one of Jim Europe's most passionate dreams – produce a successful black musical for Broadway.

One year later their show, *Shuffle Along*, opened at the Sixty-Third Street Theatre in New York – written, produced, directed and performed completely by black Americans. The show was such a financial success it created a demand for black-only shows on Broadway, revolutionizing American musical theater.

At the time of his death James Reese Europe was only thirty-nine years old and at the forefront of the burgeoning jazz movement. One can only speculate about what further contributions he might have made to American culture he had not been murdered. On the threshold of a brilliant career Europe may have become one of the most important figures in the world of popular music on par with Gershwin, Handy, Ellington and Armstrong.

Eubie Blake said sadly, "He was our benefactor and inspiration. Even more, he was the Martin Luther King of music."

Tommy Benford of the Jenkins Band sadly recalled the murder of Jim Europe as related to him by his former drum instructor, Steve Wright:

Steve Wright said that Jim Europe never liked Herb,

that they were always arguing. He was always picking on Herb. Herb once said, "One of these days, I'm going to cut your throat." And the particular day came ... Herb killed Europe with a little penknife. He cut his throat.

Prophetically, the back page of the Pathé Recording catalog predicted: "Jim Europe's jazz will live forever!" And it has; in 1996 Memphis Archives, a record company dedicated to preserving America's rich musical heritage, released a carefully re-mastered compact disc of the rare Pathé recordings. In the promotional catalog, they proclaimed that Europe was:

> ... the world's greatest exponent of syncopation. You hear every moan of the trombones, and every roar of the saxophones, every shrill note of the clarinets. The swing, the rhythm and the fascination of the Jazzing makes you want to dance! You can't sit still!

In late February 2000, a busload of aging legionnaires carefully ambled up a slippery, wet grassy hill at Arlington National Cemetery. They were from the 1st Lt. James Reese Europe American Legion Post 5 in Washington, D.C. They laid a wreath at the headstone engraved with "Lt. James Reese Europe - Feb. 22, 1881 - May 14, 1919." Europe has a larger headstone than most - it was erected in July 1943 to replace a small government-issued 1919 grave marker.

Post commander Thomas L. Campbell said:

> Our post was named in honor of James Reese Europe in 1919, but to my knowledge, no one ever stopped to put a flower on his grave. Frankly, we did"t know much about him until we read a story about him in the American Legion magazine about a year ago. I thought it was time we did something to show some appreciation for the man whose name is on our post.

Anglo-American Exposition.   "Altogether."   The Famous Piccaninny Band.

Jenkins Band, Anglo-American Expo postcard – "The Famous Piccaninny Band.
*Photo courtesy of the Charleston Jazz Initiative, Avery Research Center
for African American History and Culture, College of Charleston.*

FOURTEEN
Charlestonia

"We can only conjecture about the sound of the early Jenkins' Orphanage Bands. They played a robust music that loosened up the formal ragtime arrangements. The Jenkins Band's zestful way of re-phrasing melodies in a more rhythmically exciting way certainly left its mark on listeners."   - John Chilton, *A Jazz Nursery*

THROUGHOUT THE GREAT WAR, THE JENKINS BANDS continued traveling across America. There was an endless supply of young boys ready to step in and replace a departing older player. The bands continued to perform at a high level.

Herbert 'Peanuts' Holland, born 1910, was one of those young boys. Peanuts became a master trumpeter, playing with Alphonse Trent, Lil Hardin, Jimmy Lunceford, Coleman Hawkins and Fletcher Henderson. He spent more than a decade in Europe, recording more than forty albums for European labels. He recalls how he came to join the band:

A Jenkins Band came to Norfolk, Virginia, my home town, and I just followed that band, I wanted to play one of those instruments. One boy there was playing nice cornet, another boy too, they were Cladys (Jabbo) Smith, and John Murphy. So I went to my aunt, and asked her, "Don't you think it would be possible for you to send me to this school?" She said, "I've already spoken to the man who is carrying the banner." So it came about ... everything was arranged, and she put a tag on my little suit and put me on the train. When I got to Charleston there was someone there with a horse and buggy to meet me. Took me to Jenkins Orphanage, but there weren't any bands there then, they were all out on the road. So I hung around, wishing and waiting for the bands to come back, so maybe I could join one of them.

Peanuts soon got his wish. He was assigned with the Number Two Band, playing cymbals.

I used to beat the cymbals, twist them, roll them and everything. So, one day in Jacksonville, Florida, we were playing on a street corner and some guy gave the manager a cornet, seems like he was reading my mind, so he gave the coronet to me. So the coronet players were then Cladys [Jabbo] Smith, John Murphy and myself - I wasn't doing much. Jabbo, oh, he was still my idol, from the very first time I saw him. We would be on the street playing … and he would play an octave higher, oh boy, that was something, that was tops, and the people would applaud and applaud. After Jabbo left, I took over leadership of the band, which meant calling the number and setting the tempo, and I often tried to do that 'Bubbles', but I just couldn't make it to save my life, until way later. After I had left the band I tried it on a job in Albany, New York and I made it!

During the early 1920s, touring brought the Jenkins Band to Chicago for several weeks. For Jabbo and Peanuts the highlight of that trip was a chance to see Louis Armstrong perform. Armstrong had been a strong influence on most musicians of the era and on the Jenkins kids in particular. They were all aware Armstrong had learned to play the coronet as a young kid in a Waif's home brass band in New Orleans. For the Jenkins kids, Armstrong was proof positive that one could make it as a musician.

It's interesting to note that, with the exception of Henry "Kid" Rena, there are few other jazz musicians from the Colored Waif's Home Brass Band who managed to have successful musical careers. Compare this to the success of the Jenkins band; for more than thirty years, dozens of professional jazz musicians were trained in the "jazz nursery," illustrating how magical and unusual the Jenkins Band actually was.

Perry Bradford mentioned the Jenkins band in his autobiography, *Born with the Blues*. Bradford was a singer, songwriter, pianist, vaudeville and minstrel performer who changed American music when he convinced Okeh Records to release the first Blues record in 1920. For several years Bradford had been positive that there was a market for black music aimed at black consumers but no one at the New York white-owned record companies were willing to take the chance. Through the years Bradford recorded and performed with several Jenkins musicians in his band including: Jabbo Smith, coronet; Gus Aiken, coronet; Bud Aiken, trombone and Bill Benford, tuba. He commented that the Jenkins kids were trained to:

> ... play such wonderful, traditional Afro-American music ... please bear in mind this happened four years before Sidney Bechet went to Europe with Will Marion Cook and Lattimore's Syncopated Orchestra.

John Chilton, the English music historian who first popularized the term "jazz nursery" in connection with the Jenkins Bands, speculated on what style of music they were playing in the early days:

> We can only conjecture about the sound of the early Jenkins' Orphanage Bands. If they had made recordings we could go a long way toward establishing what their role was in the story of early jazz. They played a robust music that loosened up the formal ragtime arrange-

ments, and produced emphatic syncopations when playing marches and two-steps. By 'ragging' marches and popular tunes of the day, I think the early bands imparted a 'jazzy' phrasing to their performances, more polyrhythmic than polyphonic. However, I do not think, that at any stage in the pre-1910 era were the players encouraged to improvise solos. The Jenkins Bands' zestful way of re-phrasing melodies in a more rhythmically exciting way certainly left its mark on listeners.

Fred Norman, trombonist and arranger spoke of hearing the band during the early days. "They were swinging like crazy then."

James P. Johnson remembered the rhythmic aspect of the Jenkins Band:

> There was another band that played New York and other Northern cities in the years 1910-1916, they could really swing. That was the Jenkins Orphan Asylum [sic] Band from Charleston, S.C. They played marches, and minstrel and cotillion tunes with real syncopation and swing. 'Traps' McIntosh, in my opinion, the greatest drummer of all time was trained there, as was Herbert Wright and Gene Anderson whose specialty was drumming on the wall.

Leonard De Paur, composer and conductor gave a description of the Jenkins Band in *The Book of Jazz*:

> I remember when I was child, those kids used to come up as far north as Trenton and just play on the street corners in the most non-descript uniforms you ever saw - some sort of the jacket with brass buttons and pants with stripes. They would just stand around in a circle and the leader was somebody who could dance like hell - he didn't have to have any talent more than the ability to say '1, 2, boom!' and then go into a routine of his own which would highlight the performances. But they

did move around all over the country and they played the most positive ragtime you have ever heard.

The Jenkins' players also thought they had something special. Jabbo Smith said that the band "created excitement wherever it went." Tommy Benford recalled:

> We played all types of music. Any type of music you can mention, we played-from rags to marches to hymns; different songs, different types of music. Everyone you know who came out of that school was a wonderful musician ... We used to swing when we played overtures, talk about swinging, we used to swing on *Poet and Peasant.*

Jabbo and Benford both admit that jazz was *not* taught at Jenkins. However, the effects of jazz crept in via the playing of kids who "escaped" for a period and then returned after playing in bands up North. Jabbo recalled when Gus Aiken returned to the Orphanage after a brief dash of freedom, he had learned the art of tongue-fluttering and growling on the trumpet.

Soon every brass player at Jenkins was practicing those skills. It was a skill Jabbo would brilliantly demonstrate ten years later on the Duke Ellington recording of "Black and Tan Fantasy." Jabbo recalled that on one of his 'escapes' from the Orphanage he heard Sidney De Paris on trumpet and was floored by his playing. But Louis Armstrong was always seen as the pinnacle of success and artistry. All the Jenkins kids revered him.

Cat Anderson, who entered the Orphanage ten years after Jabbo left, said:

> There were records at the school, but in those days the only ones that interested me were Louis Armstrong's.

In school, all the trumpet players played *Shine* and made a hundred C's with the F on the top.

On May 16, 1918 Edmund Thornton Jenkins was awarded the Charles Lucas Prize for Composition at the Royal Academy. His studies had continued unabated during the War. During his fifth year at the Royal Academy Will Marion Cook's Southern Syncopated Orchestra played at London's Philharmonic Hall. Jenks looked upon Cook as the type of musician he aspired to be.

The appearance of the Southern Syncopated Orchestra was a major musical event in London. The fifty musicians of the orchestra included two Jenkins Orphanage Band veterans, Ed and Jacob Patrick. It also included several other musicians with Jenkins connections. William Arthur Briggs was a West Indian from Charleston who had studied music with Eugene Mikell. A drummer named Buddy Gilmore and a cornet player E.E. Thompson had performed in the Hellfighters Band with Jim Europe, Eugene Mikell, Amos Gaillard and the two non-brother Wright drummers. Jenks was able to meet with his former band mates from Charleston and learned of Jim Europe's murder by the young Herbert Wright.

Jenks continued his studies, and began to perform concerts, shows and dances with a group referred to as A Coterie of Friends. He knew that his best road for financial success was through music, be it classical, or with the more popular dance/jazz music that was sweeping across Europe. He was learning the hard lesson Will Marion Cook had twenty years earlier: Breaking through the European classical music ceiling wouldn't be easy for a serious black composer.

Jenks realized he was a unique musician in England – classically trained, but also with deep roots in the ragged style of the Jenkins Band and the new "hot" music. He was one of the few musicians in England who could play classical music as well as the new syncopated style, and to a much higher standard than most.

The Coterie of Friends performed a concert at Wigmore Hall in London on December 17, 1919. The publication *West Africa* described the concert as a tribute to the greatest musical composer of the African race, Samuel Coleridge-Taylor.

> Mr. Edmund T. Jenkins, who will be the first coloured conductor, other than Coleridge-Taylor himself, to render his work before a British audience. Miss Coleridge-Taylor, the late composer's daughter, will contribute a musical monologue, set to music by her father.

> PROGRAMME
> *Symphonic Variations – On an African Air*
> Song – *Hiawatha's Vision* (soloist Mrs. W.A. Michael)
> *Scenes From an Imaginary Ballet*
> Concerto in G minor (violin solo: Winifred Small)
> Monologue – *The Clown and the Columbine* (Gwendolen Coleridge-Taylor) with violin, cello and piano
> *Folk Rhapsody* written by Edmund Jenkins
> Songs – *Sons of the Sea* and *Beat, Beat Drums* (soloist Mrs. Michael)
> March – *Ethiopia Saluting the Colours*

The program notes, written by Wendell Bruce James, stated:

> Mr. Jenkins, though as yet little known to the musical world at large, has obtained an enviable reputation among those who do know him, as one of the rising hopes of his race in the sphere of Art Music. An

American by birth, he had a brilliant career at the Royal Academy of Music in London. The work played today under his baton may justly be regarded as the first-fruits of his undoubtedly high talent.

James also wrote about Jenkins's *Folk Rhapsody,* or *Charlestonia, A Folk Rhapsody,* as it became officially titled:

After a short introduction, based upon an original theme, we hear the Solo Horn a characteristic Negro melody. This at once begins a dialogue with the Solo Violin, the latter playing the well-known Negro folk song, or spiritual "Swing low, Sweet chariot." With tempo moderato we arrived at another well-known air, "Nobody knows de trouble I see, Lord." These three themes form the melodic back-bone of the whole work, and we have them alone, or in combination, during the progress of the whole piece, up to the brilliant climax with which is terminates. This composition is, as a Folk Rhapsody should be, full of rhythmic and characteristically racial vitality.

In November 1919 the Original Dixieland Jazz Band played nightly at the Palais de Danse in west London's Hammersmith. England was jazz crazy. Many of the black musicians of the Southern Syncopated Orchestra saw a great opportunity for making money. It was fashionable for a white English dance band to hire one of two black musicians to make a point to the audience that this was "genuine" dance music. Hundreds of these types of bands toured from one side of England to the other.

Because of his school duties, Jenks was unable to tour, so he organized a dance band to perform nightly at the chamber music hall in the roof of the Queen's Hall. Jenkins performed with pianist Harold Ivy. The crowds were large and Jenks made fifty pounds a week, roughly $1000 in 2012 currency. They were joined by pianist Jack Hylton, who later became one of the most popular band leaders in England during the 1930s and 40s. Hylton described the Queen's Hall scene as:

> A most curious band that operated there ... a real ragtime affair, busking choruses in woeful harmony to a background of kitchen furniture noises ... there were two saxophonists and a long-neck banjo player. Virtually the only schooled musician in the outfit was a coloured clarinetist by the name of Jenkins, who was actually a professor on his instrument at the Royal Academy and could read [music].

In the early summer of 1920, Jenks returned home to America during his summer vacation from the Royal Academy. He sailed on the *Imperator* from Southampton. In an article he wrote for *The Academite,* Jenks discussed some of the fellow distinguished travelers he met who were also traveling first class: Vincent Astor, son of John Jacob Astor IV, who died on the *Titanic* in 1912; various members of the Vanderbilt family and W.T. "Big Bill" Tilden, the greatest tennis player of his time who won fourteen tournaments, including ten Majors.

Jenks arrived in New York City on August 8. It was his first time home in six years and the change in black America was immediately apparent to Jenks. He visited friends in Boston and in his *Academite* article he offered observations of this new change in American culture:

> From Boston ... I next visited Washington, and on through to Charleston in South Carolina. It was no other than the great composer, Antonin Dvorak, who said that the only national music America has consists of the Negro Folk Music, which the master himself

used so effectively and tellingly in his wonderful symphony No. 5 in e minor ... It is, therefore, but natural that I should comment upon the remarkable progress the coloured population of America had made, and is still making, in the realms of Art, as in all other phases of life.

Although life for black Americans in New York and Boston seemed greatly improved, when Jenks arrived in Charleston he realized his hometown had not progressed. He was now more European than Southern; his measured and cultured demeanor fit perfectly in London and Paris, but in Charleston he would be seen as a dandified and uppity Negro putting on airs.

At this time in America there were hundreds of "riots," confrontations between whites and blacks. The Hollywood film *The Birth of a Nation*, revived interest in the Ku Klux Klan. During 1920 there were more than 100 Klan attacks in the South. In Charleston the uneasy balance between the whites and blacks was kept in check by both sides performing an uneasy thrust-and-parry social dance,

As if that was not enough to make Jenks uncomfortable, he arrived in Charleston during the oppressive summertime. He was dismayed that "not only the concert halls, but even the theatres, were closed" due to the heat. To pass the time, Jenks used any musical outlet available to him. Lucius Goggins, a former resident of the orphanage, recalled that Jenks played the piano "day and night." On September 9, 1920, he performed a concert at his father's church, the Fourth Tabernacle Baptist.

E.C. Lockhart wrote to Rev. Jenkins in 1926 and said:

During my visit to Charleston about six years ago it was

my privilege to see him [Jenks] in all the glory of young manhood. His face showed a peculiar radiance which reflected the artist. His affability was delightful. His English characteristics which were no doubt unconsciously cultivated from contact were superb. He was brilliant, scintillating – bubbling with music, which seemed to hold his soul captive.

Ku Klux Klan march in Washington, DC., circa 1920.
Courtesy of the Library of Congress

Jenks' visit to Charleston was likely the first time he was introduced to his half-sister, a fourteen-year old black British girl named Olive Jenkins. Earlier that year, Rev. Jenkins brought Olive home from England, wishing her to grow up among a prosperous black American family. With her English family,

Olive had been the only Negro in Wigan, England. The shock of being transplanted from England to the American South must have been difficult for the teenager. To the people within the world of the Orphanage, Olive was a curiosity; she talked with an English accent and carried herself properly and formally like a lady.

She was also somewhat of an awkward presence for Ella, a constant reminder of her pre-marital sexual relationship with Rev. Jenkins. Ella decided to pass Olive off as just another orphan, but in a show of Christian charity, she announced she would formally adopt the young English girl - her own daughter. In Charleston, the social pressure to keep up a polite façade was immense.

Jenks returned to the London Royal Academy in October 1920 for his seventh and final term, relieved to be back in Europe, a world in which his future seemed limitless. As he wrote to his father, "Though I was born in the South, you yourself have admitted it would be impossible for me to live in safety there now."

Former Jenkins black lamb Tom Delaney had been working for almost ten years as a saloon singer and "whorehouse professor." His first big break came when he was thirty-two years old, in 1921. Delaney's song "Jazz Me Blues" combined risqué lyrics about sex with a swinging ragtime feel. The song attracted the attention of professional musicians and, more importantly, people who owned recording studios. They were always looking for songs to record, especially now that there was money to be made with "black" songs.

Perry Bradford finally convinced a New York

record company to record a "black blues" song. In 1920 Mamie Smith recorded Bradford's "Crazy Blues." It sold more than a million copies in less than a year. Suddenly, "black blues" songs were hot.

Tom Delaney met a young singer named Ethel Waters. She performed in vaudeville shows for years as a dancer billed as "Sweet Mama Stringbean." Waters, however, preferred singing to dancing, and on March 21, 1921, she recorded two of Delaney's songs for the Pace & Handy Music Company, "Down Home Blues" and "At The Jump Steady Ball." A twenty-three year old former chemistry student named Fletcher Henderson played the piano for the session. "Down Home Blues" became a hit. Pace & Handy paired Waters and Delaney together and sent them out on tour, Waters on vocals and Delaney on piano.

Two months later an act called Lillyn Brown and Her Jazz-Bo Syncopaters recorded "Jazz Me Blues." That was followed quickly by an instrumental version of the song by the Original Dixieland Jazz Band. Both versions sold thousands of copies. Through the years more than 100 of Delaney's songs were recorded by the most popular artists of the day. "Jazz Me Blues" became a standard recorded by Duke Ellington, Louis Armstrong, Bix Beiderbecke, Count Basie, Jack Teagarden and Benny Goodman.

It didn't take the Jenkins Band kids long to learn of the success of one of their alumni. It was not just Louis Armstrong who could make the big time from a waif's school band. Now one of their own had done it!

In 1925 Delaney recorded a song titled "Parson Jones (You Ain't Livin' Right.)" Accompanying himself on the piano Delaney sang:

Parson Jones, you better watch your step / 'Cause you sure ain't living right.
You better stop your slipping and dodging around / These sisters' house at night.

You ought to be ashamed to preach from that pulpit,
Cause you ain't nothing but a hypocrite.
Parson Jones you better watch your step / 'Cause you
sure ain't living right.

LP cover featuring Tom Delaney photo (bottom right). *Author's collection*

There is nothing to indicate Rev. Daniel Jenkins
ever heard this song, or if he did, what his opinion
was of the tune.

The Jenkins Bands were spread out across the
eastern United States throughout the year, bringing
in more than $10,000 annual income for the Orphan
Aid Society. Each band traveled with a chaperone,
often a minister, a cook and a valet to care for the
uniforms and instruments. The chaperone also carried
a letter of introduction from the mayor of Charleston
to be given to the mayor or police chief of each town at
which they stopped. In 1923, the letter read:

Jenkins letterhead, 1923, reflecting the Jim Crow attitude of the time. The implied racist message of the letterhead is: The Jenkins Orphanage was run by a black man, but there were responsible white citizens monitoring the Orphan Aid Society, assuring donations were used properly. Even after thirty years of success, Rev. Jenkins was still not fully trusted by the white citizens of Charleston. *Reconstructed by the author*

City of Charleston

Executive Department, July 12, 1923
To the Mayor, Board of Alderman and the Officials of any City in the United States:

This is to certify that Rev. D. J. Jenkins, President and Founder of the Jenkins Orphanage of this city, has been conducting an orphanage for over thirty-two years, having since connected with it a reform school and industrial farm and a rescue home for girls only. Reports show that he had handled and trained over three thousand little Negro boys and girls. They have been sent here from all portions of the country to be reformed. This he had done practically entirely on voluntary contributions.

There are four brass bands connected with the work, known as the Jenkins Orphanage Bands. We would appreciate anything you may do for him in letting his boys give entertainments and play upon the public streets of your city. It is raising money for a purely charitable work on a small basis, and I will assure you that he has ever managed to keep the order and conduct of his bands so that they have not become a nuisance, but rather a pleasure for the citizens to hear them play.

Rev. Jenkins had a Board of leading white citizens to keep up with the accounts and advise whenever necessary.

Very respectfully,
JOHN P. GRACE
Mayor

Not every member of the Jenkins Band was actually an orphan. Frederick William "Freddie" Green was born in Charleston in 1911. As a child he became friends with some of the Jenkins' kids and learned to read music from one of the orphanage's music instructors. Freddie learned to play the banjo and ukulele. He was so good he was allowed to join the band. He remembered:

> I used to stop whatever I was doing and follow the Jenkins band all over the city. I figured if I could get away – I knew I wouldn't be able to make it in Charleston, not playing music. I had to get away. And because of the fact I had been to New York – I had been there and had seen, and I had heard, and I knew whatever it was, it had to come from New York. And I went with the Jenkins band, we stopped in New York and I just stayed in New York, and I didn't go back.

By that time, Rev. Jenkins and Ella had moved into a four-story, five thousand square foot brick house at 34 Magazine Street, across the street from the City Jail, just around the corner from the Jenkins Orphanage House. They also owned a town house in Harlem at 147 132nd Street, a place for the bands to live during their extended stays in the North. The reverend also purchased a summer home in beach resort town of Asbury Park, New Jersey.

They were living a grand life. Ella was able to purchase fine clothes. They had a cook and house-keepers that traveled with them. Some blacks in Charleston grumbled about the lifestyle. Most respectable people, black or white, were struggling to keep afloat, but the Jenkins' were living a high life, dining on fine food prepared by a cook while the orphans were still eating cornbread and molasses.

Across town an artistic revival was stirring within the white community. In October 1920 the Poetry Society of South Carolina was founded by local writers DuBose Heyward, Josephine Pinckney, Beatrice Witte Ravenel and two Northern transplants, Hervey Allen and John Bennett. Their stated goal was to recall "Charleston's past in print." Part of this artistic renaissance in Charleston was also driven by the visual artists who illustrated the quaint nature of Charleston's landscape through watercolors and etchings. The Charleston Etcher's Club was formed as a parallel organization with the Poetry Society.

The membership rolls of both groups included the same names. The Poetry Society decided to set their membership dues at the exorbitant cost of five dollars per year, which guaranteed membership was open only to the socially acceptable of Charleston's blue blood upper elite. These groups helped create the still-accepted romantic view of Charleston: a sepia-toned-dashed-with-watercolor portrait of a place where, in the words of poet Amy Lowell, "history touches legend."

Both groups discovered that much of their crea-tiveity was inspired through the exploration of the African "Gullah" culture which was as integral a part of Charleston's fabric as heat, rice and white aristocracy.

This cultural renaissance led by Heyward and the Poetry Society lured "high-class winter colonists" to spend several months a year in the Lowcountry. Charleston, a city which was pushed aside by America after the Civil War, was now purposefully coming out of its cocoon. Although there was much opposition for the "opening of Charleston" from some locals, Meigs Russell, manager of the Charleston Chamber of Commerce declared, "There is no source from which new money can be brought in here except through the medium of tourists."

Charleston, after a long exile, was sneaking back into mainstream American culture for the crassest of reasons – money.

FIFTEEN
The Roaring 20s

"How you gonna keep 'em down on the farm after they've seen
Paree?"   - lyrics of a 1918 popular song by Joe Young & Sam M. Lewis

HUNDREDS OF THOUSANDS OF YOUNG AMERICANS,
black and white, served in France during World War
I. The survivors flocked to see fabulous shows at
famous Paris establishments like the Moulin Rouge
and Cafe de Paris. For less than a "buck", soldiers
could drink French wine, eat a meal, and watch wild
floor shows featuring scantily clad chorus girls. When
they returned home to America, they looked for
similar entertainment.

Millions of these young Americans had seen the
hell of war *and* the gay life of Paris. They concluded
that smoking and drinking were good for you!
American women bought into patriotic fervor and
aggressively entered the workforce to support their
country, but discovered that settling down in
peacetime America was more difficult than expected.
The humdrum routine of pre-War American life held
little interest for the younger generation, the
Pollyanna land of rosy ideals; they could not act as if
nothing had happened. They had broken the mold of
society. Dressing up and going out on the town
became a way of life.

After World War I, night clubs became a central
part of American culture. Not restaurants, not

ballrooms, but night clubs. Night clubs were different because they exclusively offered adult entertainment with booze and music central to the experience.

There was always a "cigarette girl" dressed in a short skirt, toting a tray with various brands of cigars and cigarettes. Waiters in tuxedos served up exotic-looking drinks. But best of all, there were chorus lines of luscious dancing girls and bands playing hot jazz.

Flappers, the new modern woman of the 1920s.
All images, *Courtesy of the Library of Congress*

Women were more anxious than men to avoid returning to society's rules and roles after the war. The passage of the 19th Amendment to the Unites States Constitution in 1920 gave American women the right to vote. It also emboldened them to push against other boundaries of society.

Pre-war, a proper young woman did not date. She

waited until an acceptable young man with honorable intentions showed formal interest. However, a large part of an entire generation of young men died in the war, leaving young women with less possible suitors. These women decided that they were not willing to waste their young lives waiting idly for the arrival of spinsterhood; they were going to enjoy life. They became America's first modern women. They were called Flappers. But what exactly *was* a Flapper?

The term "flapper" first appeared in Great Britain after World War I. It described young girls, still somewhat awkward in movement who had not yet entered womanhood. F. Scott Fitzgerald, in his short stories and novels, described the ideal flapper as "lovely, expensive, and about nineteen." John Held, Jr., a cartoonist and illustrator for leading magazines of the time, accentuated the flapper image by drawing young girls wearing unbuckled galoshes that would make a "flapping" noise when walking. In William and Mary Morris' *Dictionary of Word and Phrase Origins*, it states,

In America, a *flapper* has always been a giddy, attractive and slightly unconventional young thing who, in [H. L.] Mencken's words, 'was a somewhat foolish girl, full of wild surmises and inclined to revolt against the precepts and admonitions of her elders.'

Pulitzer Prize winning novelist Willa Cather wrote, "The world broke in two in 1922 or thereabouts." Young women of the 1920s ushered social and sexual liberation into the middle class sensibilities. For the first time in public, "proper" women presented themselves as sexual beings.

They wore make-up - rouge, powder, eye-liner, and lipstick - something that was only done by supposedly "loose" women. The flapper attitude was characterized by stark truthfulness, fast living, and sexual behavior. Flappers seemed to cling to youth as if it were to leave them at any moment. They took risks and were reckless ... they smoked. Something only men had done previously. Their parents were shocked.

Smoking wasn't the most outrageous of the flapper's rebellious actions. Flappers drank alcohol, at a time when the United States had outlawed alcohol. Some even carried hip-flasks full so as to have it on hand. Flappers had a scandalous image ... rouged and clipped, careening in a drunken stupor to the lewd strains of a jazz quartet.

Without doubt, national Prohibition helped create the jazz craze of the 1920s and fueled the rise of the flapper. Prohibition brought jazz into gangster-run nightclubs, the only venues that served alcohol and hired black musicians. These speakeasies allowed whites and blacks to mingle socially for the first time on a grand scale; it also attracted audiences from all social classes, seduced by the booze, the music and the increasingly suggestive jazz dances. The mixing of races and widespread belief that jazz incited sexual activity pushed the keepers of High Standards into a moral frenzy.

Ann Shaw Faulkner, president of the General Federation of Women's Clubs, asked the question, "DOES JAZZ PUT THE SIN IN SYNCOPATION?"

America is facing a most serious situation regarding its popular music. The blame is laid on jazz music and its evil influence on the young people of to-day. Jazz disorganizes all regular laws and order ... It is harmful and dangerous and its influence is wholly bad ... Jazz was originally the accompaniment of the voodoo dance, stimulating half-crazed barbarians to the vilest of deed ... the weird chant, accompanied by the syncopation of the voodoo invokers, has also been employed ... to stimulate brutality and sensuality. Many scientists have demonstrated that it has a demoralizing effect on the human brain.

In a couple of 1921 articles in *The Ladies' Home Journal* titled "The Jazz Path of Degradation" and "Unspeakable Jazz Must Go!" Mr. John R. McMahon, a dance instructor wrote:

> Our Middle West is supposed to be a citadel of Americanism and righteousness. Yet a survey of its length and breadth shows that it is badly spotted with the moral smallpox known as jazz. Those moaning saxophones and the rest of the instruments with their broken jerky rhythm make a purely sensual appeal. They call out to the low and rowdy instinct. All of us dancing teachers know this to be a fact … if Beethoven should return to earth and witness the doings of a jazz orchestra, he would thank heaven for his deafness …
>
> Jazz dancing is a worse evil than the saloon and scarlet vice. Abolish jazz music … or any form of dancing that permits the gentleman to walk directly in front of his partner. The road to hell is too often paved with jazz steps.

Fenton T. Bott, from Dayton, Ohio held the position of "Director of Dance Reform" in the American National Association Masters of Dancing. His opinion of modern jazz dancing was:

> This strikes especially at the youth of the nation, and the consequences are almost too obvious to be detailed. When the next generation starts on a low plane, what will its successors be?

A. J. Weber from Brooklyn, New York, was a member of the Dancing Masters' Association. He declared:

If the jazz is not reformed the first thing we know there will be a national law prohibiting all public dancing. It will be just like the story of the saloon. The metropolitan area stands in need of all the reform that can be applied. The jazz is simply rotten. It must go and leave room for clean and wholesome dancing.

On October 28, 1919, Congress enacted legislation called the National Prohibition Act, better known as the Volstead Act which set the starting date for nationwide prohibition for January 17, 1920.

The first documented infringement of the Volstead Act occurred in Chicago on January 17th, 1920 at 12:59 a.m. According to police reports, six armed men stole $100,000 worth of "medicinal" whiskey from two freight train cars. This trend in bootlegging liquor created a domino effect among criminals across the United States. In fact, some gang leaders were stashing liquor months before the Volstead Act was enforced. The ability to sustain a lucrative business in bootlegging liquor was largely helped by the minimal police surveillance at the time. According to Charles C. Fitzmorris, Chicago's Chief of Police during the beginning of the Prohibition period, "Sixty percent of my police were in the bootleg business."

Section 29 of the Act allowed 200 gallons (the equivalent of about 1000 750 ml bottles) of "non-intoxicating cider and fruit juice" to be made each year at home. Initially "intoxicating" was defined as anything more than 0.5%, but that was soon struck down which effectively legalized home wine-making. For beer, however, the 0.5% limit remained until 1933, often called "near beer."

"Near beer" was a term for malt beverages that contained little or no alcohol which were mass-marketed in the United States. The most popular "near beer" was named Bevo by Anheuser-Busch. The

Pabst Com-pany sold "Pablo", and Schlitz brewed "Famo". By 1921 production of near beer had reached over 300 million gallons.

The Volstead Act also contained a number of exceptions and exemptions that were used to evade the law's intended purpose. The most common way to legally obtain alcoholic beverages during Prohibition was through a physician's prescription, purchasing the liquor from a pharmacy. Physicians could prescribe distilled spirits - usually whiskey or brandy - on government prescription forms. The government allowed the limited production of whiskey and the distribution of wine to churches for sacramental purposes.

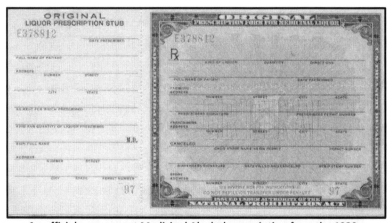

An official government Medicinal Alcohol prescription from the 1920s. Used during Prohibition to acquire prescription alcohol, usually whiskey, for strictly medicinal purpose. *Public Domain*

The Volstead Act stipulated a trial for any individual charged with an alcohol-related offense. Unfortunately, the legal system did not anticipate that most jury members would be unwilling to convict these "criminals." In New York alone, the first 4,000 arrests ended in less than five hundred indictments, which led to only six convictions, and ultimately not a single jail sentence.

National prohibition of alcohol - the "noble experiment" - was undertaken to reduce crime and corruption, solve social problems, reduce the tax burden created by prisons and poorhouses, and improve health and hygiene in America. It had the opposite effect. It caused an explosive growth of crime and increased the amount of alcohol consumption. Prohibition was ultimately ineffective because it was unenforceable.

Federal agents disposing of confiscated booze.
Courtesy of the Library of Congress

Bootleggers smuggled liquor from overseas and Canada, produced their own, or just stole it from government warehouses. People started hiding their liquor in hip flasks, false books, hollow canes, and anything else they could find. There were also illegal speakeasies which replaced saloons after the start of prohibition. By 1925, there were over 100,000 speakeasies in New York City alone. Charleston, S.C, boasted more than 250 illegal "Blind Tigers" for a population of 60,000. Charleston Mayor John P. Grace stated that the illegal Blind Tigers were "too much a part of the web of life" to be closed down, so the saloon owners handed out more than $50,000 a month in bribes to various state and city officials to "look the other way." Grace stated that "It is the government's job to prevent crime, not sin."

During Prohibition, because the manufacturing of and importing alcohol was illegal, people needed to find ways to avoid being caught. Beer had to be transported in large quantities, which made secrecy impossible, so the price of beer soared. Thus Americans began to drink less of it. Instead, they began to drink more hard liquor, which was more concentrated, easier to transport and less expensive. Americans began to consume more potent drinks and became more inebriated by drinking less. The major danger with that was that illegally-made alcohol products had no production and safety standards.

Although the goal of prohibition was to make alcohol more difficult to obtain, liquor actually became more easily available. The bootlegging business was so immense that customers could obtain alcohol by walking down almost any street. Speakeasies were often hidden in basements, office buildings, and warehouses and only admitted those with membership cards. They had the most sophisticated alarm systems possible to avoid being shut down. Barber shops would offer a daily shave and haircut, complete with a pint of hair tonic!

Booze flowed across American like water over Niagara Falls. Soon, gangsters weren't content with just supplying the booze; they wanted to get some of the rest of the action: girls, gambling and jazz. One of these ambitious New York City gangsters was a savvy young English immigrant, Owney Madden, called "that banty little rooster from hell." Madden had a very simple business model. He would walk into a club, and after a short "conversation" in the back room, the owner suddenly discovered he had a new business partner. In 1923 Madden took over the Club Deluxe at 644 Lenox Street in Harlem. It was owned by former heavy-weight boxing champion Jack Johnson. Madden renamed it the Cotton Club and it quickly became the Mob's most prominent showplace in New York.

The Cotton Club had an "all-white" customer policy - only the performers were allowed to be black The club's floor shows reinforced the racist imagery of the times, often depicting blacks as savages in the "darkest Africa" or as "darkies" in the plantation South. The club also imposed a color restriction on the chorus girls who performed in skimpy outfits: they were described as "tall, tan, and terrific," at least 5 feet 6 inches tall, light-skinned, and under twenty-one years of age. In the fall of 1923, the club opened with a high stepping line of the most beautiful "sepia skinned" chorus girls in the city. The music was hot jazz, the shows had the best choreography, and soon white customers poured uptown to Harlem every night to join the party.

During its years of operation, the Cotton Club spawned a generation of top flight talent. In 1927, Duke Ellington's orchestra was hired, and was replaced a few years later by Cab Calloway's band. It also introduced the world to a 16-year old singer named Lena Horne.

Tommy Benford retraced his odyssey from the Jenkins Orphanage Band to playing in the clubs in New York:

When I got away the last time I worked in a hotel in South Carolina … then my brother came by to get me to join another Circus. Then we joined a Carnival … and I left Chicago with a road show, Edgar Marton's Burlesque Show. That was a terrific show, lasting two to two and a half hours, with singing and dancing – real entertainment. We were in the pit the whole time and we played before the show started, during the show, and sometimes during the intermission as well. We only traveled with three musicians.

When we got to Pittsburg I got a call from my brother asking me to come on to New York as my sister's marriage had just broken up and he figured we should all be together, so I quit and went to New York.

We had a family get-together and talked about what we were going to do. "Can you read music?" my brother asked. "Sure, I can. Why ask me that? You know we learned that at school," I told him. "I just wanted to make sure, as I've got us a job at Leroy's."

That was one of the top clubs in Harlem at 135th Street and 5th Avenue, and Gene Aitken (sp) had the band there. Bill [Benford] was on tuba, Frazier Smith on guitar, Jake Green on trombone and Steve Wright on drums. Buddy [Gene Aiken] played trumpet and trombone.

Leroy's was quite a big place and they put on different acts; singing, dancing, comedians and so on, just like today, but it was all new then. They started at 9 in the evening and went on until 4 or 5 in the morning.

One of the clubs that challenged the Cotton Club in popularity was Small's Paradise. Ed Smalls was born in Charleston and moved to New York as a young man. Legend has said that he was kin to the legendary Robert Smalls, an African slave who, during the Civil War, stole a steamer in Charleston harbor and delivered it to the Union navy. Robert Smalls later became one of the first black Congressmen in 1865. Another legend states that Ed Smalls was also related to the notorious Sammy Smalls, "Goat Cart Sam," a crippled beggar who was often seen drunk on the streets of Charleston being pulled around in a goat cart. Sam usually frequented gambling saloons and whorehouses. "Goat Cart Sam" was about to become a legendary and universal character known as Porgy, the title character of Dubose Heyward's lyrical novel of black life in Charleston.

Both stories are untrue, legends with no facts to back up their creation, not unusual in Charleston.

Ed Smalls opened Small's Paradise on October 22, 1925. It was housed in a large basement at 2294½ Seventh Avenue at 135th Street and could accommodate 1500 patrons. It offered extravagant floor shows and the Charlie Johnson Orchestra played the hottest jazz music in Harlem. The Paradise also featured a slew of flamboyant, Charleston-dancing gay waiters who served Chinese food and bootleg liquor to the small tables. During those early years, the Charlie Johnson Orchestra featured two former Jenkins Orphanage trumpet players: Gus Aiken and Jabbo Smith, who had just recently "escaped" from the orphanage.

Within in a year of playing at the Paradise, the eighteen-year old Jabbo was considered the hottest trumpet player in New York. Two years later, Jabbo recorded "Black and Tan Fantasy" with the Duke Ellington Orchestra, replacing an ill, most likely too-drunk-to-play, Bubber Miley on the session. The Duke was so impressed by young Jabbo he offered the hot shot trumpet player a job in his band at the Cotton Club. Jabbo turned him down. "He offered me ninety dollars," Jabbo said, "but by that time everybody claimed I was the best in New York and I was getting a hundred and fifty a week."

In the book *Jazz Anecdotes,* Rex Stewart remembers a night in Harlem:

> Jabbo Smith tried on several occasions to prove he was better on trumpet than King Louis. He was never able to convince any of the other musicians, but he certainly tried hard.
>
> One such occasion comes to mind. It was an Easter Monday morning breakfast dance at Rockland Palace, Harlem's biggest dance hall. Jabbo was starring in Charlie Johnson's band from Small's Paradise, but Don Redman's band, featuring Satch, (Armstrong) from Connie's Inn was the top attraction.
>
> Jabbo was standing out front, and I'll say this, he was *blowing* – really coming on like the Angel Gabriel himself. Every time he'd fan that brass derby on a high F or G, his buddy from Small's would yell, "Play it, Jabbo! Go ahead Rice!" [Everybody from Charleston called each other Rice. It was the hometown nickname.] When Johnson's set ended with Jabbo soaring above the rhythm and the crowd noise, everybody gave them a big hand. I could tell from the broad grin on Jabbo's face that he felt that once and for all he'd shown Satch who was king.

The major difference between Small's Paradise and the Cotton Club was that Small's was always integrated, drawing an audience of local and out-of-town blacks as well as the well-to-do whites from downtown. The Cotton Club was refined and the Paradise was hot! The mixed crowd of customers vied for space on the postage-stamp-size dance floor, sweating and gyrating, bumping into each other, flinging their arms and stomping their feet, creating an exuberate atmosphere filled with abandon and sexual tension. And by far, the most popular dance was the Charleston.

Newspaper article about the dangers of doing the Charleston.
Author's collection

SIXTEEN
Doin' The Charleston

"Jazz dancing is degrading. It lowers all the moral standards."
- J.R. MacMahon, 'Unspeakable Jazz Must Go!'
Ladies' Home Journal, December 1921

IN MAY 1921 NO ONE IN NEW YORK PAID ATTENTION TO announcements that a new all-Negro show called *Shuffle Along* was opening at the 63rd Street Theatre, a dilapidated hall mainly used for rehearsals and lectures. The hall required extensive renovations just to become a mediocre facility for a musical.

No one gave the show much chance for success. It had been ten years since there was a successful all-black show on Broadway. The composers and cast of *Shuffle Along* were virtual unknowns and the out-of-town word-of-mouth reports about the show were tepid. When the show finally opened on May 23, 1921, in the shabby theatre on the fringe of Broadway, the production was $18,000 in debt. Composer Eubie Blake recalled:

> It was really off-Broadway, but we caused it to be Broadway … it was the price of the ticket that mattered. Our tickets cost the same as any Broadway show. That *made* it Broadway!

Theatre historian John Kenrick discussed the legacy of *Shuffle Along*:

Judged by contemporary standards, much of *Shuffle Along* would seem offensive ... most of the comedy relied on old minstrel show stereotypes. Each of the leading male characters was out to swindle the other.

Shuffle Along was not just embraced by black audiences. Whites flocked to it because it became "de rigueur for anyone wishing to be au courant," as historian David Krasner explains:

African American audiences realized that a certain degree of bowing and scraping was necessary for the success of the performer, and so they accepted performers of their own race 'blacking up.' *Shuffle Along* was one of the first shows to provide the right mixture of primitivism and satire, enticement and respectability, blackface humor and romance, to satisfy its customers.

When the show closed fourteen months later after 504 performances, it was the most successful black musical ever on Broadway.

The two leads, Flournoy Miller and Aubrey Lyles, became major stars and appeared on Broadway in new shows every year throughout the 1920s. Other members of the cast and chorus – Florence Mills, Josephine Baker and Paul Robeson – became international stars over the next few years. The show's big hit song "I'm Just Wild About Harry" has become an American standard and made the composers, Sissle and Blake, two of the most successful songwriters of their time. President Harry Truman chose the tune in 1948 as his campaign theme song.

Writer Langston Hughes claimed he chose to attend Columbia University in 1921 just so he could see *Shuffle Along*. He also credits the show for giving:

… a scintillating send-off to the Negro vogue in Manhattan It gave the proper push – a pre-Charleston kick – to the vogue that spread to books, African sculpture, music, and dancing.

Sheet music cover for "I'm Just Wild About Harry" from *Shuffle Along*.
Courtesy of the Library of Congress

James Weldon Johnson also credited *Shuffle Along* for breaking the barriers of rigid segregation in New York theatre, a tradition that relegated blacks to the balcony. *Variety* noted that on opening night "colored patrons were noticed as far front as the fifth row." In an effort to soothe the anxiety of white patrons wishing to attend the show, they also stated that "the two races are rarely intermingled."

Over the next three years nine Negro musicals opened on Broadway, including *Runnin' Wild*. The music for that show was composed by James P. Johnson and featured his song "Charleston" accompanied with a line of fast-dancing chorus boys.

Shuffle Along had featured some Charleston-style dancing, but it was not yet recognized or called as such. The chorus line performing the dance steps were referred to as "the Fastest dancers ever seen" or "a Colored Cast Revue."

In 1922, Charleston-style dance steps were featured in the Ziegfeld Follies at the New Amsterdam Theater. Ned Wayburn, composer of "Syncopated Sandy" and the choreographer for the Ziegfeld shows met a dancer through Sissle and Blake who taught him the signature Charleston steps. Wayburn choreographed a few variations, paired the dance to a couple of Sissle and Blake songs and the Charleston dance sensation begin to pick up momentum.

That same year a stage play called *Liza* introduced the Charleston dance done by Rufus Greenlee and Maude Russell, but the show was largely ignored. Then, on October 29th, 1923, Flournoy Miller and Aubrey Lyles introduced their second Broadway show *Runnin' Wild* with songs by James Johnson and Cecil Mack. The choreographer, Elida Webb, later falsely claimed to have invented the dance. Yet, the first act of *Runnin' Wild* ended with the "Charleston" performed by Elizabeth Welsh, backed by a group of chorus boys called the "Dancing Redcaps."

James Weldon Johnson wrote when the dance was introduced in *Runnin' Wild*:

> They did not wholly depend upon the orchestra – an extraordinary jazz band – but had the major part of the chorus supplement it with hand and foot patting. The effect was electrical and contagious. It was the best demonstrating of beating out complex rhythms I have ever witnessed; and, I do not believe New York ever

before witnessed anything of just its sort.

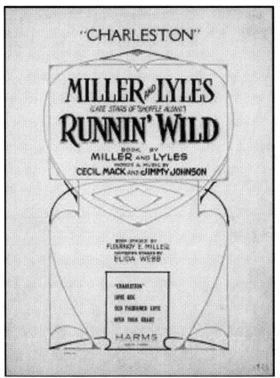

Sheet music cover for "Charleston" from *Runnin' Wild.*
Courtesy of the Library of Congress

Roger Pryor Dodge, in his book *Hot Jazz and Jazz Dance* says:

> The famous single-step, the Charleston, suggests the rhythm 4/4 but does not explicitly state it. The Charleston rhythm … pervades all music, and for our purposes is predominant in ragtime. Nevertheless the Charleston rhythm had not, up to the time of James P. Johnson's composition *Charleston* become unmistakably identified. While ragtime sheet music and piano rolls are records of the past, the elusive elements of the dance are lost. Whether the dancers actually used a Charleston rhythm before James P.'s piece I do not know. Since that time and with the help of a music strongly accenting this

rhythm, the dancers still do not actually follow it, but give the impression that they do only because we associate the step with a music having this rhythm. Maybe James P. made point of constantly holding to this rhythm because of the impression he got from the dancers, or very likely with the music in a slower tempo some dancers did more than just give an impression of the rhythm and did accent it. Certainly the dance was not evolved to fit James P.'s composition; rather, James P. derived his music from his impression of the dancers, with the possibility that some of them actually may have followed the musical rhythm. Thus our visual impression of the step is influenced by the Charleston rhythm in the music so that whatever the dancer is doing we assume he is still following the musical rhythm.

The Charleston dance step may have a longer history than most think. The Branle of 1520 is presumed by most dance scholars to be similar to the Charleston. Dance historians speculate the Ashanti People of Africa were the originators since some of their tribal dances incorporated what could be viewed as Charleston-style steps and movements.

But Willie "the Lion" Smith in his autobiography mentions a black Charleston dancer named Russell Brown:

> His dance was a Geechie step like those I had seen in "The Jungles" [a name often used in the 1910s for the San Juan Hill District of New York]. He was given a nickname by the people of Harlem … they would holler at him, "Hey Charleston, do your Geechie dance!" Some folks say that is how the dance known as the Charleston got its name. I'm a tough man for facts, and I say the Geechie dance had been around New York for many years before Brown showed up. The kids from the Jenkins Orphanage Band of Charleston used to do

Geechie steps when they were in New York on their yearly tour.

Willie "the Lion" Smith. *Courtesy of the Library of Congress*

It can safely be accepted that the origins of "the Charleston" are most likely a combination of all of the above, particularly the line that runs from the Ashanti African tribal dances directly to the southern plantations of the 18th and 19th centuries. What cannot be denied is that by the end of 1923, everybody in the country was doin' the Charleston.

Nothing else epitomizes the spirit and joyous exuberance of one the most tumultuous decades in American history as the Charleston dance. Other dance crazes have had their fifteen minutes of fame: the Waltz, Tango, Hokey-pokey, Twist, Hustle,

230 / Mark R. Jones

Macarena, and Breakdancing.

None of them, however, managed to influence and infect an entire generation so thoroughly the way the Charleston did. Almost 100 years later, the image of the Jazz Age is always a Flapper doing the Charleston. No other American decade can be so neatly summed up in one simple image.

By 1923, the entire world was Charleston mad!
All images, *Courtesy of the Library of Congress*

Tin Pan Alley songwriters turned out hundreds of "Charleston" songs. Charleston dancing contests became a regular part of dance halls and hotels everywhere, from big cities to small towns. One of the classic scenes in American cinema is the Charleston dancing contest in *It's A Wonderful Life* with James Stewart and Donna Reed falling into the swimming pool as the floor opens up. Hollywood stars Joan Crawford and Ginger Rogers got their first breaks into show business by winning national Charleston dance contests. Hospitals across America began to admit patients complaining of "Charleston knee."

Congressman T.S. McMillan of South Carolina shows Misses Sylvia Clavans and Ruth Bennett how to do the Charleston. *Courtesy of the Library of Congress*

Many non-dancing jobs of the 1920s required black employees to be competent to dance or teach the Charleston in order to be hired. There were hundreds of advertisements in the New York papers looking for a waiter, a maid, a cook, or a gardener with the stipulation: "Must be able to Charleston!"

However, not everyone was infected with the Charleston fever. In London, sixty teachers of ballroom dancing learned how to "Charleston" and pronounced it "vulgar," until Edward, Prince of Wales, learned it and performed it very skillfully in public. Most people in England then embraced the dance. If it was good enough for the Prince it was good enough for them.

However, the Vicar of St. Aidan's thought:

any lover of the beautiful will die rather than be
associated with the Charleston. It is neurotic! It is
rotten! It stinks! Phew, open the windows!

In 1925, tragedy struck. The press found a
physician in Seneca, Kansas, who claimed that "pretty
Evelyn Myers," age 17, had died of peritonitis brought
on by dancing the Charleston too violently. *Variety*
Magazine reported in Boston, the vibrations of 100
people in a Charleston dance contest collapsed the
floor of Pickwick Club. The disaster killed fifty
people. The newspaper headline screamed:

> WAS THIS BUILDING STAMPED DOWN
> BY 'CHARLESTON' DANCERS?

More than 200 people - police, fireman and
volunteers - worked for twenty hours digging through
the rubble of the Pickwick Club to free the trapped
victims. Following the catastrophe, the Boston
mayor's office issued an edict barring the Charleston
from public dance-halls. Other cities followed suit,
banning the dancing of the Charleston for safety
reasons, but nothing could stop the Charleston
stampede. The more the authorities preached against
it, the more popular the Charleston became.

Mayor Frank Borden, Jr, of Bradley Beach, New
Jersey, outlawed the dance from the city-owned
ballroom. He cited "broken shins" as his reason. "I
have no objection to a person dancing their feet and
head off, but I think it best that they keep away from
the Charleston."

Richard Zober of Passaic, New Jersey also banned
the Charleston in his town. "I think it would be safer
and better for all concerned," he said.

On September 16, 1925, New York City police Sgt.

George Smith was making his evening rounds on Broadway when he spotted a disturbance – a gang of kids on the sidewalk. Smith called for help from two nearby traffic officers. He pointed out the problem.

Newspaper article about the Pickwick Club disaster.
Author's Collection.

"See those kids over there? See what they're doing? They're dancing the Charleston, that's what they're doing. You gonna just stand there?"

Police rushed into the crowd of 200 spectators and the dancers took off running down side streets. Cops managed to arrest two dancers; they were brought to the stationhouse amidst a chorus of jeers, boos and catcalls from the crowd.

Under grilling, the suspects admitted they made a minimum of $2 a night dancing the Charleston on the streets. Sometimes they had real music for accompaniment. Other times, like tonight, they made do with a few harmonicas and some energetic hand-clapping. One suspect said he had banked $200 from his Charleston dancing. The other said he supported his widowed mother with his ill-gotten money.

The dancers' parents were summoned and warned that if these fellows were caught dancing again, the parents would be responsible. If they persisted, they would be sent to the Children's Society.

The crackdown on Charleston street dancing was about as effective as the crackdown on booze at Prohibition speakeasies. Charleston dancing on street corners, the *New York Sun* reported, was a nightly occurrence all over town, from "downtown to Washington Heights."

It was also contagious. By early 1926, the new dance craze spread to the ballrooms of Park Avenue, where black musicians Lucky Roberts and Paul Bass were in high demand to give private Charleston lessons to rich folks.

Among their clientele, who occasionally would bring Roberts and Bass with them south to Palm Beach during the winter social season, were Mrs. William Dick, who had survived the sinking of the Titanic that claimed her first husband, John Jacob Astor; Mr. and Mrs. Edward F. Hutton, Mr. and Mrs. Florenz Ziegfeld; Mr. and Mrs. Philip Doubleday; and Herbert Pulitzer. Clearly the difference between being a common outlaw and a celebrated mentor in the Charleston biz was location, location, location - though it was discreetly noted in several newspaper stories that the Charleston as danced by society matrons was a different form of motion than the version danced at 49th and Broadway.

An article syndicated by the International Feature Service cautioned its readers about the Charleston:

> From coast to coast the "Charleston" has caught the country swaying to its curious rhythm. No dance, since jazz first came into vogue, has created such a furor. Enthusiasts ecstatically stamp to its syncopated measures, while others, equally in earnest, denounce it. But the controversy that is carried on everywhere concerning this latest mania has failed to stem its tide of popularity. America is "Charleston" mad.
>
> There were many similar cases cited to substantiate this supposition. The description in the Bible of the taking of Jericho tells how, when the seven priests, preceded by a force of armed men, compassed the city seven times "the wall fell down flat." Even to-day when soldiers march across a bridge they are required to break step, for engineers assert that the strongest bridge built cannot withstand the strain of rhythmic vibration. A violin chord, if tuned to exactly the right pitch, will shatter a vase. It is regarded by some, therefore, as not only a possibility but a fact that the "Charleston" was responsible for the Boston tragedy.
>
> But for each one who believes the "Charleston" to be a dance of death, there are thousands who blithely trip its measures and proclaim it the most harmless, though fascinating, stunt that has yet been introduced.

Emil Coleman, a famous orchestra leader, declared that the "Charleston" is "the most characteristically American of any of the modern dances whose peculiar accent in time is the musical expression of the native [black] temperament."

One female evangelist in Oregon called the Charleston:

> ... the first and easiest step toward hell. The modern dance cheapens womanhood. The first time a girl allows a man to swing her around the dance floor, instinct tells her she has lost something she should have treasured. What she usually lost was her corset. Most of these girls were forced by their mothers to wear foundation garments, but the flappers hated them. They discourage men and made it uncomfortable to do dances like the Black Bottom and the Charleston.
>
> Therefore, as soon as they arrived at parties they retreated into the ladies room and 'parked their girdles.' Once liberated, the girls were free to indulge in the slow fox trot or to break loose doin the faster, jazzier numbers.

Some ballrooms gave up trying to discourage the frantic Charleston all together. They just posted large signs on the dance floor that read: PCQ – PLEASE CHARLESTON QUIETLY!

SEVENTEEN
Porgy & the Charleston Renaissance

Bare, splay feet padded upon the cobbles; heads were thrown back, with lips to instruments that glittered in the sunshine, launching daring independent excursions into the realm of sound. Yet those improvisations returned to the eternal boom, boom, boom of an underlying rhythm, and met with others in the sudden weaving and reveling of amazing chords. An ecstasy of wild young bodies beat living into the blasts that shook the windows of the solemn houses. Broad, dusty blue-black feet shuffled and danced on the many cobbles and the grass between them.   – from *Porgy* by Dubose Heyward.

IN 1922 A PETITION WAS SENT TO CHARLESTON CITY Council, signed by thirty-seven white residents of nearby Church Street and St. Michael's Alley, which called for the immediate evacuation of the all-black residents of Cabbage (Catfish) Row. The petition detailed unsavory behavior of the black residents including prostitution of black women with white sailors, knife and gun fights, unsanitary conditions and "the most vile, filthy and offensive language."

During the spring of 1924, Dubose Heyward, founder of the Poetry Society of South Carolina, began to work on "a novel of contemporary Charleston." Heyward was the descendent of Thomas Heyward, Jr., a signer of the Declaration of Independence. Dubose Heyward was part of Charleston's aristocratic heritage where family bloodlines were more important than the bank account.

During the early 1920s Dubose Heyward gained a reputation in American literary circles as a talented, serious poet. Charleston society was rightly proud of Heyward's success and reputation. The perception at Charleston tea parties was that his forthcoming novel of "contemporary Charleston" would be a drawing room drama, or a comedy of manners. Everyone was anxious to read it, assuming it was going to be about "them." They never imagined a lyrical folk novel about the Gullahs of Charleston.

For many white Charlestonians, the ubiquitous presence of Gullahs was as common as palmetto trees – just another part of the scenery, present on each street but rarely acknowledged. Heyward lived on Church Street, a Colonial-era neighborhood that after Emancipation became quite un-gentrified. Whites descended from the elite families of Charleston society now lived in close quarters, side-by-side, with ancestors of their former slaves. The once pristine houses and gardens were now covered with shabbiness created by decades of dwindling fortunes and cultural depression.

Heyward became fascinated by the odd story of Samuel Smalls. The Charleston *News and Courier* featured a small item on the police blotter:

> Samuel Smalls, who is a cripple and is familiar to King Street, with his goat and cart, was held for the June term of Court of Sessions on an aggravated assault charge. It is alleged that on Saturday night he attempted to shoot Maggie Barnes at number four Romney Street. His shots went wide of the mark. Smalls was up on a similar charge some months ago and was given a suspended sentence. Smalls had attempted to escape in his wagon and was run down and captured by the police guard.

Heyward finished a first draft of a novel based on Smalls. He gave the manuscript to his friend, John Bennett, to read. Bennett was astonished at the story. "There had never been anything like it," he said.

The story was set in a location Heyward called "Catfish Row," two run-down tenement buildings one block from Heyward's home on Church Street. Nestled between the two tenements was 87 Church Street, a classic brick Georgian double house that was the home of Heyward's ancestor, Thomas Heyward, Jr, signer of the Declaration. By the turn of the 20th century the two tenements were notorious for their crime and violence.

Charleston, S.C., 85-91 Church Street, circa 1910. These once fashionable pre-Revolutionary structures deteriorated into slums at the turn of the 20th century. (L-R) Cabbage Row, Thomas Heyward House and Catfish Row.
Courtesy of the Library of Congress

Dubose Heyward's novel published in September of 1925, was titled *Porgy*, the story of a crippled beggar on the streets of Charleston. During a dice game, Porgy witnesses a murder committed by a rough, sadistic man named Crown, who runs away from the police. During the next weeks Porgy gives shelter to the murderer's woman, the haunted Bess, in the rear courtyard of Catfish Row, a rundown tenement on the Charleston waterfront. Porgy and Bess fall in love. However, when Crown arrives to take Bess away Porgy kills him. He is taken in by police for questioning for ten days. He is released because the police do not believe a crippled beggar could have killed the powerful Crown. When Porgy returns to the Row, he discovers that while he was away Bess fell under the spell of the drug dealer Sportin' Life and his "happy dus". She has followed Sportin' Life to a new future in Savannah and Porgy is left alone brokenhearted.

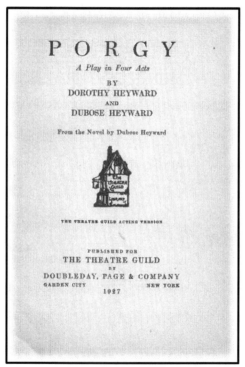

Cover of script for *Porgy. Author's Collection*

The novel became a national best-seller and received rave reviews. Dubose Heyward was praised for portraying "Negro life more colorful and spirited and vital than that of the white community," and for creating a character that is "a real Negro, not a black-faced white man" who "thinks as a Negro, feels as a Negro, lives as a Negro."

In Charleston, the reaction was polite, but less positive. Some acknowledged the truth - it was a powerful book, while others claimed "the paper was wasted on which it was writ." Most people were disappointed, and shocked, when they discovered *Porgy's* main characters were black, not white. White characters were little more than walk-on caricatures.

Lost among the initial praise and criticism is that at its heart, *Porgy,* is a memorial to the old way of life in Charleston. Blacks are second class citizens, living lives of limited freedom, still expected to be subservient to the whites. *Porgy,* however, examines this world from the viewpoint of the blacks. Portrayed with realism, they were nonetheless far removed from the "new Negro" who could be seen daily on the streets of Harlem, and was appearing in the writings of New York writers. In Charleston blacks and whites suffered from the same malaise.

One year after its publication, *Porgy* was read by George Gershwin. Gershwin's 1924 Broadway musical, *Lady Be Good!* ran for 330 performances and established him as one of the most popular songwriters in America. While his second hit show, *Tip-Toes*, was on Broadway, Gershwin read *Porgy* in one sitting. He immediately wrote to Heyward proposing the two men work together on an opera based on the story.

Heyward was astonished - and then excited. Gershwin was one of the most powerful, successful and talented people in the New York musical world. He contacted Gershwin and was told the composer wanted to do the opera but his work schedule was booked solid for the next several years. Heyward decided to go ahead and write a nonmusical stage version of *Porgy*.

Dubose Heyward's wife, Dorothy, was a prize winning playwright. They met in 1922 at the MacDowell Colony, an artist's retreat in New Hampshire, and Heyward was immediately smitten. They married in New York in 1923 at the same time, Dorothy's play, *Nancy Ann,* won Harvard's Belmont Prize, beating out Thomas Wolfe's *Welcome to My City*. First prize was $500 and a Broadway production of the play. Meanwhile, MacMillan Publishing had accepted a volume of Heyward's poetry for publication. The young couple spent the first months of their marriage living apart, Dorothy in New York working on the play production and Heyward on a speaking tour about poetry across the South.

Heyward's decision not to wait on Gershwin, but to go ahead with a dramatic stage version of *Porgy*, was an important one. After all, he already had the perfect collaborator living under the same roof, his wife. Together the Heywards turned the novel into a stage play. Gershwin was fully supportive of the effort. He told Heyward that a stage version of the story could more easily be transformed into the libretto for the proposed opera.

Dorothy added most of the dialogue of the play, smoothing the Gullah dialect from the novel into more recognizable English. By the summer of 1926 the play was written and submitted to three professional production companies in New York. One week later, it was accepted by the Theater Guild, but the Heywards were not optimistic the play would ever be produced. They had one unshakable demand which could easily be the death knell of the production – they wanted black actors, not white actors in blackface. The original director resigned due to their demands. The play was set aside.

In early 1927 a young Armenian director named Rouben Mamoulian wanted to direct *Porgy* - with a black cast. Trained as a lawyer, Mamoulian and his sister fled Russia during the Bolshevik Revolution to London and began to work in West End theaters. He arrived in America at the invitation of George Eastman (of Eastman-Kodak) to work for the American Opera Company. It was there that he attracted the attention of the Theatre Guild, who asked him to stage *Porgy*.

Over the next thirty years, Mamoulian came to be known as "the mad Armenian" due to his frantic energy. He directed more than twenty Hollywood movies and several successful Broadway plays, including the original *Oklahoma* (1943) and *Carousel* (1945). *Porgy,* however, was his first opportunity to be in charge of a Broadway production.

To prepare, Mamoulian traveled to Charleston to soak up the atmosphere and learn about the Gullah culture. Because Heyward and Dorothy were on a European vacation, Mamoulian was shown around Charleston by Heyward's mentor, author John Bennett. On his second day in Charleston, Mamoulian was taken to the Jenkins Orphanage for an after dinner private concert. Several women sang spirituals and then members of the Jenkins Band performed. Mamoulian was amazed by the band's "melodious discordance" and the "infinitesimally small darkey boy who led the band."

Before he left Charleston the next day, Mamoulian persuaded Rev. Jenkins the band should appear in the *Porgy* production. On opening night, October 10, 1927, the Jenkins Band made their second appearance in a major New York City stage production. At the beginning of the second act, when the cast travels to Kittawah Island for the picnic they

244 / Mark R. Jones

were led onstage by the Number One Jenkins Band playing "Sons and Daughters Repent Ye Saith the Lord."

Within a week, *Porgy* was playing to Standing Room Only audiences. When it closed after 367 performances it was considered an overwhelming success, with more box office than its main competitor, Eugene O'Neill's *All God's Chillun Got Wings.* During its run *Porgy* employed more sixty black performers in a serious drama, unheard of on Broadway at that time. It was also another pay day and exposure for Rev. Jenkins and the orphanage. When the touring version of the play traveled across America in 1929 the Jenkins Band was with them, charming audiences and raising the profile of their Orphanage.

Five years later, George Gershwin's heavy work schedule finally gave him the time to devote his energy on the operatic version of *Porgy*. In late February 1934 he reported to Heyward that "I have begun composing music for the first act, and I am starting with the songs and spirituals first." He then asked Heyward to join him in New York so the work could be expedited. Over the next two months, while living in a guest suite of Gershwin's famous fourteen-room house at 132 East Seventy-second Street, Heyward wrote the lyrics for almost a dozen Gershwin compositions, including "Summertime," "A Woman Is a Sometime Thing," "Buzzard Song," "It Take A Long Pull to Get There," "My Man's Gone," "It Ain't Necessarily So" and "I Got Plenty of Nuttin'." The opera was beginning to take shape.

During his last year at the Royal Academy, 1921, Edmund Thornton Jenkins worked hard to convert the Queen's Hall small rooftop hall into a proper night club. He helped put together a small band to play during the evening. The band members included: Bert Heath, trumpet; Jesse Stamp, trombone; Bert Worth, alto saxophone; Edmund Jenkins, clarinet and alto saxophone; Dick De Pauw, violin; Bert Bassett, banjo; Wag Abbey, drums and Jack Hylton, piano. Hylton later became one of the most popular entertainers in England during the 1930s and 40s.

This band, billed as The Queen's Dance Orchestra, recorded four songs for His Master's Voice (HMV) Records. Each musician was paid five pounds. The songs were released on two, double-sided ten-inch discs, numbered B-1236 and B-1237. *Idol of Mine* (Jenks, saxophone) with *Turque* (Jenks, clarinet) and *The Wind In The Trees* (Jenks, saxophone) with *I'm Wondering If It's Love* (Jenks, sax).

Queen's Dance Orchestra / Jack Hylton Jazz Band. Edmund Thornton Jenkins in the rear on saxophone, Jack Hylton on piano.
Courtesy of Pete Faint, JackHylton.com

The records sold enough copies because the band was brought back to the studio for another recording session. Recording as Jack Hylton's Jazz Band on July

8, 1921, they recorded four more songs: *The Love Nest* (Jenks, sax), *Mon Homme – My Man* (Jenks, sax), *Billy* (Jenks, sax) and *Wang Wang Blues* (Jenks, clarinet).

Over the next year Jack Hylton's Jazz Band recorded more than twenty records. By English standards these were "jazz" records but by American standards they were merely mild dance tunes. Many of the white English musicians were also starting to resent black American musicians, feeling as if they were taking their places on the bandstand and in the studio. *The Dancing Life*, a London music magazine stated:

> The 'darkie' question, as it concerns dance orchestras, seems to be getting still darker. Everybody knows that Englishmen can play every bit as well as South Americans [meaning blacks from the American South], and sometimes better, and it is always annoying to see a coloured orchestra playing when there is so much English talent available."

Margaret Butcher, in her book, *The Negro In American Culture, (1972)* writes:

> As a child, [Edmund] Jenkins had been a member of his father's Charleston [South Carolina] Orphanage Band and had acquired a hold on Negro idioms and jazz accent that persisted after years abroad following his graduation from the London Royal College of Music.

Shortly after these recording sessions Edmund Thorton Jenkins completed his time at the Royal Academy. He was elected an Associate of the Royal Academy of Music (ARAM), a distinguished honor. He had served as a sub professor of clarinet and completed courses in harmony, composition, voice, clarinet, oboe, bassoon, organ and piano. He was proficient on the cornet, trombone, trumpet, violin, bass clarinet, alto sax and also demonstrated the ability to compose for a full orchestra.

Jenks decided to move to Paris. He was dissatisfied with the bland records he recorded with Jack Hylton's Jazz Band; he knew he could do better. The Paris music scene was thriving for black American musicians. Parisians had been introduced to American "hot" music by the Hellfighters Band in 1918 and remained jazz-mad. In the fall of 1921, Jenks moved to Paris and found an apartment in the Seventeenth Arrondissement.

One of the most romanticized periods of American history is the Lost Generation in Paris of the 1920s. Dozens of American writers and artists, mostly white, were so disillusioned by the war they chose to live an impoverished bohemian existence in Paris as they honed their art, drank, danced and debauched. F. Scott Fitzgerald, Gertrude Stein, Ernest Hemingway, Henry Miller, John Dos Passos and T. S. Eliot all spent years in Paris being ignored by the Parisians who considered these American writers barely worthy of their notice. Black American musicians however, were considered true artists.

Jenks had little trouble finding work in the Parisian clubs. He was the best musician in every band he played. He lived and worked in a low-class neighborhood filled with rough saloons and whore-houses, populated by slumming Americans, drunk and rowdy soldiers, pimps, drug dealers and well-heeled Russians expatriates who had fled the Bolshevik Revolution. The Parisian night club scene was filled with opium, booze and sex. Unlike their American counterparts, most Frenchmen enthusiastically embraced the hedonistic 1920s lifestyle. Jenks easily slipped into the life. He made large sums of easy money playing for dancers until four o'clock in

248 / Mark R. Jones

the morning. He purchased a car, a Talbot Darracq which cost him the equivalent of $3500. He rarely made it home until dawn where he would sleep until dusk and then begin his nightly sojourns again. He had given up any attempt at writing "serious" music.

One of his jobs was with the Art Hickman Orchestra. Hickman was a white American musician who had come to Paris to cash in on the jazz craze. When Hickman was called back to America, he tapped his twenty-eight year old clarinetist to become the black conductor of his white jazz dance band.

During that time Jenks also renewed his friendship with his musical inspiration, Will Marion Cook, when the Southern Syncopated Orchestra performed in Paris for a time. On March 7, 1923, Cook wrote a letter to Rev. Jenkins:

> Dear Rev. Jenkins,
> Want to congratulate you on your son Edmund T. Jenkins with whom I had a most wonderful association while in Paris. He is possibly the best Musician in the coloured race; the very best instrumentalist in any race, and one of the most perfect Gentlemen I have ever had the pleasure of knowing.
> Will Marion Cook

This must have been heady praise for Jenks, particularly since Cook considered himself "the greatest violinist in the world."

Will Marion Cook returned to America to create a new Broadway show. The interest in black musicals had waned after 1910 and Cook, despite his enormous success as the musical force behind most of the good black shows, was forced to move on to other things to make a living. But the overwhelming success of *Shuffle Along* created another opportunity to work on Broadway and Cook was determined to cash in. In

1923, Jenks received a letter from a theatrical agent in New York hiring him for $125 a week to play in Cook's new show. It was a pittance compared to what he was making in Paris, but Jenks was intelligent enough to realize the Parisian nightclub life was a creative dead end. There was money to be made, but nothing to challenge him artistically.

Jenks traveled first class to New York, and at enormous cost, brought his beloved Talbot Darracq automobile in the cargo hold of the ship. He was determined to make a splash in America. Most musicians his age did not have a fancy European car. Cook's show was titled *Negro Nuances*, starring Paul Robeson and Alberta Hunter with "an orchestra of twenty-five, under the direction of Edmund T. Jenkins and Will Marion Cook."

The show bombed and closed almost immediately. Jenks floundered for several months, looking for other opportunities in America. He wanted to launch a music publishing company and when that venture failed to generate any financial interest, he wanted to establish a black music school and symphony. He traveled to the major urban centers in the North looking for backers, but no one was interested. He was told repeatedly that dance music was what white audiences wanted to hear from black musicians.

He also managed to visit his English half-sister, Olive Jenkins, who was attending Hartshorn Memorial College in Richmond, Virginia. He performed a piano recital for the students while he was there.

By this time Jenks was almost broke. He left his car in America to be sold and booked second class passage back to Paris. He was disappointed with the Paris scene when he returned. The decadent night club lifestyle had turned more outrageous. American dancer and singer Josephine Baker used her stardom from *Shuffle Along* to catapult herself to international fame. She appeared on the Parisian stage completely nude, except for a pink flamingo feather between her legs.

Black American performers were more in demand than ever, but Jenks had no stomach for returning to that lifestyle. His time in America, and the realization of the limitations of his life there rekindled his creative spirit. He took only enough nightclub jobs to pay his rent, devoting his energy to writing an operetta called *Afram*. Set in the South, it was the tale of an African prince and princess from rival tribes who are in love. Both are captured into slavery and sold to different plantations in America. After years of tragedy and suffering the two are ultimately reunited.

Jenks also pulled out his "Folk Rhapsody" from his school days which he expanded and renamed "Charlestonia: A Folk Rhapsody." In 1925, Jenks conducted a full orchestration of the piece in Belgium. The concert met with rave reviews. Jenks wrote his father, asking for a loan of three thousand dollars so he could continue to work on *Afram*.

On July 15, 1926, Edmund Thornton Jenkins was admitted to the Hospital Tenon in Paris. The diagnosis was appendicitis and he underwent surgery. After being returned to his bed he fell onto the floor sometime during the night where he remained undiscovered for several hours. He contracted pneumonia and his condition worsened. However, for some inexplicable reason, he was released from the hospital and sent home.

Two months later, the coroner's report read:

The twelfth of September nineteen hundred and twenty-six at 21:15, there died at 4 rue de la Chine, Edmond Thornton Jenkins, living in Paris at 27 rue de Lecluse, born at Charleston (North America) aged 32 years, composer of music, son of Daniel Jenkins and of

Lena James, couple without any profession living at the said Charleston, bachelor. Reported 13ᵗʰ September 1926 at 13:10 on the declaration of Pierre Rivassoux, age 40, employee at 4 rue de la Chine, Paris.

The American consul in Paris cabled Rev. Jenkins to inform him of his son's death. The six hundred dollar cost of having his body embalmed and shipped to America was paid by Rev. Jenkins. The funeral was held in Charleston on Thursday, September 30, 1926 at the New Tabernacle Fourth Baptist Church on Palmetto Street. The Jenkins Band marched through the Humane Friendly Cemetery and played a dirge at the gravesite. Jenks was buried next to his mother, Lena Jenkins.

As Jenks' former music professor at Morehouse College Benjamin Brawley stated:

Let us remember this: he not only knew music but at all times insisted on its integrity. For him there was no short cut to excellence. He wanted the classic and he was willing to work for it. He felt, moreover ... that there was little creative work in the mere transcribing of Negro melodies. For him it was the business of a composer to compose, and he did so ... The music of the Negro and of the world suffered signal loss in the early death of Edmund T. Jenkins of Charleston, South Carolina.

Lucien White, music critic of the New York Age wrote:

The race has cause to mourn the passing of one of the most promising young race artists since the untimely death of Samuel Coleridge-Taylor.

The world lost a young musician when he was about to embark on what he considered his life's work – the composition of "serious" music. It's ironic that

252 / Mark R. Jones

the so-called Lost Generation of white American writers in Paris lost very little. Most of them went on to fame and fortune, more revered today than during their lifetimes. Many of their works are required reading for American school children in the 21st century. Jenks, however, was truly one of the Lost, a lost lamb. He possessed an enormous talent, trained and honed for success against all convention of his time and ungraciously cut short by frustrating circumstance. Who knows what riches American culture lost upon the death of Edmund Thornton Jenkins?

Hopefully, somewhere in a concert hall in the Everafter, Jenks and Big Jim Europe are writing and conducting unheard symphonies, operas and dance tunes.

Stephen Sondheim in *Invisible Giants: Fifty Americans Who Shaped the Nation But Missed the History Books*, wrote:

> DuBose Heyward has gone largely unrecognized as the author of the finest set of lyrics in the history of the American musical theater - namely, those of *Porgy and Bess*. There are two reasons for this, and they are connected. First, he was primarily a poet and novelist, and his only song lyrics were those that he wrote for *Porgy*. Second, some of them were written in collaboration with Ira Gershwin, a full-time lyricist, whose reputation in the musical theater was firmly established before the opera was written. But most of the lyrics in *Porgy* - and all of the distinguished ones - are by Heyward. I admire his theater songs for their deeply felt poetic style and their insight into character. It's a pity he didn't write any others. His work is sung, but he is unsung.

In June 1934, George Gershwin arrived by train in Charleston with his cousin, artist Henry Botkin. They drove out to Folly Beach where Heyward had rented a cottage at 708 West Arctic Avenue.

Folly Beach was a remote, sparsely developed barrier island ten miles from Charleston. It was a vastly different world from Gershwin's New York neighborhood, in the middle of rollicking night life and luxurious accommodations. Life at Folly Beach was at best simple and at worst, primitive. The surrounding marshes were filled with gators and other wild exotic creatures. Crabs and snakes entered houses freely. Heat and humidity often reached equatorial proportions. In his letters Gershwin complained that the heat "brought out the flys, and knats, and mosquitos," leaving there "nothing to do but scratch." Two weeks later, the *Herald-Journal* (Spartanburg, S.C.) filed this story:

GERSHWIN, GONE NATIVE, BASKS AT FOLLY BEACH. Charleston, June 30.

Bare and black above the waist, an inch of hair bristling from his face, and with a pair of tattered knickers furnishing a sole connected link with civilization, George Gershwin, composer of jazz music, had gone native. He is staying at the Charles T. Tamsberg cottage at Folly Beach, South Carolina.

"I have become acclimated," he said yesterday as he ran his hand experimentally through a crop of dark, matted hair which had not had the benefit of being combed for many, many days. "You know, it's so pleasant here that it's really a shame to work."

Two weeks at Folly have made a different Gershwin from the almost sleek creator of "Rhapsody in Blue" and "Concerto in F" who arrived from New York City on June 16. Naturally brown, he is now black. Naturally sturdy, he is now sturdier. Gershwin, it would

254 / Mark R. Jones

seem intends to play the part of Crown, the tremendous buck in "Porgy" who lunges a knife into the throat of a friend too lucky at craps and who makes women love him by placing huge black hands about their throats and tensing their muscles.

The opera "Porgy" which Gershwin is writing from the book and play by DuBose Heyward, is to be a serious musical work to be presented by the Guild Theater early next year, is an interpretation in sound of the life in Charleston's "Catfish Row"; an impressionistic dissertation on the philosophy of negro life and the relationship between the negro and the white. Mr. Heyward, who is staying at Lester Karow's cottage at the beach, spends every afternoon with the composer, cutting the score, rewriting and whipping the now-completed first act into final form.

"We are attempting to have an opera that is serious and dramatic," Mr. Gershwin said. "The whites will speak their lines, but the negroes will sing throughout. I hope the audience will get the idea. With the colored people there is always a song, see? They always find something to sing about somewhere. The whites are dull and drab."

It is the crap game scene and subsequent murder by Crown which may make the first act the most dramatic of the production. A strange rhythm and an acid, biting quality in the music create the sensation of conflict and strife between men and strife caused by the rolling bones of luck.

"You won't hear the dice click and roll," he said. "It is impressionism, not realism. When you want to get a great painting of nature you don't take a camera with you."

Jazz will rear its hotcha head at intervals through the more serious music. Sporting Life, the negro who peddles "joy powder" or dope, to the residents of Catfish Row, will be represented by ragtime.

"Even though we are cutting as much as possible, it is going to be a very long opera," Mr. Gershwin said.

"It takes three times as long to sing a line as it does to say it. In the first act, scene one is 94 pages of music long and scene two is 74."

There is only one thing about Charleston and Folly that Mr. Gershwin does not like. "Your amateur composers bring me their pieces for me to play. I am very busy and most of them are very bad – very, very bad," he said.

George Gershwin. *Courtesy of the George Grantham Bain Collection, Library of Congress*

Heyward took Gershwin on forays to the neighboring James Island, which had a large Gullah population. They visited schools, and especially churches. Gershwin was particularly fascinated by a dance technique called "shouting," which entailed beating out a complicated rhythm with feet and hands to accompany the spiritual singing. Heyward wrote:

> The most interesting discovery to me, as we sat listening to their spirituals ... was that to George it was more like a homecoming than an exploration. The quality in him which had produced the "Rhapsody in Blue" in the most sophisticated city in America, found its counterpart in the impulse behind the music and bodily rhythms of the simple Negro peasant of the South.
>
> I shall never forget the night when at a Negro meeting on a remote sea-island George started 'shouting' with them. And eventually to their huge delight stole the show from their champion 'shouter.' I think he is probably the only white man in America who could have done it.

The first version of the opera ran four hours, with two intermissions, and was performed privately in a concert version at Carnegie Hall, in 1935. The world premiere performance took place at the Colonial Theatre in Boston on September 30, 1935. This was the traditional out-of-town performance for any show headed for Broadway. The New York opening took place at the Alvin Theatre in New York City on October 10, 1935 and ran for 124 performances, impressive for an opera, and but woefully short for a musical. The reviews were decidedly mixed.

Brooks Atkinson wrote in the New York *Times*, October 9, 1935:

> After eight years of savory memories, Porgy has acquired a score, a band, a choir of singers and a new title, *Porgy and Bess*, which the Theatre Guild put on at the Alvin last evening ... Although Mr. Heyward is the author of the libretto and shares with Ira Gershwin the credit for the lyrics, and although Mr. Mamoulian has again mounted the director's box, the evening is

unmistakably George Gershwin's personal holiday …
Let it be said at once that Mr. Gershwin has contributed
something glorious to the spirit of the Heywards'
community legend.

It was called "crooked folklore and halfway opera"
by Virgil Thomson. Whereas, Lawrence Levine stated:
"*Porgy and Bess* reflects the odyssey of the African
American in American culture." Most critics
complained about the form of the show - was it opera,
or was a musical?

Broadway production of *Porgy and Bess.* Note the similarities of the set
to the real Cabbage - Catfish Row in Charleston (pg. 239)
Courtesy of the Library of Congress

Gershwin himself anticipated those reactions. In
the *New York Times* in 1935 he said:

Because *Porgy and Bess* deals with Negro Life in America
it brings to the operatic form elements that have never
before appeared in the opera and I have adapted my
method to utilize the drama, the humor, the
superstition, the religious fervor, the dancing and the
irrepressible high spirits of the race. If doing this, I have
created a new form, which combines opera with
theater, this new form has come quite naturally out of
the material.

The argument still rages.

People in Charleston, however, wasted little time taking advantage of *Porgy and Bess* for profit. As the first American folk opera, composed by one of America's greatest composers, and based on a story written by a native son, the opera was a boon for Charleston marketing. The Chamber of Commerce paid for the placement of historical markers on structures throughout the city and the subsequent opening of the Cooper River Bridge gave motorists direct access to the city via Route 40 and the Atlantic Coast Highway. The 1922 petition to clean up Cabbage - Catfish Row was given new life. New York landscape artist, Loutrel Briggs, was the driving force behind the petition. He wanted to save the Row. He wrote:

> DuBose Heyward, with an artistry to which my unskilled pen cannot do justice, has preserved for posterity the picturesque life of "Catfish Row," and I have attempted to reclaim, with as little external change as possible, this building and restore it to something of its original state in revolutionary time.

The *New York Times Magazine* headline of the Cooper River Bridge opening read: ALOOF CHARLESTON CALLS TO OUTER WORLD. *The Chicago Tribune* wrote:

> In a world of change, Charleston changes less than anything ... Serene and aloof, and above all permanent, it remains a wistful reminder of a civilization that elsewhere has vanished from earth.

With the Great Depression gripping America, Charleston was in no financial position to deny any money. The pre-Revolutionary residential area of Heyward's former neighborhood – Church and Tradd Streets - became a haven for tourist shops, catering to the much-disdained, but much-needed Yankee trade. Ladies of "quality" from Charleston's "first families," opened coffee houses and tea shops, serving as "lady guides" on walking tours down the cobblestone streets and brick alleys. Their version of Charleston was completely focused on the glory days of the past, discussing "servants" not slaves, architecture not secession, George Washington not Jim Crow. They were trying to preserve, or more realistically, resurrect, what Rhett Butler described in *Gone With The Wind* "the calm dignity life can have when it's lived by gentle folks, the genial grace of days that are gone."

Led by two community boosting mayors, John P. Grace and Thomas Stoney, this refocusing of history transformed Charleston in the 21st century. The 1930s preservation and tourism campaign solidified Charleston's image as "America's Most Historic City," making it the darling of upscale tourists. In 2012, readers of the international travel magazine *Conde Nast* voted Charleston the #1 Tourism City in the World.

Kendra Hamilton, descendent of former Jenkins orphan, Lonnie Hamilton, III wrote:

The ironies of the situation are compelling. Charleston becomes daily more segregated, the chasm between rich and poor ever deeper and wider, as in the salad days before the war. The tourist-minded city fathers become daily more ingenious at smoothing down the ugly truths of the city's history so as to increase its appeal to people whose impressions of the South owe more to Scarlett O'Hara than Shelby Foote. And yet, the city's most readily identifiable cultural emblems – from Porgy to "the Charleston" – have African-American roots.

During the 1930s and 40s, DuBose Heyward's former home at 76 Church Street became the Porgy Shop. This store sold antiques, china curios and other fine furnishings that had nothing to do with the opera, the play, or the novel. It certainly had nothing in common with its namesake, a poor, violent, black beggar turned into a folk hero.

The Porgy House, 76 Church Street, DuBose Heyward's home turned into a gift shop. *Courtesy of the Library of Congress*

In another ironic twist, the "first families" of Charleston who made money from this skewed, picturesque version of history did not even allow a version of their most famous commodity to be performed in its home setting until 1970, thirty-four years after its debut. Indeed, Charleston often goes out of its way to soften its African history. In the 1991 video, *Charleston, S.C.: A Magical History Tour*, Mrs. Betty Hamilton, daughter of artist Elizabeth O'Neill Verner, discusses her mother's 1920s era paintings as capturing "the Gullah South Carolina niggra with their simplicity and their sweetness."

In 1952 a new international production of *Porgy and Bess* was mounted, featuring a twenty-four year old newcomer named Leontyne Price as Bess, and the veteran Cotton Club song-and-dance man Cab Calloway as Sportin' Life. This production was a theatrical triumph in Vienna, Berlin, and London and also a hit when it returned to New York's Ziegfeld Theater. The black press, however, launched a furious attack of the opera. James Hicks, a reporter with the Balti more *Afro-American*, called the opera as "the most insulting, the most libelous, the most degrading act that could possibly be perpetrated against colored Americans of modern times." William Warfield noted:

> In 1952 the black community wasn't listening to anything about plenty of nothing being good enough for me. Blacks began talking about being black and proud.

In 1954 there was an effort to produce *Porgy* in Charleston but it ran into trouble. South Carolina law at the time forbade the "mixing of the two races in places of amusement" for "historic reasons of incompatibility." Local black performers refused to perform in front of a segregated audience and the show was canceled. It wasn't until 1970 during South Carolina's tri-centennial festivities that an amateur production of *Porgy and Bess* was approved and ultimately performed in Charleston in front of an integrated audience. It was the first amateur production of the opera allowed by the Gershwin estate, but by that time, the opera had acquired a dubious reputation.

During the 1960s the Civil Rights and black power movements transformed America. *Porgy and Bess* became an embarrassment to many black activists. Harold Cruse wrote that:

> *Porgy and Bess* belongs in a museum and no self-respecting African American should want to see it, or be seen in it.

Such is the love-hate relationship of *Porgy and Bess*, and the ebb-and-flow of cultural acceptance, that endures to this day. However, in 2012 the story was reborn for Broadway. Titled *The Gershwins' Porgy and Bess* and starring four-time Tony-award winner Audra MacDonald, the new show was not without controversy. The producers changed some of the story and music to make it more appealing to modern audiences. The operatic-styled recitatives were replaced by spoken dialogue. Eight-time Tony winner, Stephen Sondheim, also complained that the new title completely ignored Dubose Heyward's significant contribution to the work.

The show closed on September 23, 2012 after 322 performances, making it the longest production of *Porgy and Bess* ever staged. [Editor's note: The production was nominated for ten Tony Awards in 2012 and won the Best Musical Revival. MacDonald won a fifth Tony-award for her performance as Bess.]

Generations have either been delighted by Heyward's story and Gershwin's music, or insulted by the mythical myopic portrayal of southern blacks, but at the heart of the discussion is one overwhelming, indisputable fact: without the African southern culture, the story and music of *Porgy and Bess* could have never been created. And in Charleston, South

Carolina – which has the historic distinction of being American's largest slave port and the most ardent defender of the "peculiar institution" – the most striking and pervasive symbol of America's African musical heritage is the nearly forgotten influence of the Jenkins Orphanage bands.

2013 view of the Old Marine Hospital, 20 Franklin Street. Currently the Charleston Housing Authority. *Photo by author.*

EIGHTEEN
The End of an Era

I remember when I was child, those [Jenkins] kids used to come up as far north as Trenton and just play on the street corners in the most non-descript uniforms you ever saw - some sort of jacket with brass buttons and pants with strips. They would just stand around in a circle and the leader was somebody who could dance like hell - he didn't have to have any talent more than the ability to say "1, 2, boom!" and then go into a routine of his own which would highlight the performances. But they did move around all over the country and they played the most positive ragtime you have ever heard.

- Leonard De Paur, composer and conductor,
from *The Book of Jazz*.

WITH THE ONSLAUGHT OF THE DEPRESSION, THE exuberance of the Roaring 20s gave way to a more somber reality. Bank accounts of the Jenkins Orphanage thinned. Many people who used to donate to the cause were now forced to keep whatever money they had to themselves. Another page of history turned.

In the pre-dawn morning of March 17, 1933, one hundred and seventy-seven children were evacuated from the Jenkins Orphanage when a fire swept through the second floor. Part of the wall collapsed and several rooms were gutted. The old orphanage was no longer habitable. The fire also destroyed the majority of the Orphanage's historical records, a monumental loss that has only become more tragic over time as various historians, writers and archivists have attempted to piece together the story of the orphanage and its music.

The year before the fire, Rev. Jenkins assumed the $7000 mortgage of the building next door, formerly part of the South Carolina Medical College After the fire the children moved into that building. However, fallout from the fire was not that easily overcome or ignored. A series of local newspaper articles detailing the fire were critical of the orphanage empire. It brought to public notice the long-term complaints of white families who lived around the Orphanage compound - loud music, extreme noise, petty crimes and runaway waifs.

Some of Rev. Jenkins' success can be traced to Charleston's official historic disinterest in the welfare of black children. As long as the leading white citizens could provide token financial support to the Orphan Aid Society, their Christian duty was fulfilled. But now, the residents of the neighborhood called for a public meeting to discuss the orphanage issue, which quickly became a whites-only rally. No black citizens were invited. Fire chief John Wohlers denounced the orphanage for poor electrical wiring and inadequate fire escapes. Stories of crime and disturbances were aired publically. The white citizens voted to "condemn the orphanage."

Several relatives of former orphans also came forward to complain of stories of beatings and abuse by the orphanage staff, and there were the oft-repeated grumblings that the reverend and his wife were living an elevated lifestyle on the backs of charitable donations. The city of Charleston ordered an official inquiry to determine if Rev. Jenkins and his wife Ella were guilty of negligence and malfeasance. In 1934 the Charleston Bureau of Social Welfare appointed a "Committee to Investigate the Conditions in the Jenkins Orphanage." John Bennett wrote about the investigation in his diary:

The Jenkins Orphanage investigation seems a futile thing, saying little drastic, recommending less. Rev. Jenkins intimates he cures tuberculosis by giving the patient a horn in the band and making him blow it. Nothing at all appears to have come from the loud accusations of self-enrichment by Jenkins of which we heard so much, from the usual Negro sources mostly.

During this period *Time* magazine ran a story about the success of the orphanage. The reporter interviewed Rev. Jenkins at his Harlem home.

TIME. August 26, 1935.
JENKINS BANDS
The end of the War between the States (or the War of the Rebellion) brought freedom to tall, blue-black Daniel Joseph Jenkins, born a slave in 1861and soon orphaned. Turned off a plantation in Charleston, S.C. he said: "I took God for my guide. I got a job on a farm and two pounds of meat and a quart of molasses a week to live on." One day he came upon half a dozen shoeless, shivering pickaninnies huddled by a railroad track. He gave them his last dollar.
Daniel Jenkins became a Baptist minister. Soon Preacher Jenkins preached a sermon on "The Harvest Is Great but the Laborers Are Few" persuading his congregation to help him found an orphanage for poor black moppets. That was 1891. Daniel Jenkins proceeded to rid Charleston of roaming, thieving "Wild Children:" In two buildings in the city and farms and schools outside it, he had cared for more than 536 orphans at a time, today less than 300 in his charge. Of the thousands of Negroes turned out by the Jenkins Orphanage at 14, he claims that less than ten have ended up in jail. Grizzled, black-garbed and ailing at 74, Daniel Jenkins is Charleston's No. 1 Negro citizen, prosperous enough to have been touched for a loan by a white Charlestonian in the early days of the War. The fame & fortune of the Jenkins Orphanage, however, did

not come from piety alone. Taking a leaf from Booker T. Washington who successfully raised money through his Tuskegee Singers, Daniel Jenkins early began to exploit small Negroes playing band music.

Having on his hands a number of undernourished, rickety and tuberculosis youngsters, Jenkins optimistically decided "My children's lungs would get strong by blowing wind instruments." He obtained some battered horns, organized a band which he sent North in 1893 to play on street corners for whatever passersby would give. So successful was the band that is has never since missed a trip. In 1905 it played in Teddy Roosevelt's inaugural parade. It appeared at the St. Louis Exposition, the Anglo-American Exposition in London. It has toured the U.S. from coast to coast, played in Paris, Berlin, Rome, London, Vienna. Divided into sections as the kids grew older and learned to play better, the Jenkins Band once had five units simultaneously on tour.

Today, its 125 players, age 10 to 18, earn from $75,000 to 100,000 a year for the Orphanage. Once boys & girls used to play together in the band, but says Daniel Jenkins, "They got too fresh and I had to separate them." Now the girls play in their own bands or sing to the boys' accompaniment. Each band-section is chaperoned and guided by a ministerial graduate of the Orphanage. Boys wear dark blue uniforms and girls wore simple print dresses.

In winter, Jenkins bands play in schools, churches, halls throughout the South and West. In the summer they head North. This year 65 of 125 bandsters were chosen, divided into Bands No. 1 and No. 2. Last week Band No. 1, with twenty-one year old Freddy Bennett as leader, played in Providence, R. I., moved to Hartford, Conn. Under the guidance of William Blake, who has been with the Orphanage for 38 years, Band No. 2 had been in Saratoga, N.Y. where the horse-racing season opened early this month [TIME, Aug. 12]. Day & night at the race track, at baseball games on the spa's Broadway the hard-working youngsters played spirituals, sweet ballads and hot arrangements of tunes like *Dinah* and *Sweet Sue* on their rusty cornets, trombones, French horns, drums. Bystanders were especially taken with Band No. 2's impish 12-year-old leader who juggled his baton and shimmied vigorously.

Rich old Rev. Daniel Joseph Jenkins in his institution's Northern headquarters in New York's Harlem, scrutinized detailed weekly reports of his band's doings. Collections in Saratoga, even with five youngsters passing hats and wheedling coins from bystanders, were good only when someone with a kind heart produced a windfall. Last week Daniel Jenkins sent Band No. 2 back to Charleston, where No. 1 would rejoin it, playing its way southward by way of Philadelphia, Baltimore, Washington, Richmond and Durham. Daniel Jenkins is soon returning South. "I ain't got long to stay here," he cackles. "But I'll carry on till Jesus calls me home."

Rev. Jenkins wrote letters to several newspapers refuting the Orphanage's income stated in the *Time* article. He claimed the band was bringing in less than five thousand dollars, not one hundred thousand. Jenkins' claims were probably more accurate. The Depression had hit America hard; people in soup lines didn't have much interest in giving money to a black orphanage. The orphanage was also down to just two bands. After a forty year run of almost constant success, Rev. Jenkins, like the rest of America, was falling on hard times. The Roaring 20s became the Depressed 30s. Charleston City Council proposed the orphanage be given over to public control and that Jenkins resign. He refused and defended himself in a letter:

I plead guilty to failing to consider the recommend-dations made to me to turn over the Jenkins Orphanage and all property to the city. I have been a member of the National Conference of Social Workers for over twenty years. I am no stranger to every move made for the welfare of children. But God is not dead. I must prove true to God first, secondly to my fellow men, and thirdly to my heart and conscience – no more, no less.

The City of Charleston had another plan. The Federal government under President Roosevelt was now providing money for housing projects to be constructed across the country. The city council had its eye fixed on the neighborhood surrounding the Orphanage and the city jail for a construction project. They planned to evict poor, mostly black residents of Franklin and Magazine Streets and Cromwell Alley, raze the dilapidated houses and build a new housing project for whites. The orphanage was the main obstacle in their way; indeed it was most likely the only reason the city authorities were hesitant to take action. Fate, however, gave the city an opportunity.

Rev. Daniel Joseph Jenkins died on July 30, 1937, eleven days after he suffered a cerebral hemorrhage. He was seventy-five years old and had been the head of the Orphan Aid Society for forty-five years. Ironically, both of the bands were away on tour in New York and Boston and could not return to Charleston in time for the funeral. His obituary in the *News and Courier,* July 31, 1937, in part read:

REV. JENKINS DIES; KEPT ORPHANAGE
Negro Institution Founder Sent Brass Bands to Europe Three Times
The Rev. D.J. Jenkins, founder of the Jenkins Orphanage, whose brass bands have toured the United States and crossed the ocean three times to Europe, died last night after a long illness. He was seventy-four years old.

Jenkins founded the orphanage December 16, 1891, and built it into an institution which has taken care of 5000 negro boys and girls in the intervening forty-five years. The orphanage has its main building in Franklin Street, maintains two farms and publishes a newspaper (The Messenger). Boys learn printing, carpentry, shoe making, chair caning and automobile mechanics. Girls are taught to do housework.

In Charleston the orphanage is known best for its bands. There are two now, frequently there have been four, which play at street corners to the energetic directions of a diminutive conductor. These bands have been familiar sights in cities all over the United States, going as far west as Los Angeles. Charlestonians have reported seeking them in many out-of-the-way places. Their silver donations go to the orphanage fund.

In 1914, the Rev. Jenkins took the band to England to represent the negro race at the Anglo-American exposition in London celebrating a century of peace between the nations. The band played before the Queen of England.

The war broke out and Jenkins was able to assist several prominent Charlestonians stranded by the money confusion. They were unable to cash checks but he was paid in gold and loaned money for them to get out of the country.

The Jenkins band marched in the inaugural parade when President Taft was inaugurated and at the St. Louis Exposition.

Seventy children in the three groups, now are on the road, playing and singing in Boston, Saratoga (for the races) and New York city.

Jenkins had a flow of language both oral and written calculated to wring the hearts of prospective donors, and he received contributions from some of the most eminent people in the United States. His letters to the newspapers asked alms for his "Little Black Lambs" were powerful pleas that were read by generations of Charlestonians.

Besides being president of the orphan society Jenkins was pastor of the Fourth Baptist church for forty-six years.

Rev. Daniel Jenkins' grave at the Unity and Friendship Society Cemetery, Charleston, S.C. *Photo by author*

The *New York Times* also ran an obituary of the "Orphan Man" and his widow, Ella, was flooded with letters and telegrams of condolences from people all over the world. She quickly realized that their church, the New Tabernacle Fourth Baptist, was too small to accommodate the sheer volume of people who would most likely attend the funeral so it was moved to the larger Morris Street Baptist church. More than 2000 people attended.

In 1982, in an interview with *Cadence* magazine, Jabbo Smith remembered Rev. Jenkins:

> He's about the most famous person, to me. Martin Luther King was all right, but brother D.J. Jenkins was the man.

Rev. Jenkins died without a will so the probate court appointed his wife Ella Jenkins as the administrator of his estate. Her "adopted" English daughter, Olive, was left out of Ella's dispensation to the family. The rift between mother and "daughter" would never be healed.

A year after Rev. Jenkins's death, the orphanage was financially floundering. Under Ella's direction, two longtime associates of the orphanage, Rev. John and Sarah Dowling, ran the day-to-day operations but money was getting thin. No one could raise money the way Rev. Jenkins had, and the Depression had ravaged the country for almost a decade.

Ella released control of the Orphan Aid Society to the city of Charleston who promised to build a new facility out of town. The new Jenkins Orphanage was finished in 1938 at a cost of $33,000. The compound consisted of four barracks constructed eight miles north of the city on former farm land. Almost immediately, the buildings began to leak and the plumbing stopped working. Ella served as adminis-trator for several years before retiring. She died in Charleston, May 1975.

After the Orphanage moved from Franklin Street, most of the surrounding neighborhood was leveled by the city of Charleston with two exceptions - the City Jail and the Marine Hospital at 20 Franklin Street, the original orphan house. The fire-damaged wings were demolished but the main building was left intact.

In 1973 the Marine Hospital was declared a National Historic Landmark for two reasons: One, its architect was Charleston native Robert Mills who later became famous for his designs in Washington, DC - the Washington Monument, U.S Treasury Building and the Patent Office; two, the birthplace of the Jenkins Bands.

The Jenkins Institute for Children is located on Azalea Drive in North Charleston, South Carolina. The Institute is a low management residential care facility for children whose primary need is physical and emotional nurturing.

Historic markers currently on 20 Franklin Street.
Photo by author

After relocating outside the city, the Jenkins Bands rarely marched through the streets of Charleston. By the 1960s, stories of the Jenkins Band had all but disappeared from the history of Charleston, and from the fabric of American music. For most of the 20th century, the history of Charleston as related in published books, newspapers and magazines consisted of little more than sepia-toned memories of the genteel past. In one of the more glaring examples of the band's forgotten legacy there is not a single member of the Jenkins Band in the

South Carolina Entertainment and Music Hall of Fame, even though such luminaries as TV personalities Vanna White and Leeza Gibbons have been inducted.

Current entrance to the Jenkins Institute on Azalea Drive, North Charleston, S.C. *Photo by author*

During Charleston's golden age of white luxury and leisure, Africans grew the crops, cooked the food, raised the children (black and white), and built the houses and churches. Yet somehow, this invisible caste also managed to help invent America's most enduring contribution to world culture – jazz music.

In the 21st century the African/Gullah culture is finally being given overdue acknowledgment for their rich contributions to Lowcountry life. The Jazz Artists of Charleston perform concerts that often include songs made famous by members of the Jenkins Bands and other local early jazz and blues musicians.

In 2012 Charleston was named the #1 Tourist City in the world by *Conde* Nast magazine. It is also one of the top culinary destinations in the world. Every Charleston restaurant heavily features African-style food. What used to be "southern soul food" is now called low country cuisine and praised all over the world.

From rags to ragtime and from Charleston to the world, orphans of the Jenkins Band composed the soundtrack for the 20th century.

Historic Markers on Azalea Drive next to the Jenkins Institute entrance.
Photo by author

PART FOUR:
LEGACY OF THE LAMBS

NINETEEN
Cladys "Jabbo" Smith
cornet, trumpet, vocals. 1908 – 1991

"I don't know who that is, but he just invented be-bop!"
— Dizzy Gillespie in a *Downbeat* blindfold test after hearing
songs recorded by Jabbo Smith in 1929.

JABBO SMITH NEVER BECAME A LEGEND, BUT SOMEHOW managed to become legendary. He was born on December 24, 1908 in Pembroke, Georgia, the son of a barber and church organist. When Jabbo was four his father died and he moved to Savannah with his mother, who found it increasingly difficult to care for him. Jabbo got his nickname from a kid named James Reddick after "an ugly Indian in a William S. Hart movie." At age six, Jabbo was placed in the Jenkins Orphanage when his mother could no longer provide for him financially. Jabbo remembered:

> The orphanage building was once the old marine building, and that building took care of sick seamen …

There were tombstones in the back ... The kids who played there thought the place was haunted, and naturally – with tombstones and kids running around playing tag – they always felt it was a spooky place. And then the city jail was right next to it, which also filled the kids' heads with stories of kidnappings.

The first thing they do is send you out on the farm for two years ... So the young kids, they send them out to the farm. So you get a farm life out there, then you come on back to town and get back to people ... Well, they call you a yard boy when you come back from the farm to come to the city in Charleston. You didn't do nothin' until the guy calls you and they tell you what you're going to do – shoemaker or baker or anything. They tell you. "You come here. You come here." So they was pickin' for the band. I guess that was Mr. Jenkins's way of doing it, because people lived down town so he got us so all could play all the instruments – all the brass instruments. And so anyway, I learned the trombone and things like that.

By 1924, after nine years of playing with the Jenkins Band and running away about a dozen times only to be dragged back, the sixteen-year old Jabbo Smith ran away for good. He ended up in Philadelphia living with a half-sister and playing at the Waltz Dream Ballroom with the Harry Marsh Band. From there he moved to Atlantic City and ran into his former Jenkins band mate, Gus Aiken, who was working the Drake and Walker Minstrel Show. Gus got Jabbo hired on with him.

In 1925, Jabbo met band leader and pianist Charlie Johnson who invited him to New York. Johnson was the leader of the Paradise Orchestra, house band at Smalls Paradise in Harlem. Jabbo jumped at the chance because:

It had Sidney de Paris, who was my idol. I liked the way be blew his horn and the ways he used mutes. I never acquired his style, but he influenced me … he also had Benny Carter and Edgar Simpson … and the great drummer George Stafford. Ed Smalls, who owned the Paradise, adopted me. He was from Charleston, and all eighteen of his waiters were from Charleston.

Soon eighteen-year old Jabbo Smith was the hottest trumpet player in New York City. His flamboyant playing style and brash personality made him a natural performer. Women loved him and he was out on the town nightly with a different girl on his arm.

Jabbo Smith. *Drawing courtesy of Joe Mathieu*

In 1927 Duke Ellington asked Jabbo Smith to fill-in at a recording session for the always-ailing alcoholic Bubber Miley. That session resulted in one of the all-time great Ellington tracks, "Black & Tan Fantasy." Jabbo's playing from that session is considered the definitive version of the Ellington standard. Jabbo remembered:

> The night before I recorded with Duke, somebody stole my horn. I had to go to a music store and get a replacement, and the mouthpiece was way too big. I had a hell of time hitting that opening high C in my solo.

Gunther Schuller in *Early Jazz* says this about Jabbo Smith:

> He was above all an astonishingly consistent player and musician – a musician's musician, which I am sure is the reason Jabbo Smith was never a great public success. Every one of the arts is full of examples of great technicians and intelligent artists who do not quite catch on because their work is too advanced or sophisticated technically, while at the same time they lack just enough of the personality quotient which is so necessary to communicate with a broad public.
>
> His playing is always dramatic and unconventional; making a dull record seems to have been impossible for him. He had a vivid imagination and evidently, by virtue of a natural embouchure and an excellent technical foundation, could realize anything that came to his mind. His endurance and range were formidable, and I believe he must have outclassed Armstrong in these respects in 1929.

Jabbo turned down the chance to replace Bubber Miley in the Duke Ellington Orchestra over money. Charlie Johnson paid Jabbo one hundred and fifty dollars while Duke offered only ninety. Instead, Duke hired Freddie Jenkins, another hot young trumpet player who also claimed to be kin to Rev. Daniel

Jenkins, which has never been proven.

Four months later, Jabbo professionally was on thin ice. He remembered:

> I was undependable, and I was late a lot for the show, which hit at nine o'clock. And it was two bits in the pot for the Christmas party every time you were late. So Ed Smalls told me to just get there by midnight and everything would be fine. The musicians didn't like anyone getting such special treatment, particularly a kid. Charlie called a meeting and said, "You, Jabbo, bring yourself in at nine, or that's it. The composer [producer and director] Con Conrad had been after me to join the band of *Keep Shufflin'*, so I quit.

Keep Shufflin' was another successful Miller and Lyles Broadway musical revue, basically of a sequel of *Shuffle Along* and *Runnin' Wild*. The music was composed by James P. Johnson and Fats Waller. Jabbo joined the orchestra and recorded some of oddest songs of his career with Johnson, Waller and Garvin Bushell. Calling themselves the Louisiana Sugar Babes, the line-up was: Jabbo on cornet; Bushell on clarinet; Johnson on piano and Waller on organ. They recorded "Persian Rug," "Thou Swell" and two songs from *Keep Shufflin'*, "Sippi" and "Willow Tree."

The show went on the road and Jabbo traveled with it. However, in 1929, the show ran into a major roadblock. Arnold Rothstein, the notorious New York Jewish gangster and major financial backer of the show, was murdered. Rothstein, infamous as the man who "fixed" the 1919 Chicago "Black Sox" World Series, has been the inspiration of many a Hollywood gangster character - including Meyer Wolfsheim in Fitzgerald's *The Great Gatsby* and Nathan Detroit in *Guys and Dolls* and on the HBO series, *Boardwalk Empire*, Rothstein's character is portrayed by actor

Michael Stuhlbarg.

Keep Shufflin' immediately closed after Roth-stein's murder, stranding the cast and crew in Chicago. Jabbo found a job playing at the Sunset Café where he attracted the attention of Mayo Williams at Brunswick Records. Williams saw Jabbo as someone who could tap into the market of Louis Armstrong fans. Jabbo quickly formed a quintet from local musicians called the Rhythm Aces. From January to August 1929, the Aces recorded nineteen sides in which Jabbo displays extraordinary virtuosity and exemplary musicianship on trumpet, trombone and vocals. Possibly, because the work was so advanced and sophisticated, the records did not sell well, and until the 1980s, were largely forgotten. Jabbo remembered the recordings:

> The Rhythm Aces was Ikey Robinson's, it was just a pick up band. That's what I was sayin' about those guys back then, they didn't have to have all this music. It didn't have to be written down, we could go to the studio and I could hum these things to these cats and everybody got it from there. They were fabulous, 'cause they had fabulous musicians, like Lawson Buford, Omer Simeon and Ikey Robinson and Cas Simpson, just fabulous cats.

Of much more importance however, was that these records attracted the attention of trumpet player Roy Eldridge, who began to adopt some of Jabbo's technically explosive, chance-taking speed in the high register and explorative style into his own playing. According to Roy Eldridge's own account he lost a "musical battle" to Jabbo in 1930 when:

> Jabbo Smith caught me one night and turned me every way but loose ... he wore me out before the night was

through. He knew a lot of music and changes ...

Whitney Balliett in *Jelly Roll, Jabbo & Fats* (1983) wrote:

Jazz categorists have long declared Jabbo Smith a second-rate Louis Armstrong, which is like calling Scott Fitzgerald a follower of Hemingway. Armstrong was guided by rhythmic and melodic considerations, but Smith was directed largely by technique. Armstrong was lyrical and poetic ... Smith's style was never completely balanced. He kept poking at his technical boundaries, playing high notes and wild intervals and thirty-second note runs that had never been played before. This was particularly true after he arrived in Chicago and challenged Armstrong, who he had known only from recordings. Before that, in New York, Smith's playing was sly and sinuous and lyrical. It was the first cool jazz improvisation ... He grew agitated on the Brunswick recordings and his once creamy melodic lines jump and zigzag ... He goes after intervals and arpeggios that Armstrong could not have managed either. He shows off.

The Brunswick records were designed to compete with Armstrong's Hot Fives and Hot Sevens. The instrumentation of trumpet, clarinet, piano, banjo, and bass is similar ... His dynamics are superb, he is leaping and mercurial, he is full of sorrowing blue notes, and he delivers several scat-sung vocals that surpass Armstrong. There are many intimations: Roy Eldridge breaks; legato runs that suggest the Henry Allen of 1933; fast muted runs that resemble Dizzy Gillespie. The Brunswicks [sides] are among the best of the early jazz recordings.

As the Depression gripped the country during the 1930s, Jabbo Smith gradually withdrew from serious music activity. He ran an eight-piece band in Chicago and Milwaukee from 1930-36, recorded sporadically.

Then he played with the Claude Hopkins Big Band.

In 1939 Jabbo briefly led a group at the World's Fair in New York and gigged in a Newark, New Jersey club called the Alcazar. It was at the Alcazar that Jabbo met a seventeen-year old Newark singer. He encouraged the young woman to enter the talent show at Harlem's Apollo Theater. She won and became known worldwide as The Divine One, Sarah Vaughn.

By the 1950s Jabbo was out of music completely, living in Milwaukee, Wisconsin. He married, raised a family and ran an Avis Car Rental Agency. He was soon forgotten by the musical world.

In 1968, Gunther Schuller wrote five glowing pages about Jabbo Smith in *Early Jazz* which introduced him to another generation of jazz players and journalists. In the mid-1970s impresario George Wein invited Jabbo to New York to receive an award as one of the greatest living musicians in jazz history.

Jabbo Smith began practicing the trumpet again thanks to the encouragement of Swedish clarinetist Orange Kellin, who invited him to New Orleans to play in his band. In 1979 Kellin became the musical director of a Broadway musical revue titled, *One Mo' Time*, a pastiche of 1920s musical shows, like *Shuffle Along, Runnin' Wild* and *Keep Shufflin'*. All the songs in the new show were from the 1920s. Kellin hired Jabbo to play in the orchestra. One of the show's highlights was when Jabbo walked on stage to perform his own song, "Love." The show got mixed reviews; Jabbo, however, became the darling of Broadway for several weeks, getting rave reviews for his singing and showmanship

After *One Mo' Time* closed, Jabbo played the New York jazz clubs and worked with Thad Jones and Don Cherry. He also toured in Europe with the Hot Antic Jazz Band, a group of French musicians. Led by trumpeter Michel Bastide these musicians were Jabbo fanatics and spent three years mastering Jabbo's 1929 repertoire which they performed onstage. They were thrilled when Jabbo agreed to come on tour and record with them.

Author's collection

Lorraine Gordon, who owned the Village Vanguard night club in New York, became a supporter, patron and friend of Jabbo Smith in the 1980s. She was instrumental in getting Jabbo's 1961 recordings released. She said:

> John Steiner is a jazz collector of importance in Milwaukee. He loves jazz. He's always followed Jabbo's career. He made these recordings when Jabbo hadn't been playing. He took him out to the University of Chicago with Marty Grosz and others and put it down,

but he didn't do anything with it. Maybe he didn't think they were good enough. He left them on the shelf for twenty years. When I visited John with Jabbo in Milwaukee – he had an enormous record collection – he just played a little snatch of this. I said, "Is this Jabbo?" I'd never heard these. He said yes. So he sent me a cassette of more of it.

For two years I asked what he was going to do with them. He was going to sell them to someone else. I said, "Look, I'm willing to buy them." It took two years to get him to sell me the tapes, which I then put out as records, even though they may be rough and not thoroughly rehearsed. To me, it was the most valuable legacy I'd ever heard of Jabbo in those years.

There was nothing of Jabbo in '61. I didn't care if Jabbo just played two notes on it – it's so important. Perfect they're not: I left everything on the records – all the takes, starts, starting again, bloopers. I just thought it was a historic document to have.

Over the next few years Gordon remained close to Jabbo and was with him during his final days of performing. She remembered:

He suffered a couple of strokes. Three days before he went on with Don Cherry at the Vanguard, during rehearsal he suffered a minor stroke and went totally blind. We had him in and out of many hospitals. But come the night of the opening, Jabbo was there and he sang. He performed six nights, and he could barely see. Nobody really knows that. So I say he's a real showman.

In May of 1990 Jabbo moved into the Village Nursing Home in New York and died in January 1991 at age 82, ending one of the most influential careers in jazz history. Jabbo Smith's career peaked before he was twenty-one years old. His love of money, girls and booze probably had much to do with his lack of commercial success. Bassist Milt Hinton was quoted in "Hear Me Talkin' to Ya?" by Nat Hentoff and Nat Shapiro, in 1955:

> Jabbo was as good as Louis [in 1930]. He was the Dizzy Gillespie of that era. He played rapid-fire passages while Louis was melodic and beautiful ... He could play soft and he could play fast but he never made it. He got hung up in Newark ... He had delusions of grandeur and he'd always get mixed up with women ... If he made enough for drinks and chicks in any small town like Des Moines or Milwaukee, that would suffice.

Jabbo may have also been the only trumpet player in the world who could claim to have bested Roy Eldridge in a "cutting session" in 1930. As Jabbo's career faded Eldridge grabbed the hot trumpet mantle from Louis Armstrong and exerted a strong influence on the playing of young Dizzy Gillespie. Thus Jabbo Smith is a key link in the development of modern jazz trumpet playing: Louis Armstrong→ Jabbo Smith → Roy Eldridge → Dizzy Gillespie → Miles Davis → Wynton Marsalis.

All in all, not a bad legacy ... and what a life!

JABBO SMITH DISCOGRAPHY

♪ *The Complete Set, 1929-1938.* Challenge Label.
♪ *Hot Jazz In the Twenties, Vol.1.* Collectable Records.
♪ *Hot Jazz In the Twenties, Vol. 2.* Collectable Records.
♪ *Ace of Rhythm.* Pearl Records.
♪ *Jabbo Smith's Rhythm Aces. The Ultimate Jazz Archive 5, 1929-1938.,*
These are all collections of the original nineteen

Brunswick recordings with a few other random sides from the 1930s. Any of these are a MUST HAVE for any jazz fan.

♪ *The Complete Hidden Treasures Session.* Indie Europe /Zoom Records.

These are the 1960s recordings that Lorraine Gordon released. Ragged and unorganized, but sporadically spirited and fun. Portrait of the artist as an old man.

TWENTY
Thomas P. "Tommy" Benford
drums, 1905-1994

"The first band I was ever in … played jazz and blues!"
- Tommy Benford

TOMMY BENFORD WAS AN ACTIVE, WORKING PROFES-
sional jazz drummer for seventy years. He was born in
Charleston, West Virginia in 1905. He never knew his
mother and his father died when Tommy was five. He
and his older brother Bill were sent to the Jenkins
Orphanage in Charleston, S.C. In Whitney Balliett's
1982 book *Jelly Roll, Jabbo and Fats*, Benford talked
about his life at the orphanage:

> It was a big brick building at No. 20 Franklin Street.
> The Reverend Dr. Jenkins was a wonderful person, and
> we were treated very well. They had three different
> bands, with twenty-five or so members in each. I
> started out on alto horn … peck horn we called it, then
> they tried me on the baritone horn, then on trombone
> and trumpet, but I didn't like any of those things
> because when I was young I always liked to laugh and
> talk a lot and eat, and it you were blowing a horn you
> couldn't do those things. So I asked if I could try the
> drums because my daddy had been a drummer and a
> tuba player. So in the end I took up the drums and
> brother Bill took up the tuba.
>
> The bands played blues and overtures and
> marches, and they traveled all over the country giving

concerts ... Musically, they started you right at the bottom at the orphanage and worked you through the rudiments until you knew your instrument back and forward. Some first-rate musicians came out of the orphanage – my brother Bill, Gus Aiken, who played trumpet with Sidney Bechet, Cat Anderson, who was with Duke Ellington so long, and Jabbo Smith, who recorded with Ellington and had Chicago on its head in 1929 with his trumpet playing. People say he was the first Dizzy Gillespie, and they're right.

They had kids in the school from all parts of the world – England, France, Germany – and from all parts of America. That's where I was brought up, and that's the school I love.

We made it into the top band, the Jenkins Orphanage Number One Band they called it. Bill and I were in that band along with the three Aitken [sp – Aiken] brothers, Lucius, Gene and Gus ... and we played all those marches and overtures – *Poet and Pleasant, William Tell* and so on ... That band was so far advanced, and this was around 1914 to 1916. They used to call us a jazz band, and we used to feature blues too ... so the first band I was ever in my life played jazz and blues!

Tommy Benford switched to drums at the Orphanage and his teacher was Herbert Wright, who later murdered Lt. Jim Europe.

I studied with Steve Wright and with Herbert Wright. They were not brothers, but they used to work with Jim Europe in the 15th Infantry Band. During the War they used to make like machine guns on their drums ... now you're talking about drummers!

Tommy Benford ran away from the Orphanage at age sixteen to join his brother with the Green River Minstrel Show. He then arrived in New York in 1920, playing at the Garden of Joy, an outdoor cabaret at

Seventh Avenue and 139th Street. For the next five years Benford worked in the clubs in New York, becoming one of the best jazz drummers in the city.

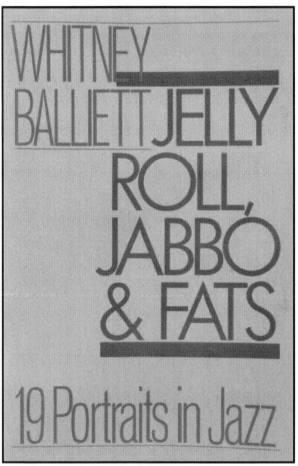

Author's Collection

He became an expert timekeeper, very important when most music was for dancing. He was one of the earliest drummers to move timekeeping from the bass drum to a "ride" cymbal, using the bass for off beats and "bombs." He became expert at using snare-drum rims, and he perfected his snappy brush work. In 1924 he played in the Duke Ellington Orchestra for a month, subbing for an ailing Sonny Greer. It was during this time he gave drumming lessons to a teenaged wunderkind named Chick Webb.

I let him [Webb] sit in at the Hoofer's Club, and it used to drive Willie the Lion crazy, because Chick still didn't have it together.

However, Benford's main legacy as a jazz drummer was three years later, when he met Jelly Roll Morton.

It was in the spring of 1928 that I first met Jelly Roll Morton. I was playing in my brother's band at the Rose Danceland up on 125th Street, and this particular night this fellow came in the club and wanted to know if he could come up and do a number with the band – we didn't know who he was at the time. Seems he's met one of the guys out on 7th Avenue and wanted to know which band was playing in there. So he came up and spoke to the proprietor and asked if he could do a number. He told him, "Yes, he could sing a song," but my brother Bill got quite upset and said that Jelly couldn't do anything unless *he* said so – it was *his* band.

Jelly had a whole lot of music with him – printed orchestrations – and he gave Bill one of his sheets and asked if the guys could read. "What kind of band do you think I've got?" Bill said. "Give me the music, I'll pass it out."

I don't remember which tune it was, but it was one of Jelly's own, and we played it. Jelly went crazy about the band and came back up there nearly every night. We found out later that he'd been going all 'round New York taking in the different bands, but we were the one he really liked. He said we were terrific and asked if we wanted to make some records with him – he had a contract with Victor … we were agreeable providing the money was right. So, a couple of days later he brought in the contract and we started rehearsing. We did that in the mornings – the dance hall finished at

1:00 am – it wasn't a night club so weren't too tired.

We rehearsed in a little night club on 7th Avenue called the Hoofer's Club. Nothing goes on in those places during the day, so they were always available for rehearsals, and we went there for a couple of days from 10:30 until 2:00, and Jelly was very particular, he knew just what he wanted. He played piano himself and had Omer Simeon come in on clarinet.

I remember that Jelly was very particular about the tempos he wanted, and right at the beginning of the rehearsals he said to me, "Watch my foot, I'll give it to you, and you hold it there."

When the first records did come out Jelly was working with us and he wanted to take the band out on tour to promote the records. Jelly was alright, he did everything properly and always asked my brother before he did anything with us. So when he wanted to go on the road, Bill told the guys and some wanted to go, and some of us didn't … we had a nice easy number where we were.

When the Depression hit America, Benford headed to Europe to work. Over the next thirty years he recorded hundreds of songs with more than a dozen different bands. The most famous session was led by Coleman Hawkins on saxophone, Benny Carter on trumpet, Django Reinhardt on guitar, Stephane Grappelli on piano and Tommy Benford on drums. Together they recorded what is considered to be one the greatest versions of the Fat Waller standard, "Honeysuckle Rose."

After World War II, Benford continued working with band leaders associated with older styles, including Snub Mosley, Bob Wilber, Jimmy Archey and notably, Noble Sissle. He toured Europe in a revue called the Jazz Train, directed by saxophonist Eddie Barefield. For the last several decades of his life he worked with the Harlem Blues and Jazz Band and toured Europe regularly. His last years were spent playing with Bob Green's World of Jelly Roll Morton, playing the songs he had recorded fifty years before. In 1982 Benford said:

> If I had my life over again, I'd want the same thing all over. They taught us everything there [Jenkins Orphanage], and they turned out some wonderful musicians.

TOMMY BENFORD DISCOGRAPHY

♪ *The Jelly Roll Morton Centennial: His Complete Victor Recordings.* Bluebird Records, 1990.
There are various collections of Jelly Roll Morton available but this five-disc boxed set is the best value with great sound clarity. Disc 2 contains most of the songs that Tommy and Bill Benford recorded with Morton.

♪ *Coleman Hawkins All Stars.* Hallmark Records, 2009.
These are the sessions with Reinhardt, Grapelli and Benny Carter. Benford plays on four of the ten tracks: "Crazy Rhythm", "Out of Nowhere", Honeysuckle Rose", and "Sweet Georgia Brown."

TWENTY-ONE
Frederick "Freddie" William Green
guitar, banjo, vocals, 1911-1987

"Rhythm guitar is like vanilla extract in cake. You can't taste it when it's there, but you know when it's left out." - Irving Ashby

IN A *DOWNBEAT* ARTICLE IN 1939 BILLIE HOLIDAY WAS ASKED about marriage and she said:

> I've loved three men. One was a Marion Scott, when I was a kid. He works for the post office now. The other was Freddie Green, Basie's guitar man. But Freddie's first wife is dead and he has two children and somehow it didn't work out. The third was Sonny White, the pianist, but like me, he lives with his mother and our plans for marriage didn't jell. That's all.

Freddie Green had the longest job in jazz history - guitar player in the Count Basie band from 1937 until his death fifty years later.

Freddie was born Charleston, South Carolina in 1911. He lived at 7 Dalts Court near Rutledge Avenue. Freddie's first musical memories were at home. His father played the pump organ and his mother sang in the AME Church choir. He played the ukulele and sang baritone in barber-shop quartets as a kid. They performed Irish songs on the street corners of Charleston for nickels and dimes. He was also a good dancer. That's how he first ran into the

Jenkins Bands

> They used to come into my neighborhood. The minute I heard that brass I used to stop whatever I was doing and follow them all over the city … There was a group called the Nighthawks in Charleston and the trumpet player's father was one of the teachers at the Jenkins Orphanage. His son was Samuel Walker. He was a terrific trumpet player so he had this group. I think it was trumpet, drums, saxophone, and piano … Most of the bands back in those days had banjos.

Freddie Green's father died and at the age of twelve Freddie moved to New York City to live with his maternal aunt. They had an apartment in Harlem, on 141st Street, between Seventh and Eighth Avenues, close to The Rhythm Club. That was where Freddie heard Jelly Roll Morton for the first time. He attended PS-51, located near 141st Street and Edgecombe Avenue, but left school at age sixteen.

> My aunt used to give house rent parties in Harlem. And she used to hire a guy to come in and play the piano. His name was Rock. He was a stride piano player. I really enjoyed the way he played. My aunt would keep drinks on the piano for him.
> I made a friend with one of the guys in the neighborhood who was supposedly the baddest guy in the neighborhood. I think we had a fight one day. And after a while, I think I kind of knocked him down. And everybody was amazed that I did that to the bad guy. So then he and I were real close friends. And he was the leader of the gang on the block. We used to go around on different corners, that's when the Charleston was out and I could always dance. So he had a ukulele and we used to go on corners and dance.

Freddie Green returned home to Charleston for

his mother's funeral. His former neighbor from Dalts Court, Leotha Elmo, met him at the train station. She became Freddie's girlfriend and later, his wife. He recalled how he became a professional musician:

There was a professor of brass instruments at Jenkins. Professor Blake was his name. We became good friends. I used to go to his house. He was a graduate of Howard University. He was a tuba player. On Sundays we would go through his library where his music books would be, and he'd help me. We would use a blackboard. We would go through the routine of scales, and what not.

My father-in-law was a contractor [in Charleston] and I used to help him quite a bit doing odd jobs and what-not … I tried all kinds of jobs and I was never pleased with whatever I did until music came.

We had our first kid. Then I left Charleston. The Jenkins [Orphanage] group had a show. They were going to tour the state of Maine. I left with them [as a non-resident of the orphanage and a grown man] and went up to Maine with this show they had. Went on the road with them with my banjo. We toured the state of Maine playing in Grange Halls, whatever they had up there in order to accommodate this traveling show. It was something! I don't think we got paid. We played for contributions and the like.

The band had two alto saxes, one tenor sax, two trumpets, two trombones, one tuba, one banjo [Freddie] and drums. We used to have to get up around noon and play all through the streets … a parade, you know. We were in the small towns of Maine. And we had dress uniforms that we wore.

The Jenkins Band stopped in New York and Freddie decided to stay. He sent for Leotha and their son to join him.

During the early 1930s Freddie had two jobs in New York, working at a factory upholstering chairs

298 / Mark R. Jones

during the daytime, and playing in a dance trio at night.

> I was working in a club called the Yeah Man Club. I knew how to play the ukulele. And the banjo, well, I could tune it, you know what I mean (laughs). Then I got a few books on banjo chords. As soon as I picked up the banjo, the guitar came in (laughs).
>
> At the Yeah Man I was playing banjo. And the manager of the club said "Well, everybody's playing guitar now. You have to get a guitar, okay?" I got one from a music store on 47th Street. King's Music Store. I bought it on time.

In 1937 Freddie was hired at the Black Cat Club in Greenwich Village for eleven dollars a week. Record producer and talent scout, John Hammond was a regular customer at the Black Cat. Hammond later achieved mythical status for his keen eye of spotting talent. Through the years he was given credit for "discovering" Billie Holiday, Pete Seeger, Count Basie, Aretha Franklin, George Benson, Bob Dylan, Bruce Springsteen and Stevie Ray Vaughn. In his autobiography *John Hammond on Record* he discussed his first impressions of Green:

> One of my favorite clubs was the Black Cat, a mob-owned joint. The band included two cousins, the drummer Kenny Clarke and the bass player Frank Clarke, but it was the guitarist that interested me the most. His name was Freddie Green, and I thought he was the greatest I had ever heard. He had unusually long fingers, a steady stroke, and unobtrusively held the whole rhythm section together. He was the antithesis of the sort of stiff, chugging guitarist Benny Goodman liked. Freddie was closer to the incomparable Eddie Lang than any guitar player I'd ever heard. He was perhaps not the soloist that Lang was, but he had a

beat.

Hammond had brought the Basie Band from Kansas City to New York and he thought a good rhythm guitar was the missing piece for the band's sound. Green auditioned in Basie's dressing room at Roseland. When the Basie Band left for Pittsburgh the next day, Freddie Green was on the bus and he stayed on it for the next five decades.

In 1938 the Count Basie Orchestra became one of the leading dance bands in America, due in part to what has been called "the All-American Rhythm Section": Count Basie, piano; Jo Jones, drums; Walter Page, bass and Freddie Green, guitar.

As the years passed, Freddie Green's importance to the Count Basie Band increased. The numerous nicknames he acquired are good illustration of his musical stature: "Esquire" – because he was such a cool gentleman; "Pepper" or just "Pep" short for "Pepperhead", because his head was shaped like a pepper; "The Fourth Wheel", short for "the fourth wheel on the Basie band wagon", "Quiet Fire" and "Mr. Rhythm." Count Basie called Freddie Green "my left hand."

Buck Clayton, trumpet player with Basie explained, "Basie never did play much with his left hand, so Freddie substituted for it." Basie's adopted son, Aaron Woodward III said, "… everyone knew Freddie's position was of equal importance to Dad's."

Quincy Jones, who arranged for Basie as a young man before becoming more famous as Michael Jackson's musical mentor and producer, said about Freddie:

> That man is a sort of spirit. He doesn't talk loud and he doesn't play loud. But man! You sure know he's there.

The brass and reeds can be up there shouting away, but there's Freddie, coming right through it all, steady as a rock and clear as a bell. He's something special. What he represents is the only one of its kind in existence.

Freddie Green's 1955 classic swinging LP. *Author's collection*

Saxophonist Paul Quinichette once observed of Green:

He's got it right there, in his wrist. What he has is the key to a musical era, an unmatched mastery of big band rhythms.

Green did not live the stereotypical life of jazz musicians. He ate smartly, rarely drank or smoked. Even while on the road with the Basie band, he rose at 7 or 8 a.m. each morning to take a long walk or play golf. Singer Joe Williams, recalling his own philandering youth, says:

> At a critical time, Freddie took me aside and advised, "Take some and leave some. Don't try to get it all. You'll enjoy it more and you'll last much longer, no matter what it is." Since it came from Freddie Green, who doesn't say that much, he only had to say it once, and I've never forgotten it.

When Charlie Christian introduced the electric guitar with the Benny Goodman in 1939, the jazz world changed dramatically. Freddie, however, continued to use his acoustic guitar on stage. Harry Edison recalls:

> Charlie Christian and he [Freddie] were very close friends, and Christian gave him an amplifier. But whenever Freddie would lay out of the band to take his solo, the whole rhythm section used to fall apart. It got to the point where we had to do something about it. So one night I would remove the plug from Freddie's amplifier wire and it wouldn't work. Next night Herschel Evans would break a wire in it so it wouldn't play, and Freddie would have it fixed … So finally we took all the guts out of the amplifier. Freddie got ready to play one night and there was nothing but a box. Naturally he got furious but nobody paid him any attention. So he reached a point where he said, "Well, to hell with it. I won't play anymore solos." So that's the reason he's not a soloist today. He probably could have been one of the best at that time, but we had to sacrifice him for the good of the band.

One of the greatest Freddie Green stories was how Freddie re-hired himself to play with Basie in 1950. After World War II most of the big bands were struggling to make money. So, Basie, like other top bands, was forced to downsize. He put together a small group that included Clark Terry, Buddy DeFranco, Bob Graf, Jimmy Lewis, and Gus Johnson. They worked a month at the Brass Rail in Chicago. Everyone in the audience was surprised that Freddie Green was not with the group.

When the sextet met in New York for their next gig, Green was sitting on the bandstand with his guitar. Clark Terry recalled the dialogue between Basie and Green:

Basie: "Say, Pep, you're not on this gig, are you?"

Green: "You're workin', aren't you? After I gave you the best years of my life, you think you're going to leave me now?"

So the sextet became a septet and Freddie Green remained the anchor of the rhythm section until his death. During his career Freddie Green performed worldwide, made over 1,000 recordings with the Basie band, and appeared as a sideman on over 700 recordings by other jazz artists. The list of artists he recorded with are a Who's Who of the 20th century: Mildred Bailey, Emmett Berry, Ruby Braff, Kenny Burrell, Benny Carter, Buck Clayton, Al Cohn, Harry Edison, Duke Ellington, Herb Ellis, Karl George, Benny Goodman, Lionel Hampton, Woody Herman, Billie Holiday, Illinois Jacquet, Jo Jones, Joe Newman, Paul Quinichette, Jimmy Rushing, Pee Wee Russell, John Sellers, Sonny Stitt, Joe Sullivan, Jack Teagarden, Joe Turner, Earl Warren, Dicky Wells, Teddy Wilson, and Lester Young.

Through the years Freddie Green also became the gauge of quality. Byron Stripling, trumpet player with Basie said, "If an arranger comes in and his work is jive, Freddie just shakes his head and it's all over."

According to Dennis Wilson (trombone), all new Basie Band members had to deal with:

... the intimidation of Freddie Green. You never know if Freddie likes you. It worries you until that mystical, magical day when he finally says a couple of words to you. Then you know you're okay, and you realize he hasn't been testing you; he's been allowing you to test yourself.

When Count Basie died in 1984 almost every publication in the world offered a eulogy. Freddie Green simply said: "I've been with the band since 1937, what am I to do now?"

Thad Jones, the popular trumpeter and Basie sideman, was chosen to take up the reins of the Basie Band after the Count's death. He commented:

I don't think it's possible to speak of the Basie band without Freddie Green. He's the link that keeps the tradition alive. He's the dean, the guy we look to for that spiritual thing.

In the May 1983 issue *of Guitar Player,* Jim Hall wrote:

If you pruned the tree of jazz, Freddie Green would be the only person left. If you have to listen to only one guitarist, study the way he plays rhythm with Count Basie.

One of the longest and quietest careers in musical history came to a conclusion on March 1, 1987. Freddie Green died of a heart attack after playing a Basie show in Las Vegas. Tributes and obituaries poured in from all over the world. Several days later, what was intended to be a surprise tribute to Green in Los Angeles organized by jazz critic Leonard Feather was turned into a memorial featuring the Basie band, vocalist Sarah Vaughan, and guitarist Kenny Burrell. Los Angeles mayor Tom Bradley declared March 19 Freddie Green Day.

Sonny Cohn said, "The most important part of your body is your heart. It keeps everything else going. That's what Freddie does."

Dennis Wilson, a trombonist and composer-arranger with Count Basie said, "It's as if in the Bible they said, 'Let there be time', and Freddie started playing."

Freddie's son, Al Green, eulogized his father:

> Dad had a quiet dignity about him, with a demeanor of an elder statesman, unassuming, diplomatic, and fair. I spent three days with Dad to celebrate his Grammy nomination as a member of The Swing Reunion album. As we got dressed for the affair that evening, he asked if I would help him with his bow tie, a kind of reversal of roles that we both acknowledged warmly. After the Grammys when we were departing, we kissed and embraced, (not knowing that it would be for the last time), he said, "I really enjoyed this time we got to spend together. It was special."
>
> You've lost Mr. Rhythm. We've lost our Dad. I've lost my hero.

Freddie once discussed about his role in the Basie band:

> The main thing is the Basie band. I get a joy out of keeping the band together and supplying the soloists with a foundation. That's more soloing to me than soloing. I've played rhythm so long that it's just the same as playing solos as far as I'm concerned. The rhythm guitar is very important. A performance has what I call a "rhythm wave", and the rhythm guitar can help to keep that wave smooth and accurate. I have to concentrate on the beat, listening for how smooth it is. If the band is moving smoothly, then I can play whatever comes to mind, but that doesn't happen too often.

I feel responsible for keeping my part in the structure going, as from the original band. I do what I do. That's enough. It's given me a whole lot of joy, pleasure, good feeling. And some bad feeling which goes with everything – you've got to take the bitter with the sweet. I'm part of it, and I'm doing a job, and that's it. I realize that the public likes the band. And I appreciate it. And I think that's what keeps us going. I go along. After all, you have to live.

FREDDY GREEN DISCOGRAPHY

Selected Count Basie Recordings:

♪ *The Complete Decca Recordings, 1937-39.* Verve, 1992
♪ *Count Basie Live – 1938 At The Famous Door, NYC.* Jazz Hour Records, 1997
♪ *April In Paris.* Polygram Records, 1956
♪ *The Complete Atomic Basie.* Blue Note Records, 1958
♪ *Chairman of the Board.* Blue Note Records, 1958

Other Recommended Recordings:

♪ *Mr. Rhythm* – Freddie Green. Fresh Sound Records.
These are the only recording sessions available with Green as band leader. As one would expect, its filled with sharp, tight arrangements of swinging songs, all propelled by Freddie's steady rhythm guitar playing.
♪ *Billie Holiday – The Legacy.* AMG, 1991.
This three-boxed set offers more than 50 songs that cover Lady Day's career. Twenty-three of the songs feature Freddie's very audible guitar strumming.

Cat Anderson. *Courtesy of the William P. Gottlieb Collection, Library of Congress*

TWENTY-TWO
William Alonzo "Cat" Anderson
trumpet, 1916-1981

"One note higher and only a dog could hear him."
- Don Walsh, *Variety* magazine. December 27, 1944.

CAT ANDERSON, WHOM WYNTON MARSALIS CALLED "ONE of the greatest high note trumpet players ever," was born in Greenville, South Carolina. He lost both parents when he was four years old and was sent to the Jenkins Orphanage in Charleston. Cat recalled:

All the upbringing I remember was received there. I even got my nickname there. When I was small, there was a fight every day. I could never win those fights, and I got tired of being whipped. One day, I ran up against the bully of the yard. There would be about four hundred of us out there, playing ball and shooting marbles. Although he didn't fall, this guy must have stumbled, and then I was on his back, scratching and tearing at him. He'd been beating me up for five or six years, but when I finished he was lying on the ground. "Hey", the kids all around said, "you fight like a cat!" The tag stayed with me right to today, although my real name is William Alonzo Anderson, Jr.

By the time he was ten years old, Cat could play several instruments, trombone, cornet and trumpet. He recalled:

The Number One and Number Two bands used to

travel a lot ... always with a superintendent from the school in attendance. They would play dance music, overtures, and marches on the street, and after each tune the superintendent would make a speech, and tell what the school was for and what it was doing. Then a hat would be passed through the audience. It was the same principle as the Salvation Army's. The bands were usually fifteen or sixteen pieces, sometimes more.

I first went out on the road in 1929. It was a wonderful experience, like going to a ball game. We would travel three months, go to school three months and then maybe head north for another three. One time, when we got into New York, all the trumpet players ran away, I was playing trombone then, but I told the superintendent that I would play trumpet if he got me one. He did that, and because one of the missing boys had been leader, I now became leader of the band.

The players in the band had a regular curriculum - school, music lessons and they also had to work some time on the farm. As they became older, they could go out at night, so Anderson began to play weekend jobs around Charleston to earn spending money.

We were all good buddies in Band Number Five, and we formed a band so that we could play dances. It began at a picnic, where we were setting riffs and each taking a "Boston" as they called solos then. It sounded good. There were about fourteen of us, and we started getting country jobs and work back of town. One Monday they said there would be no school and that most of us had to go up to the farm and pick cotton. The guys in the older bands didn't have to go and the next day they started calling us "The Cotton Pickers." The name stuck, and eventually we became the Carolina Cotton Pickers. We didn't know anything about McKinney's Cotton Pickers then because even when we were out playing the streets of cities like Boston,

Providence, and New York, we had to be in bed by sundown. So we didn't know what was going on in the music field. There were records at the school, but in those days the only ones that interested me were Louis Armstrong's.

We decided to try our luck in Texas, but we sat there two months and didn't play a job. We couldn't get any work. We were new and didn't have any transportation ... The school sent a bus to fetch us back.

For most of his professional career, Cat Anderson was famous for his incredible high note trumpet playing. Even though he was a master musician who could play beautiful muted passages and was expert with the plunger, his mastery of the "scream trumpet" gave Cat his notoriety. Capable of playing three octaves above high C, Anderson was rivaled only by Maynard Ferguson. David Von Drehl in the *Washington Post* wrote:

Maynard never courted an elite audience. Instead, he distilled his superhuman trumpet virtuosity into a very specific, excessive, showy, glitzy, oh-so-hormonal artistic achievement. He soared, screeched, trilled and exulted in a register so high even most professional horn players have rarely, if ever, played there. Ferguson didn't invent so-called "scream trumpet"; Cat Anderson was pealing far above Duke Ellington's band years before Ferguson broke through with Stan Kenton. But Ferguson took the stunt and made it a main event.

In Stanley Dance's book, *The World of Duke Ellington*, Anderson talked about the reason he became a "scream trumpet" player. The reason is one of the oldest in the world for musicians – girls. He recalled:

The reason I'd come to play so high was because at

school there were guys who could do it much better than I could. The used to take my girls from me with their high notes. This happened every Friday night at dances. Finally, I got angry and started playing everything in the upper register. They played after me this time. "Hey, you know what you were doing there?" they asked. It turned out that I'd been playing note for note an octave above what they did.

To play really high, you must have this need for recognition, this desire to be recognized. Then you try to find a way for yourself. They'd been coming in week after week, and outplaying me, and this drove me to discover a hidden talent. Many guys who would like to do it could do it, if they had the will power. They must think in that direction and they must sacrifice ... You must have complete determination. It may take many hours, many days, many years.

Before it happened to me, I was playing another way altogether. We had played all Louis Armstrong's things note for note ... In the school, all the trumpet players played "Shine", and made a hundred C's with the F on top. We were young and wanted to play. We weren't trying to prove anything.

When I say you have to sacrifice to accomplish it up there, I don't mean tone. There's a flaw in it unless it can be done as smoothly as you would in the lower register, where you phrase melodically. The rhythmic effect of jazz can be lost. The main thing is to make the high notes effective when you play them. You mustn't crowd in too many. Sometimes it may get out of hand. It may go sharp or it may go flat ... In my opinion, you can't think the same way up there as you do below. You've got to simplify to make it clean.

The Carolina Cotton Pickers were working in Florida, Georgia and Louisiana when Rev. Jenkins died in 1937 and Anderson decided it was time to leave the Pickers. He accepted an offer from Hartley Toots, a guitar player from Florida, for $17 a week. It was more money than Cat had ever seen in his life. When the band toured from Florida to New York it also gave Cat his first opportunity to play at Harlem's legendary Apollo Theater.

It was a territory band and not as polished as those in the East, but we went to play the Apollo Theatre in New York - a big deal. Mr. Tom Whaley ... was music director [at the Apollo] then. Now it seemed when territory bands went into the Apollo, they were given the hardest shows to play. They gave us "Mexican Hat Dance", and it was too much, because the guys didn't know the short cuts, and their reading was bad, but I was up on that kind of stuff because it was what we did in school. The day before the show was to open they decided they'd have to get another band. "This band can't cut the show," they said.

I'd only been in New York before with the school band, and this time I wanted to stay at least a week, so I told Tom Whaley, "If you give me the first trumpet parts, I can play them. I see there's a weakness there because he (the lead trumpet) has all the other things to play, but I'm a new fellow in the band and can't go over his head."

When Tom decided to switch the parts, I played all through that number and we make the week. That was in the pit. After that, we had to come up on stage and do the band's specialties. I had written a number called "Stop Now, You Did Enough to Me", and I was amazed by the applause my high trumpet playing was getting. I'd end with a high flare, and the whole band would shout "Stop now, you did enough to me!" of course, that was the kind of thing that was popular then, but I didn't have anything else to play.

Anderson also learned some of the money realities of the big time music business. Before the Apollo show, Cat was still with Harley Toots making $17 a week. However, the band was actually owned by Bill

Rivers, a Miami nightclub owner. Toots was just the musical leader. At the end of the week at the Apollo, the musicians were paid by a New York music union official. Anderson was stunned to be given $87.27.

"Is this mine?" he asked the union official.

"Oh, yes. All that's yours. Keep it. You're not supposed to kickback to anybody."

Anderson got upstairs and found out that Bill Rivers had already relieved the other musicians of all the money that was above their Florida band salary. Anderson refused.

Rivers: "You know your salary is only $17."

Cat: "The man downstairs said this money was all mine."

Rivers: "What man?"

Cat: "The union delegate."

Rivers: "You know, all the other fellows have given me their money ..."

Cat: "I'm going to keep this."

Rivers: "Then you'll have to lose your job."

There was still one more show to play and Anderson recalled:

> I played it with one hand, with my left hand in my pocket holding that money. I would have stayed with the band if he had just taken half, but he wanted too much!

Anderson stayed in New York playing in various bands until Pearl Harbor and the outset of World War II. During the War, Anderson played in a Special Services Army band at bases across America. During 1943-44 he played with Lucky Millender, then Erskine Hawkins. Hawkins was a trumpet player who somehow did not know that Anderson played "scream trumpet." After a few shows of outplaying the band leader, Cat was fired but ended up with a better job.

He joined the Lionel Hampton Band, one of the most popular bands of the time, second only to the Duke and the Count. Then, Cat Anderson was asked to join the Ellington band. Anderson recalled:

We were in Chicago, and Lionel was getting ready to go to California by train, and I found everybody would have a *chair* to ride in. No sleeper! I made up my mind I was going to join Ellington, and I got on the phone and found he was in Sioux City, Iowa. He told me he would be in the Chicago the very next day. I went to Philadelphia - in a sleeper! - the night after that, and opened with him at the Earle Theatre.

At rehearsal he switched the books so that I had all the lead parts. I listened very carefully. Instead of starting at the top, we'd start at the bottom, play two bars at the top, go to the middle of the arrangement for eight bars, then back to A. I made my sketches and had it all marked out, so I was ready. Then I found out the band wasn't using stands on the stage, so I had to lay the music out on the floor. The moment the curtains parted, all the lights went out! "How am I going to play this music?" I asked. "Baby, you'll have to learn it," one of the guys said. By the next day, I had memorized all the music in the show and didn't need to see it anymore."

At the Earle theatre, the band used to play Mary Lou Williams' arrangement of "Blue Skies." It wasn't a trumpet feature then. There was a chorus of clarinet by Jimmy Hamilton, a chorus of tenor by Al Sears, a release by Claude Jones, and Rex Stewart used to play the ending. We were at a theatre in Canton, Ohio, when Rex didn't show. After listening to it all week - and I'm a great listener to anything good, especially on trumpet - I knew his solo. So when Duke asked if anybody wanted to play it, and nobody volunteered, he said, "What about the new trumpet player?" I told him I'd try, and after the other solos I came down front and played it an octave higher. When I ended up on a double C, and the people were applauding, Duke said,

"Good, we'll keep it just like that." As luck would have it, Rex came in the stage door as I was blasting away. He didn't speak to me for fifteen years.

Cat Anderson solo LP. *Author's Collection*

"Blue Skies" became a showcase for the trumpet section with a new title "Trumpets No End," mainly because Anderson's performance convinced the Duke that the song worked better that way. It always left the crowd on their feet, screaming wildly and applauding. Cat remembers:

I feel like a giant. It makes me feel bigger than my horn. There are trumpet players who play equally well - some who play better. But I know it's attitude toward people that counts. You have to give it all your soul and body - do it as best you know how. As long as you continue to give, people appreciate it. They see what you are giving, and they're pulling for you. Even the horn players are in your corner. Sincerity must be there. Anything you want to do you can. But you can only learn by giving and asking.

Cat Anderson (left) with Duke Ellington (center).
Courtesy of the William P. Gottlieb Collection, Library of Congress

Anderson played with the Ellington Orchestra for more than twenty years, including one of the most famous concerts and recordings, the 1956 Newport Jazz Festival. At that time, the big band era had been usurped by the smaller be-bop bands, led by Charlie Parker, Dizzie Gillespie and Thelonious Monk.

Most big bands had folded completely, but Duke kept his band working, supporting the band himself through royalties earned on his popular compositions of the 1920s to 1940s. At the time of the Newport Festival, the Duke Ellington Orchestra did not even have a record deal, but the Duke still paid for the concert to be recorded.

During the concert the Duke announced that they were pulling out "some of our 1938 vintage." It was a pair of blues, "Diminuendo in Blue" and "Crescendo in

Blue." The two songs were to be joined by an improvised interval played by tenor saxophonist Paul Gonsalves. Ellington had been experimenting and reworking the songs for several years before the Newport performance. The night of the show, Ellington told Gonsalves to "blow as long as you feel like blowing."

As performed at Newport, and wonderfully documented on the one of the best-selling jazz records of all time, *Ellington at Newport*, the new version kick-started Ellington's waning career and secured the band financially for the rest of Ellington's life. Gonsalves played a 27-chorus solo backed only by bassist Jimmy Woode, drummer Sam Woodyard, and Ellington himself punctuating piano chords. Throughout the song there are several audible comments from the band members. The Duke himself is often heard urging the saxophonist, shouting "Come on, Paul — dig in! Dig in!" About five minutes into Gonsalves' solo, the sedate wine-and-cheese crowd realized they were witnessing a magical moment. They started dancing in the aisles and can be heard cheering and shouting at the band.

When the solo ended Gonsalves collapsed in exhaustion, and the full band returned for the "Crescendo in Blue" portion. The real crescendo of "Crescendo in Blue" however starts at the 13:15 minute mark, as Cat Anderson stands up and begins to play several octaves above the Orchestra for the final minute of the song. In a moment worthy of any classic rock concert, the already excited crowd is brought to the edge of hysteria by Anderson's screaming trumpet. When the song ends, pandemonium ensues for several moments as the Duke tries to quiet the crowd. It is truly one of the most classic recorded moments in jazz history.

Anderson had three different stints with the

Ellington Orchestra, from 1944 -1947, 1950 -1959, and from 1961-1971. Each break corresponded with Cat's attempt to lead his own band. During those periods, Anderson recorded several brilliant solo LPs which have fortunately been re-released on CD and MP3 formats in the 21st century. However, none of his solo ventures were financially successful and the Duke always enthusiastically welcomed him back into the Orchestra. Cat's fondest memories were of his time with the Duke:

> Words can't describe Duke Ellington. He never could find words to be cross. He never would fire anyone, either. Once you were in you were always in - a part of that family. And you were always loyal because that was the way *he* lived. Ellington left so much with us all - I just can't find the words.

After 1971, Anderson settled in Los Angeles where he continued to play studio sessions, gig with local bands, most notably with Bill Berry's Band, and he occasionally toured across Europe. He also began to tutor promising young trumpets players. During the late 70s, Anderson began to exhibit erratic behavior and mood swings, the result of a brain tumor which killed him in 1981.

One of his California students was named Paul Cacia, who remembered the first time he heard Anderson play:

> I was sitting at the old Tomorrow Land stage at Disneyland waiting to see the Kenton Orchestra when I suddenly heard a sound so high I didn't know if it was really a trumpet. I found myself running towards this sound where I came upon the Carnation Plaza Stage, down front was Cat dancing as he played "The Birth Of The Blues," in front of the Charlie Barnet Big Band. Cat was playing triple high G's so loud and effortlessly

and skipping whole octaves for effect. I met Cat that very night and made arrangements to take lessons from him. He was a warm hearted, jovial man with super human chops. I graduated from being his pupil to playing lead trumpet in his band and I had the privilege of sitting next to him in other trumpet sections. They don't make them like Cat anymore, and they never will.

CAT ANDERSON DISCOGRAPHY

Duke Ellington:

- ♪ *Ellington at Newport,* Sony Records, 1956.
- ♪ *Far East Suite*, RCA 1966.
  Wynton Marsalis calls this one of the ten greatest jazz recordings of all time.
- ♪ *Reprise Studio Recordings*, Rhino/Warner Records, 1999.
  Contains most of Ellington's post-Newport 1956 recordings.

Cat Anderson:

- ♪ *In Paris,* Inner City, 1964.
- ♪ *Cat's in the Alley,* Fresh Sounds, 2007.
  This contains Cat's first LP as a bandleader, 1959's *Cat On a Hot Tin Horn,* as well as *Cat's In The Alley.*
- ♪ *Cat Speaks*, Disques Black and Blue, 1977.
- ♪ *Plays W.C. Handy, The Definitive Black and Blue Sessions,* Disques Black and Blue, 1979.

APPENDIX

TOP 40 "CHARLESTON" SONGS

(Author's choice)

Song	Artist
1. *Charleston*	James P. Johnson The Varsity Eight Paul Whiteman Orchestra Django Reinhardt
2. *Charleston Is The Best Dance of All*	Charlie Johnson Paradise Orchestra w/Jabbo Smith
3. *Don't Forget To Mess Around (When You're Doing the Charleston)*	Louis Armstrong
4. *Sweet Georgia Brown*	Coleman Hawkins All-Stars w/ Tommy Benford on drums
5. *Runnin' Wild*	Duke Ellington
6. *Clap Hands, Here Comes Charlie*	Fletcher Henderson
7. *Lina Blues*	Jabbo Smith
8. *I'm Gonna Charleston Back to Charleston*	Coon-Sanders Nighthawks
9. *Charleston Mad*	Lovie Austin and Her Serenaders
10. *Yes Sir, That's My Baby*	Ace Brigode & His Fourteen Virginians
11. *I Love My Baby and My Baby Loves Me*	Fred Waring & His Pennsylvaninas
12. *I'd Rather Charleston*	Fred & Adele Astaire
13. *Charleston Charley*	Bert Firman and the Carlton

	Hotel Dance Orchestra
14. *Then I'll Be Happy*	Josephine Baker
15. *Cake Walking Babies From Home*	Louis Armstrong
16. *I'm Looking Over A Four Leaf Clover*	Bill Murray
17. *Charleston Baby O' Mine*	The Georgians
18. *Black Bottom*	Johnny Hamp's Kentucky Serenaders
19. *Sugarfoot Stomp*	Fletcher Henderson
20. *I Ain't Gonna Play No More Second Fiddle*	Perry Bradford w/ Louis Armstrong & Gus Aiken
21. *Fascinating Rhythm*	Savoy Orpheans
22. *Ain't She Sweet*	Gene Austin
23. *Five Foot Two, Eyes of Blue*	Art Landy and His Orchestra
24. *Happy Feet*	Paul Whiteman Orchestra
25. *The Varsity Drag*	George Olsen and His Music
26. *Everything Is Hotsy-Totsy Now*	Coon-Sanders Nighhawks
27. *I Wanna Be Loved By You*	Helen Kane
28. *Charleston Ball*	Cotton Club Orchestra
29. *Brush Stomp*	Chicago Footwarmers
30. *I Lost My Gal From Memphis*	Bubber Miley
31. *Dying With The Blues*	Jabbo Smith
32. *Alabamy Bound*	Fletcher Henderson
33. *Carolina Stomp*	Cotton Pickers
34. *Charleston Baby*	Six Black Diamonds
35. *Cotton Club Stomp*	Duke Ellington
36. *Everybody's Doing The Charleston Now*	Trixie Smith w/ Fletcher Henderson
37. *I Found A New Baby*	Alphonso Trent
38. *Hitch Up The Horses*	Savoy Orpheans
39. *Original Charleston Strut*	Eva Taylor
40. *Charleston Stampede*	Thomas Morris and His Seven Hot Babies

QUESTIONS AND TOPICS
FOR DISCUSSION

The author would love to participate in your group's discussion of this book. Please contact @ mark@MarkJonesBooks.com.

1. What is the significance of the title? Did the title take on a different meaning as you read the book?

2. The "Prelude" section is titled "The Most Important Day in American Music History." Do you think the author has a valid point? If not, why?

3. Charleston is as much of a character in the book as Rev. Jenkins and the musicians. As portrayed in the book, how is Charleston different than your modern impression?

4. Did the images in the book help tell the story? If so, how and why?

5. The illegitimate pregnancy of Rev. Jenkins and Ella Harleston and the abandonment of their child creates a moral quandary. Do you think their guilt over the situation became a motivating factor for the rest of their lives?

6. Who was your favorite character in the story? What made the person so interesting?

7. Compare the changing social attitudes toward women and blacks during the time period covered in the book. What are the similarities and differences between the struggle for racial and gender equality?

8. Can you cite any examples of modern popular music that are directly related to the music of the 1920s?

9. Has the book increased your interest in any of the subjects covered in the story?

10. What was the most surprising piece of information you learned?

BIBLIOGRAPHY

Magazines, Newspapers & Periodicals

Baldwin, B. "The Cakewalk: A study in stereotype and reality." *Journal of Social History,* 1981.

Boyd, Frank. "Harlem Rent Parties." *American Life Histories, 1936-1940.* Federal Writers' Projects.

Charleston City Directory, 1890-1930. Charleston: Sholes & Co.

Charleston News & Courier, 1891-1935.

Condell, James. "Freddie Green – Mr. Rhythm." *Coda,* April/May 1988.

Dance, Stanley and Helen. "The Freddie Green Interview." Institute of Jazz Studies, Rutgers, University, August 9, 1977.

Dexter, Dave, Jr. "Too Many Bad Kicks," An Exclusive Online Extra, an interview in Chicago with Billie Holiday. *Downbeat*, November 1, 1939.

Ferguson, Jim. "Freddie Green – Mr. Rhythm – Remembered." *Guitar Player* Magazine. 1987.

July, Owen Cordle. "Now That The Count Is Gone, More Than Ever The Basie Legacy Resides In The Wrist Of Freddie Green." *People* Magazine, March 4, 1985,

Long, Richard A. "The Outer Reaches: The White Writer and Blacks in the Twenties." In *The Harlem*

Renaissance Re-examined. Ed. Victor A. Kramer. New York: AMS Press, 1987, 43-50.

Newsom, Jon. "The American Brass Band Movement: An Overview." *The Quarterly Journal of the Library of Congress 36* (1979): 115-30, 138-39.

Smith, Hal. "Freddie Green: All-American Rhythm Guitarist." *Jazz Rambler* Newsletter; Jan/Feb 2000.

Standifer, James. "The Complicated Life of *Porgy and Bess.*" *Humanities,* November/December 1997, Volume 18/Number 6.

Stifelman, Leslie. "James P. Johnson: A Composer Rescued." *Columbia Journal of American Studies 1:1,* 1995.

Electronic

Carr, Peter, Vollmer, Al and Wright, Laurie. "Have Drum, Will Travel: An Interview With Tommy Benford." *www.doctorjazz.co.uk.*

Crohn, Burrill, director. *Trumpet Kings.* Video Artists International, Inc. 1989, videocassette.

Farrow, David & Peters, Pete. *Charleston, S.C.: A Magical History Tour* DVD. MHT Productions, Vreel Communications Hc, 2006.

FreddieGreen.org

Hamilton, Kendra. "Goat Cart Sam, a.k.a Porgy: Dubose Heyward's Icon of Southern 'Innocence'." *American Studies, xroads.virginia.edu.*

LaGuardia, Fiorella H. "American Prohibition in the 1920s." 1926. Online. Netscape. 23 April 1998.

RedHotJazz.com

Zax, David. "Summertime for George Gershwin."

Smithsonian.com, August 9, 2010.

Books

Aldrich, Elizabeth. *From the Ballroom to Hell: Grace and Folly in Nineteenth Century Dance.* Evanston, Illinois: Northwestern University Press, 1991.

Allen, Frederick Lewis. *Only Yesterday: An Informal History of the Nineteen-Twenties.* New York: Harper & Brothers Publishers, 1931.

Alpert, Hollis. *The Life and Times of Porgy and Bess: The Story of an American Classic.* New York: Alfred A. Knopf, 1990.

Andrist, Ralph K., ed. *The American Heritage: History of the 20's & 30's.* New York: American Heritage Publishing Co., Inc., 1970.

Armitage, Merle, ed. *George Gershwin.* London: Longmans, Green & Co., 1938.

Badger, Reid. *A Life in Ragtime: a Biography of James Reese Europe.* New York and London: Oxford University Press, 1995.

Baker, Jean-Claude and Chase, Chris. *Josephine: The Hungry Heart.* New York: Random House, 1993.

Ball, Edward. *The Sweet Hell Inside: A Family History.* New York: HarperCollins Publishers, 2001.

Baughman, Judith S., ed. *American Decades: 1920-1929.* New York: Manly, Inc., 1996.

Balliett, Whitney. *Jelly Roll, Jabbo & Fats: 19 Portraits in Jazz.* New York: Oxford University Press, 1983.

Bean, Annemarie, ed. *Inside the Minstrel Mask: Readings in Nineteenth-Century Blackface Minstrelsy.* Weslyan University Press, 1996.

Behr, Edward. *Prohibition: Thirteen Years That Changed America.* New York: Arcade Publishing, 1996.

Berlin, Edward A. *King of Ragtime: Scott Joplin and His Era.* New York: Oxford, 1994.

Bogle, Donald. *Heat Wave: The Life and Career of Ethel Waters.* New York: HarperCollins, 2011.

Bowen, Ezra, ed. *This Fabulous Century. 6 vols.* New York: Time Life Books, 1969.

Bradford, Perry. *Born With The Blues.* New York: Oak Publications, 1965.

Butler, Nicholas Michael. *Votaries of Apollo: The St. Cecelia Society and the Patronage of Concert Music in Charleston, South Carolina, 1766-1820.* Columbia, S.C.: University of South Carolina Press, 2007.

Chilton, John. *A Jazz Nursery The Story of the Jenkins' Orphanage Bands of Charleston, South Carolina.* London: Bloomsbury Book Shop, 1980.

_____. *Who's Who in Jazz: Storyville to Swing Street.* New York: Time-Life, 1978.

Chujoy, A., & Manchester, P.W. (eds.) *The Dance Encyclopedia.* Simon & Schuster: New York, 1967.

Clarke, Donald. *Wishing on the Moon: The Life and Times of Billie Holiday.* New York: Viking, 1994.

Cockrell, Dale. *Demons of Disorder: Early Blackface Minstrels and Their World.* (Cambridge Studies in America Theatre and Drama, No 8), 1997.

Cook, Richard, and Morton, Brian. *The Penguin Guide to Jazz on CD.* London: Penguin Books, 2004.

Crawford, Richard. *America's Musical Life.* New York: W.W. Norton & Company, 2001.

Crow, Bill. *Jazz Ancedotes.* New York: Oxford University Press, 1990.

Dance, Stanley. *The World of Duke Ellington.* New York: De Capo Press, Inc., 1970.

Dodge, Roger Pryor. Dodge Pryor, ed. *Hot Jazz and Jazz Dance.* New York: Oxford University Press, 1995.

Douglas, Ann. *Terrible Honesty: Mongrel Manhattan in the 1920s.* New York: Farrar, Strauss, Giroux, 1995.

Ellington, Edward Kennedy. *Music is My Mistress.* New York: Doubleday & Company, 1973.

Fass, Paula S. *The Damned and the Beautiful: American Youth in the 1920's.* New York: Oxford University Press, 1977.

Floyd, Samuel A., ed. *Black Music in the Harlem Renais-sance.* Knoxville: University of Tennessee Press, 1990.

Franklin, Benjamin, V. *Jazz & Blues Musicians of South Carolina.* Columbia: University of South Carolina Press, 2008.

Fraser Jr., Walter J. *Charleston! Charleston! The History of a Southern City.* Columbia, SC: University of South Carolina P, 1989.

Friedwald, Will. *Jazz Singing: America's Great Voices from Bessie Smith to Bebop and Beyond.* New York: De Capo Press, Inc., 1996

Gioia, Ted. *The History of Jazz.* New York: Oxford, 1997.

Green, Jeffery P. *Edmund Thorton Jenkins: The Life*

and Times of an American Black Composer, 1894-1926. Westport Ct.: Greenwood Press, 1982.

Grime, Kitty. *Jazz at Ronnie Scott's*. Jazz-Institute Darmstadt, 1979.

Golden, Eve. *Vernon and Irene Castle's Ragtime Revolution*. Lexington, KY.: University of Kentucky Press, 2007.

Hammond, John. *John Hammond on Record*. Ridge Press/Summit Book, 1977.

Handy, W.C. *Father of the Blues: An Autobiography*. New York: Macmillan Company, 1947.

Harris, Bill. *The Hellfighters of Harlem: African-American Soldiers Who Fought for the Right to Fight for Their Country*. New York: Carroll & Graf Publishers, 2002

Harris, Stephen, L. *Harlem's Hell Fighters: The African-American 369th Infantry in World War I*. Dulles, Virginia, Potomac Books, 2003.

Haskins, James. *Black Dance in America: A History Through Its People*. New York: Thomas Y. Crowell Books, 1990.

Hasse, John Edward. *Beyond Category: The Life and Genius of Duke Ellington*. New York: Simon & Schuster, 1993.

Hatton, Jackie. "Flappers." *St. James Encyclopedia of Popular Culture*, 2000.

Herskovits, Melville J. *The Myth of the Negro Past*. Boston: Beacon, 1990.

Hill, Laban Carrick. *Harlem Stomp: A Cultural History of the Harlem Renaissance*. New York: Little, Brown and Company, 2003.

Huggins, Nathan Irvin. *Harlem Renaissance*. New

York: Oxford, 1971.

Hutchinsson, James M. *Dubose Heyward: A Charleston Gentleman and the World of Porgy and Bess.* Jackson, Ms.: University of Mississippi Press, 2000.

_____ and Harlan Greene, ed. *Renaissance In Charleston: Art and Life in the Carolina Low Country, 1900-1940.* Athens: University of Georgia Press, 2003.

Jasen, David A. & Jones, Gene. *Black Bottom Stomp: Eight Masters of Ragtime and Early Jazz.* New York and London: Routledge, 2002.

Johnson, James Weldon. *Black Manhattan.* New York: De Capo Press, 1991.

Jonas, Gerald. *Dancing: The Pleasure, Power, and Art of Movement.* New York: Harry N. Abrams, Inc.: 1992.

Jones, Mark R. *Wicked Charleston, Volume II: Prostitution, Politics & Prohibition.* Charleston, SC: The History Press, 2006.

Kimball, Robert, and Alfred Simon. *The Gershwins.* New York: Atheneum, 1973.

Krasner, David. *A Beautiful Pageant: African American Theatre, Drama and Performance in the Harlem Renaissance, 1910-1927.* New York: Palgrave MacMillan, 2002.

Kyvig, David E. *Daily Life in the United States, 1920-1940.* Chicago: Ivan R. Dee, Publisher, 2002.

LaGuardia, Fiorella H. *The Black Tradition In American Dance.* New York: Rizzoli International Publications, Inc., 1990.

Lewis, David Levering. *When Harlem Was In Vogue.* New York: Oxford University Press, 1981.

Lott, Eric. *Love and Theft: Blackface Minstrelsy and the American Working Class.* Oxford University Press, 1993.

Malone, Jacqui. *Steppin' On The Blues: The Visible Rhythms of African American Dance.* Chicago: University of Illinios Press, 1996.

McWhirter, Cameron. *Red Summer: The Summer of 1919 and the Awakening of Black America.* New York: Henry Holt and Company, 2011.

Murray, Albert. *Stomping the Blues.* New York: Vintage, 1982.

Nathan, Hans. *Dan Emmett and Rise of Early Negro Minstrelsy.* University of Oklahoma Press, 1962.

Newby, I. A. *Black Carolinians: A History of Blacks in South Carolina from 1895 to 1968.* Columbia, SC: University of South Carolina Press, 1973.

Nketia, J. H. Kwabena. *The Music of Africa.* New York: W.W. Norton, 1974.

O'Brien, Michael, and David Moltke-Hansen, eds. *Intellectual Life in Antebellum Charleston.* Knoxville, TN: University of Tennessee Press, 1986.

Powers, Bernard E., Jr. *Black Charlestonians: A Social History, 1822-1885.* Fayetteville, Ark.: University of Arkansas Press, 1994.

Ramsy, Guthrie P. Jr. *Race Music: Black Cultures from BeBop to Hip-Hop.* Berkeley: University of California Press, 2003.

Rogers, Ginger. *Ginger: My Story.* New York: HarperCollins, 1991.

Rose, Al. *Eubie Blake.* New York: Schirmer Books, 1979.

Rust, F. *Dance and Society.* Routledge & Kegan Paul:

London, 1969.

Sadie, S. (Ed.) *The New Grove Dictionary of Music and Musicians.* Macmillan, London, 1980.

Sass, Charles W. *Old Charleston.* Richmond: The Dale Press, 1933.

Schwartz, Charles. *Gershwin: His Life and Music.* Indianapolis: The Bobbs-Merrill Co. Inc, 1973.

Schuller, Gunther. *Early Jazz: Its Roots and Musical Development.* New York: Oxford University Press, 1968.

Silvester, V. *Old Time and Sequence Dancing.* Barrie & Jenkins, London, 1980.

Simpson J.A. and Weiner, E.S.C. *Oxford English Dictionary (2nd Edition).* Clarendon Press, Oxford, 1989.

Sissle, Noble Lee. "Memoirs of Lieutenant 'Jim' Europe". African American Odyssey: A Quest for Full Citizenship, Library of Congress Collection, 1942.

Slavick, William. *Dubose Heyward.* Boston: Twayne Publishers, 1981.

_____. "Going to School to Dubose Heyward." In *The Harlem Renaissance Re-examined.* Ed.Victor A. Kramer. New York: AMS Press, 1987, 65-92.

Smith, Willie. *Music On My Mind: The Memoirs of an American Pianist.* Cambridge, MA.: De Capo Press, 1978.

Southern, Eileen. *The Music of Black Americans: A History.* New York: W.W. Norton & Company, 1983.

Stearns, Marshall and Jean. *Jazz Dance: The Story of American Vernacular Dance.* New York: Macmillan, 1968.

Sylvester, Robert. *No Cover Charge: A Backward Look*

at the Night Clubs. New York: Dial Press, 1956.

Toll, Robert C. *Blacking Up: The Minstrel Show in Nineteenth-Century America.* New York: Oxford Univer-sity Press, 1974.

Tucker, Mark, ed. *The Duke Ellington Reader.* New York: Oxford University Press, 1993.

Ward, Geoffrey and Burns, Ken. *Jazz: A History of America's Music.* New York: Alfred A. Knopf, 2000.

Watkins, Glenn. *Proof Through the Night: Music and the Great War.* Ewing, N. J.: University of California Press, 2003.

Wald, Elijah. *How The Beatles Destroyed Rock'n'Roll: An Alternative History of American Popular Music.* New York: Oxford Press, 2009.

Watson, Steven. *The Harlem Renaissance: Hub of African-American Culture, 1920-1930.* New York: Pantheon, 1995.

Woll, Allen. *Black Musical Theatre: From Coontown to Dreamgirls.* New York: Da Capo, 1989.

Wondrich, David. *Stomp and Swerve: American Music Gets Hot, 1843-1924.* Chicago: A Cappella Books, 2003.

Wood, Peter H. *Black Majority: Negroes in Colonial South Carolina from 1670 through the Stono Rebellion.* New York: W.W. Norton, 1975.

Yule, Stephanie E. *A Golden Haze of Memory: The Making of Historic Charleston.* Chapel Hill: The University of North Carolina Press, 2005.

INDEX

K

L

344 / Mark R. Jones

344 / Mark R. Jones

Charleston reaction · 258, 260
composition of · 244
premiere · 256
reception · 257, 262
Porgy and Bess, reception · 258
Porgy, character · 220, 240
Post World War I attitudes · 209
Powell, Adam Clayton · 61
Presley, Elvis · 136, 143
Price, Leontyne · 261
Prohibition · 212, 214, 215, 217
Pryor, Richard · 93

Q

Queen's Dance Orchestra recordings · 245
Queen's Hall · 199

R

Race riots, Charleston · 68, 71
Ragtime · 48, 100, 101, 102, 108, 125, 136
Reconstruction Acts · 21, 22, 23
Red Summer · 70, 117
Reed, Donna · 230
Reinhardt, Django · 293
Rent parties · 132, 296
Rhapsody in Blue · 125, 253, 256
Rhythm Aces, The · 282

Rhythm Club, The · 296
Rice, Thomas Dartmouth · 91
Robeson, Paul · 224, 249
Robinson, Ikey · 282
Rothstein, Arthur · 281
Royal Academy of Music · 154, 157, 202, 244
Runnin' Wild · 226

S

Schuller, Gunther · 16, 179, 280, 284
Shoo-Fly Regiment · 117
Shuffle Along · 188, 224, 225, 248, 250, 281
closed · 224
debut on Broadway · 223
Silver Streak · 93
Sinclair, Rebel · 78
Sissle, Noble · 116, 122, 124, 157, 158, 160, 167, 175, 176, 179, 181, 183, 184, 185, 188, 209, 224, 226, 293
Clef Club management · 118
Slave trading · 78
Sleep shifting · 131
Small's Paradise · 219, 220, 221, 278
Smalls, Ed · 219, 279, 281
Smalls, Robert · 219
Smalls, Sammy · 220, 238
Smith, Jabbo · 48, 49, 65, 135, 192, 193, 195, 220, 221, 287

T

ABOUT THE AUTHOR

Mark R. Jones is an eighth generation native of the South Carolina Low country. He is an author, historian, licensed guide and tour owner. With his wife, novelist Rebel Sinclair, Jones operates Black Cat Tours, conducting night time walking tours which cover the darker history of the Holy City. He also drives carriages and gives daytime historic walking tours.

He is the author of four other books. His first book kicked off the wildly popular *Wicked* series for The History Press, *Wicked Charleston: The Dark Side of the Holy City* (2005) which was followed by *Wicked Charleston, Volume II: Prostitutes, Politics & Prohibition* (2006). In 2007 Jones published two true crime anthologies: *Palmetto Predators: Monsters Among Us* and *South Carolina Killers: Crimes of Passion.*

If you'd like to hear some of the music discussed in this book, or for more information about Mark, his books and tours, and to inquire about a speech or presentation, go to:

MarkJonesBooks.com

Contact: mark@MarkJonesBooks.com

Made in the USA
Middletown, DE
13 December 2023

45495131R00208